Imagining European Unity since 1000 AD

Imagining European Unity since 1000 AD

Patrick Pasture

Professor of History and Director of the Master Programme in European Studies:
Transnational and Global Perspectives, University of Leuven, Belgium

First published 2015 by
PALGRAVE MACMILLAN

Palgrave Macmillan in the UK is an imprint of Macmillan Publishers Limited, registered in England, company number 785998, of Houndmills, Basingstoke, Hampshire RG21 6XS.

Palgrave Macmillan in the US is a division of St Martin's Press LLC, 175 Fifth Avenue, New York, NY 10010.

Palgrave Macmillan is the global academic imprint of the above companies and has companies and representatives throughout the world.

Palgrave® and Macmillan® are registered trademarks in the United States, the United Kingdom, Europe and other countries.

ISBN 978–1–137–48046–0

This book is printed on paper suitable for recycling and made from fully managed and sustained forest sources. Logging, pulping and manufacturing processes are expected to conform to the environmental regulations of the country of origin.

A catalogue record for this book is available from the British Library.

Library of Congress Cataloging-in-Publication Data
Pasture, Patrick, 1961–
    Imagining European unity since 1000 AD / Patrick Pasture, Professor and Director at the Centre of European Studies, University of Leuven, Belgium.
        pages cm
    ISBN 978–1–137–48046–0
    1. European Union—History.   2. European federation—History.
    I. Title.
JN30.P389 2015
341.242—dc23   2015003447

To the memory of Eric Pasture, 1928–2014

Never did the mind of man conceive a scheme nobler, more beautiful, or more useful than that of a lasting peace between all the peoples of Europe.

J.-J. Rousseau, 1761

If their reconciliation does not succeed, if the European nations do not learn to recognize the legitimacy of their distinctiveness and nurture the common European culture, if we fail to unite the peoples again through cultural rapprochement, if in this way a new war among European nations cannot be prevented, then Europe's supremacy in the world will be permanently lost.

Konrad Adenauer, 1919

Contents

Preface

The origin of this book goes back to the mid-1990s, when I attended a lecture on the history of the idea of Europe by the Dutch historian Pim den Boer. Den Boer emphasized European diversity and the universal values of tolerance that had developed in Europe. I recall that I could not understand why students from the US and Asia seemed to agree with his argument, as in many respects their countries appeared more diverse and tolerant than Europe to a globetrotter like me. That at least was how I saw myself at the time, and my assessment has only been confirmed by my experience as a historian of globalization ever since.

Many years and intellectual adventures later, I found myself compelled to revisit the issue. The 2012 Nobel Peace Prize for the EU offered the occasion and the prism for the present assessment, and a new book by the leading theoretician of 'cosmopolitan Europe' provided the trigger.

The text that lies before you expresses a vision of European history and in particular of European integration. The term 'European integration' is used here in a rather narrow sense, referring to plans, projects and ideas for federating Europe on an institutionalized basis. Hence, this book is not a general political history of the continent. It only discusses the way Europeans have thought about establishing some sort of institutionalized European format. This is not to be equated with processes of 'Europeanization' as a form of convergence in political, economic or cultural terms. Nor was it my ambition to write an intellectual or conceptual history of peace or how it has been negotiated in Europe in practice, though these will be important elements in this book. Peace is notoriously difficult to define, and stating – as historians like to do in cases such as these – that we basically follow the contemporary sources' definitions and understanding is perhaps an overly easy answer. Nevertheless, I adopt a minimalistic interpretation and define peace as the absence of violence and war. The admittedly fascinating and relevant history of how peace was understood, e.g. in association with justice and good government, is obviously interwoven with this one, but it is not the subject of this book.

The immediate purpose of the book is thus to revisit the history of European integration as a way to enhance peace on the continent. That the quest for European unity in essence can be viewed as a way to enhance peace is not surprising, given the centrality of war as a key feature of Europe's history and imagination – although some of the earliest plans for European unity aimed at creating an instrument of war rather than peace, to effectively mobilize in a crusade against Muslims in the Holy Land. European plans were aimed at offering a structure that would prevent intra-European conflict, though until the late twentieth century their designers – though often considered 'utopian' in contemporary literature – were well aware that structures alone may not suffice. For centuries, guaranteeing a certain stability and balance was already quite an achievement in itself, though certainly 'true peace' was more than that. In this context, moreover, peace is seen in its internal and in its external dimensions: it refers both to the repelling of external threats and to controlling 'internal' ones – internal on a continental level but also, to a large extent, internal for the different states. The latter surely implies considering what kind of order was intended and considered 'just'.

The basic history of ideas about European integration, which is closely related to the implementation of the so-called 'idea of Europe', has already been written more than once, though I have tried to bring it up to date with the most recent findings. These offer a divergent picture from the one that the traditional European federalist histories present. The following assessment does not contain a linear narrative of a bumpy but inevitable and eventually happy road to enlightenment and unification in which Europe functions as the 'light of the world'. It takes into account the postcolonial criticism of European complacent self-representation, as particularly argued by postcolonial writers such as the Argentine-Mexican philosopher Enrique Dussel and the British sociologist Gurminder K. Bhambra. It also includes the views of those that are excluded from the older, traditional histories; from that perspective it treats Marxist and fascist ideas about Europe on an equal footing with the classic federalist proposals, and actually looks at convergences beyond the apparent differences.

In this respect, the book actually questions Europe's almost 'cosmogonic myth' (Mircea Eliade) that represents the history of Europe as the coming of age of some particular intellectual traditions – namely Greco-Roman, Judaeo-Christian and the Enlightenment – and of European integration as the fulfilment of some great ideas and liberation from the constraints of national antagonisms – what Heinz Duchhardt recently called 'model Europe'. Postcolonial writers have seriously criticized the dominant Eurocentric narrative to be found in European studies, history and politics, and although the pendulum is apparently swinging back to such conventional stories, I have tried to incorporate a global and postcolonial perspective in my text.

Nevertheless, this book takes issue with those who suggest that in order to respect the identity and legitimacy of each period and to avoid teleology, no long-term connections can be made, that one even has to ignore hindsight – writing history 'without hindsight', as Oxford medievalist Chris Wickham suggests, is not only not possible, it is also not desirable, as we always use and need hindsight to create a meaningful and coherent narrative about the past and to give it its full significance in its own time. Teleology refers to looking for determined lines in history, and writing in a 'historicist modus' easily leads to it, but it does not exclude historical connections, transformations and what social scientists dub 'path-dependency', which is nothing other than the all too familiar 'weight of the past'. Avoiding the pitfalls of teleology, I will (at least attempt to) write a history of historical connections and continuities that were not determined, and indeed were transformed and sometimes discontinued.

But I also strongly disagree with the argument that history should demonstrate the historical legacy for the present, as advanced recently, for example, by the leading British sociologist Gerard Delanty in his application of historical sociology to the history of the idea of Europe, *Formations of European Modernity*. History is, could be or perhaps even should be relevant as it may help to understand and explain the present, but the historical practice should above all focus on the past itself in its particular context. Delanty's viewing of Europe's history through the contemporary lens of cosmopolitanism may help him to recognize the importance of intercivilizational encounters – something very laudable indeed, though his choices reveal some other problems – but it generates an image of European history that hardly takes into account its colonial and imperial heritage and hence appears more a reflection of contemporary ideals about cosmopolitanism than of historical realities, while his purpose of establishing a 'normative reference point' that 'can connect the past and the present' results in a rather smug and complacent historical assessment that I cannot describe otherwise than as fundamentally Eurocentric.

The form this book takes is largely that of a historical narrative and follows a chronological order. Admittedly, such a structure entails a serious risk of creating just the sort of linearity that I want to avoid. Dividing history into chronological chapters based on established (or less established) eras moreover contains the danger that history becomes fragmented, as chronological periodizations suggest the existence of 'closed' epochs with clearly distinguishable and interrelated features. History does not proceed in this way: besides moments of acceleration and change, there are continuities that transcend epochal divisions. Moreover, continuities often follow uneven, paradoxical and even contradictory patterns: history may even 'retreat' in certain perspectives but not in others. I have chosen two modest but practical ways to deal with this problem.

Firstly, the chronological divisions do not always follow the established periodizations. One chapter deals with the period roughly from the first half of the eighteenth century up to the Napoleonic years, which is a pivotal time of intense and profound change, starting earlier than the so-called 'Age of Revolution' of 1780–1815. Likewise, the nineteenth century is subdivided into two different periods. The second part, starting around 1850–1870 – corresponding with a period of new imperialism and economic and technological innovation – runs up to WW I. The two world wars do function as caesurae, but actually overlap with preceding and following periods. The book ends with the establishment of the main European institutions after WW II, emphasizing the many different institutions that were constituted instead of focusing on the ECSC as the starting point of a new development leading to the present EU. In one respect, it continues the narrative up to about 1960, with regard to the relationship with Africa and the colonial motivation of European integration in the 1950s, as this dimension is mostly ignored in traditional overviews.

Secondly, I leave the 'frames' of the text open. Not only do I deliberately avoid giving clear indications about the caesurae, but I also refrain from summarizing conclusions after each chapter. By leaving the chapters 'open-ended', I want to emphasize the continuities of history. Chapters nevertheless still often begin by emphasizing the emergence of new patterns within a broader context, indicating in some ways the degree of continuity as well as renewal and change, and the changes of meaning within the continuities. Sometimes, though, such reflections are inserted after a first paragraph that offers a general context.

Acknowledgements

My thoughts for this book have mainly been shaped by postcolonial studies, political science and world history. They particularly benefited from the stimulating intellectual environment of the interdisciplinary Leuven Centre for European Studies, as well as the Department of History and its research unit MoSa (Modernity & Society 1800–2000). Some colleagues volunteered to comment on parts of the present text: Hans Cools, Stephan Keukeleire, Martin Kohlrausch, Emiel Lamberts and an anonymous reviewer from Palgrave, whom I would particularly like to thank for exceptionally penetrating suggestions. Many others, sometimes inadvertently, gave me ideas that left their mark on the book. To be sure, I remain responsible for any remaining errors as well as interpretations (which certainly not all will agree with). As always, my wife and colleague Chang Shu-chin's contribution to this work goes far beyond what she would be ready to acknowledge: even if she is not overly thrilled by the historiography of European integration, her cautiously critical comments from an 'inside/outside' perspective as well as her deep and extensive knowledge of European cultural history and theory have been an immense help – not to speak of her patience. I also wish to express my appreciation for my enthusiastic editor, Jen McCall, and her collaborators at Palgrave, Francis Arumugam of Integra-PDY, as well as Chris Brennan, who assisted me in writing decent English.

I dedicate this book to my father, who passed away while I was completing this book. He was one of the most intelligent people I ever knew, but had no academic education. However, when he felt that his mind was slipping away, he concluded, with his unique wit, that now, his head in the clouds, he was finally becoming a professor. He earned the title long before, though.

References

Adenauer, Konrad. Eröffnungsfeier der Universität zu Köln. Rede gehalten bei dem Festakt im Großen Saal des Gürzenich am 12. Juni 1919, verlegt bei Heinrich Z. Gonski, Köln 1919, p. 9ff (http://www.konrad-adenauer.de/dokumente/reden/eroffnung-uni-koln, 11 November 2014).
Rousseau, Jean-Jacques. *A Lasting Peace through the Federation of Europe and the State of War*, translated by C. E. Vaughan. Constable: London, 1917 (1761), 36.

1

'Peace for Our Time': The European Quest for Peace

> My good friends, for the second time in our history, a British Prime Minister has returned from Germany bringing peace with honour. I believe it is peace for our time. We thank you from the bottom of our hearts. Go home and get a nice quiet sleep.
>
> Neville Chamberlain, 30 September 1938[1]

'Peace for our time'?

'Peace for our time', the British prime minister Neville Chamberlain was proud to proclaim on 30 September 1938, commenting on the Munich Agreement between Great Britain and Nazi Germany that he had signed earlier that day. With this agreement, Chamberlain hoped to have appeased the German Reich and to have rescued peace in Europe – a hope widely shared at the moment. The very next day, however, Hitler invaded Czechoslovakia, as the agreement did indeed permit the German annexation of the Sudetenland. The sacrifice of little Czechoslovakia, whose objections the boasting statesman ignored, obviously did not prevent WW II. Hence, Chamberlain's words are usually invoked to illustrate either the cynicism of politicians or the irony of history, but what they express above all is the deep longing for peace in Europe, which obliterated all other considerations. Europeans were already doves well before 1945, it seems.[2]

The memory of the innumerable wars and, in particular, the utter destruction and insanity of WW I and even more so the atrocities of WW II have taught Europe to see itself as a deeply divided continent, always prone to devastating wars, a situation that was finally overcome by the European integration process. That is the reason why the Nobel Peace Prize Committee in 2012 conferred its most prestigious award on

1

the EU and – significantly – 'its forerunners [because they] have for over six decades contributed to the advancement of peace and recon-ciliation, democracy and human rights *in Europe*' (emphasis added).[3] It was, incidentally, not the first time that the Norwegians had honoured European politicians for their contribution to peace on the continent: actually Neville Chamberlain's half-brother Austen Chamberlain had already received a Nobel Peace Prize in 1925, together with the American Charles G. Dawes – followed by Aristide Briand and Gustav Stresemann the subsequent year for their solution to the Ruhr Crisis in 1923–1924. The occupation of the industrial Ruhr region by French and Belgian troops had brought Europe to the brink of a new war, and the Locarno Treaty (1925) was heralded as the dawn of a new era of peace for Europe.

There are many arguments in favour of this 2012 European Nobel Prize, though. The pacification of Europe is indeed no small feat. As one of the foremost commentators on the state of Europe observed, 'we need this Europe to prevent our falling back into the bad old ways of war and European barbarism'.[4] That danger, this book will also show, is far more real than one sometimes imagines: war has been declared dead many times, by some of the most illustrious minds, but it has the very bad habit of always returning with a vengeance. Recent history has known moments where paths towards barbarism could have been cho-sen, but were, at least for now, avoided. Long may it remain so. But the award can be the start of a critical reflection nevertheless. One ques-tion is certainly to what extent the EU can be effectively considered the successor of the agencies that realized this post-war peace. I will argue in this book that while the European institutions certainly kept the peace, the institutions as such did not subdue the hatred and passion for revenge that existed after the war and they did not, at least not solely, originate from a general European wish to overcome the divisions that had provoked the war. Moreover, in its argumentation, the Norwegian committee somehow bypassed the division of Europe, which led to the situation of an 'armed peace' between 1947 and 1989. In particular, the committee also ignored many 'smaller' conflicts and, more importantly, the postcolonial wars in which European countries had been engaged, including the Algerian Liberation War (which was, legally speaking at least, an intra-European civil war and cost hundreds of thousands of lives).[5] The latter, incidentally, is symptomatic of most traditional repre-sentations of Europe, which seems systematically disconnected from its colonial past. This neglect is quite illustrative of Europe's post-war his-torical representation; that the Norwegian Nobel Peace Prize Committee consists exclusively of Europeans is significant in this respect. Europeans sometimes seem unaware that their cherished and carefully cultivated image as the harbinger of peace, advocate of human rights and 'soft power' is not always convincing to others because of its past.[6]

The following text is woven around a largely familiar story of how Europeans imagined the organization of their continent. Though this book is by no means a general history of Europe, these representations and imaginations of European unification do tell us something about European culture and identity, even if what they tell us is only related to the ideas and (self-)perceptions of a certain intellectual and political European elite. But that 'something' will nevertheless allow me to make some more general observations that I hope may help readers to look at European history in a slightly different manner, perhaps one that is more apt to the contemporary globalized world.

Proposals for a European organization, first of all, reflect the ways in which Europeans have imagined and tried to contain the many diversities that they felt confronted by within the continent, be these religious, political or ethnic, and which they learned to fear and aimed to contain. Secondly, they are also formulated with a view to Europe's position in relation to others. In this context, most contemporary references are to the world of Islam – in the wake of Sam Huntington's infamous 'clash of civilizations' – but especially since the nineteenth century, Europeans have thought far more about organizing their continent against upcoming economic powers such as the US, Japan and, more recently, the 'Asian tigers' and 'BRICS' (Brazil, Russia, India, China and South Africa).[7] In this respect, one should certainly also take into account that Europeans have tried, successfully, for a long time, to dominate, conquer and exploit peoples, lands and seas. Keeping this position of superiority and dominance has been an important motive in considering the organization of Europe as well, though not all visions of Europe have been imperialistic.[8] Nevertheless, it is no coincidence that European integration gained momentum in parallel with decolonization. Even if the relationship is less straightforward than it may appear, decolonization profoundly affected the post-war turn towards European integration as well as the way European institutions defined themselves.

But my focus in this book remains on European institutional integration history itself. It is a story of ups and downs, one that represents European integration history as a reconstruction afterwards – one that was not written on the face of the earth, but largely imagined in the light of the present – and hence a non-linear history, one of roads taken and not taken, one of dreams as well as nightmares, of vision and blindness, of learning but also, and perhaps more significantly, of forgetting – perhaps, then, a more human history.

European identity and diversity

In this book, I want to review in particular the relationship between European organization and the idea of peace in Europe. Although my focus is on plans and sketches for a (con-)federal European organization, I cannot avoid reflecting on European identity. It only makes sense to discuss ways to unite and organize Europe after one has developed some understanding of what Europe is, even though institutions and policies no doubt further foster such identity.[9] Identities do not arise in isolation, but always in interaction. That certainly applies to a term as vague as 'Europe'.

Europe is by no means a ready-made concept: not only is it, from a geographical perspective, just 'a small cape of Asia' (Paul Valéry); there were times when no such thing as 'Europe' existed in the minds of people, and since it has so existed, its meaning has shifted over time.[10] Acknowledging that Europe has no existence outside the human imagination does not, of course, imply that it is pure chimera. After all, we do use the term 'Europe' frequently, knowing what it means and assuming others do too. Nevertheless, opinions about the meaning of 'Europeanness' diverge both within and outside Europe. Moreover, all interpretations and perceptions are temporal: they reflect the ever-changing contexts in which they are articulated. This clearly comes to the fore, for instance, in the shifting boundaries allotted to the continent – though these also suggest there is some consistency in the representations as well: discussions about European boundaries oscillate around the same questions and regions again and again, since the concept is used to denote not only a territory but also a political and cultural space – the British Isles, Russia and Turkey, with the Dardanelles as an established frontier. Still, we have to ask ourselves from when has it been meaningful to speak about Europe and what is meant by it, and in the more limited aim of this book, when was the need for a European organization first advanced. Given the interactional character of identity-building, in particular in the case of collective identities, the formation of a European identity refers to both internal and external dimensions. This history of European integration particularly focuses on challenges and threats, and on plans and institutions to organize Europe as a means to assure peace: if I had focused on European identity I would have rather followed Delanty's example (at least in this respect) and emphasized interaction with other 'civilizations' (borrowing from, as well as opposition to and rejection of). Looking at plans for European unity or federalism – in all its variations – requires an assessment of the association between war, peace and the concept of Europe. It will allow me not only to highlight the strong desire for peace and the ways originally envisaged to achieve it, but also to uncover some root causes of major problems Europe has been, and still is, confronted with.

One of the most enduring representations of Europe is that of a deeply divided continent, which has nevertheless finally managed to overcome its 'curse'.[11] In this respect, the standard narrative emphasizes that Europeans developed values of toleration, freedom and equality – humanism and enlightenment are hence considered essential European features. In this perspective, it appears that Europe finally overcame its 'demons' by choosing the path of institutional integration, of a European federation: European integration as an 'escape from history'. The present EU has actually made this representation an essential dimension of its identity, epitomized in its motto 'united in diversity'.[12]

I believe this (multifaceted) representation is a myth. First, one may wonder if Europe is such a divided continent. There is no doubt that there are important diversities in Europe and that the continent is deeply divided politically.[13] But can one really make the case that Europe is (or perhaps was) more diverse than the 'melting pot' of North America (in this respect, clearly to be distinguished from the 'old continent'), the Indian subcontinent with its multitude of languages and faiths, or Southeast Asia, sometimes labelled Asia's 'noodle box' because of its intermingling of languages, ethnicities and religions? The 'diversity index' compiled by the team of Alberto Alesina and Arnaud Devleeschauwer at Harvard certainly suggests otherwise: it is rather African and Asian countries that one finds at the top of the different indices, not European ones (with former Yugoslavia being the exception that proves the rule, as well as reminding us that the eastern parts of Europe are actually more diverse than Western Europe, an issue to which we will return).[14] If one takes language as an indicator of diversity, Europe pales in comparison to India, where the number of languages runs into the hundreds.[15] Certainly, Europe nowadays has become more diverse as a result of migration and processes of social and cultural differentiation, but one should be aware that previously the continent, as a result of the Holocaust and massive ethnic cleansing during and immediately after WW II, became more homogenous than it had ever been. Moreover, it still remains debatable whether early twenty-first century 'super-diversity' (Steven Vertovec) is so much more pronounced in Europe than elsewhere.[16]

And is Europe really more apt at coping with diversity? From a postcolonial perspective, the opposite rather seems to be the case: the many postcolonial conflicts between ethnic and religious groups in Africa and Asia can often be attributed to colonial legacies – the case of Rwanda immediately comes to mind. Although there is a great deal of discussion about the pre-colonial origins of ethnic conflicts in the region of the Great Lakes, there is a little doubt that they were reinforced considerably by the British, German and Belgian colonizers and that the latter introduced borders that reflect their respective power relations but not the existing pre-colonial divisions.[17] Pre-colonial societies certainly had their conflicts, but at least the main Asian civilizations, even when separating 'civilized' people from 'barbarians', were far more tolerant towards religious, linguistic and ethnic diversities than Europe, as their definitions of identity were more inclusive.[18] Southeast Asia, for example, without doubt had known many bloody conflicts long before the arrival of European colonizers, but religion and ethnicity were rarely if ever the root cause of them, and race was arguably an unknown concept. Ancient civilizations such as Srivijaya and Melakka developed a cosmopolitan, 'multicultural' model of living together long before the first millennium AD. It was put to the test by the introduction of Islam in the fifteenth century, and largely set aside by the Portuguese, Dutch and British when they introduced their characteristic *European* policies of racist, ethnic and religious separation and segregation, setting up populations against each other. But it seems that old patterns return today. Alfred Stepan's study of contemporary 'multiple secularisms' shows how and why large and diverse nations such as India and Indonesia – the latter predominantly Islamic – adopted a far more inclusive model of state–church relations, which may be more effective in integrating huge religious diversities than the European model.[19] Likewise, governments in Malaysia and Singapore have to a large extent been able to overcome the ethnic tensions that resulted from the colonial occupation, and to reinvent a multicultural common identity for all Malaysians and make its diversity an asset, not only for tourism purposes.[20] Many African states, far more disturbed by European colonialism, were not so lucky, as the genocide in Rwanda illustrates.

Even if Europe appears a safe haven for many today, its long history of religious wars, ethnic cleansing and the Holocaust shows that the continent was rarely a model as regards coping with different ethnicities and religions. But I contend that Europe is actually not so diverse at all, especially not if one considers religion and even ethnicity as basic forms of identity: Europe became predominantly Christian from around 800, and since then people of other faiths – Muslims and Jews in particular – have essentially been defined as 'outsiders' and hence often persecuted or expelled. The divisions of Christianity in Europe remain limited after all – more limited, incidentally, than in North America, where the process of fragmentation of the Christian religion led to considerably more divergence than in Europe.[21] An exception may be the rise of atheism and secularism, but in many (paradoxical) ways they are also the product of Christianity.[22] Also with regard to ethnicity, one could make a case that Western Europe, at least, is more rather than less homogenous than some other parts of the world. Though comparable data are lacking, it is hard to imagine that European capitals and ports even in Renaissance and Enlightened Europe, after the establishment of the first global European empires, were particularly multicultural and multiethnic compared to the great African and Asian port cities in the Indian Ocean or even the main trade hubs along the ancient Silk Roads.

Without doubt, in Southeast Europe, the parts that belonged to the Byzantine and Ottoman empires were considerably more diverse than Western Europe. Under Byzantine rule, though, Christianity was the norm, which increasingly differentiated from Latin Christendom; by the eleventh century, Orthodox and Latin Christianity had parted ways completely. Byzantine Christendom largely shared western Christian exclusiveness, as it also adopted Christianity as a state religion and defined its identity in opposition to the Islamic empires in the east. However, it shared with the Romans an inclusive notion of citizenship. While the populations under Byzantine rule were mostly Christians, Jews enjoyed relative freedom of faith, although they were excluded from some official functions. With the disintegration of the Byzantine Empire, however, Orthodox Christians constituted different Orthodox churches. When 'European' Christian lands fell into Muslim hands, neither Christians nor Jews were forced to convert, as Muslims were when Christians conquered Muslim lands. Muslim empires, including the Ottoman Empire, nevertheless privileged Muslims and imposed some, at times significant, restrictions and discrimination upon non-Muslims. Hence, in large parts of Eastern and Southeastern Europe, a complex ethnic and religious hotchpotch developed as a result of conquest, migration, religious renewal – including the emergence of Protestant movements and sects from the sixteenth century – and different forms of political organization. Although these people did not always live together as harmoniously as is sometimes imagined, the region became a source of systematic religious and ethnic conflict only with and after the disintegration of the Ottoman Empire, when the region followed the western models of nationalism and became the playground of the great powers.[23]

Nation and ethnicity became the main sources of division in Europe in the nineteenth century, but these divisions appear even more relative when imagined along with the process of nation-building itself, even if they had antecedents which go back much further into history.[24] How much that was the case comes to the fore in the confrontation with non-Europeans, when race, or 'whiteness', or even Europeanness, largely prevailed over intra-European national or ethnic divisions.[25]

Hence, I argue that Europe, rather than *being* extremely diverse, is in the first place *concerned with*, even obsessed by, diversity and otherness – perhaps a large-scale example of the 'narcissism of small differences' – and that this fear has compelled it to search for ways to overcome and control diversity. These ways were indeed sought in philosophies of toleration, but far more in politics of homogenization. Most historians and political scientists in this respect refer to the politics of exclusion in nationalism and the emergence of the nation state, which are not restricted to Europe.[26] The German historian Thomas Mergel locates the origin of Europe's *Sehnsucht nach Ähnlichkeit* ('longing for similarity') in the industrialization, urbanization and development of modern nation states, which made it possible to imagine homogeneity, even if differentiation was what European societies actually experienced.[27] My argument is that this search for homogeneity has much older roots and originates, on the one hand, in the exclusive nature of Christendom – that unique association of religion and political power that emerged in late Roman times but which only came to full development in the European Middle Ages – and is to some extent a product of it (which also explains the strong emphasis on Europe's external borders and its need to distinguish itself from others) but has been, on the other hand, elevated to a political principle since the 'Wars of Religion' of the sixteenth century.[28]

Such a long-term perspective is disputed. Eric Weitz and David Nirenberg, for example, oppose locating the origins of Europe's 'path to genocide' in the Middle Ages, arguing that there was no linear connection and one should observe that there were (long) periods of stability as well.[29] The latter is true, of course, but needs to be qualified too, as I will attempt to do. In addition, I will be the first to acknowledge that racism and nationalism are in many ways fundamentally new phenomena, proper to the 'modern age', and that nationalism is not a 'secularized religion'. But, nevertheless, I will argue that the search for homogeneity largely pre-dates the idea that there should be one state for one nation. That comes to the fore particularly with respect to the idea of European unity: the European search for peace and unity, I contend, cannot be separated from the idea that diversity is detrimental to peace. Hence these European plans emphasize order and stability as conditions for peace.

As the longing for homogeneity implies politics of 'purification' and exclusion, this book also takes issue with currently popular representations of 'cosmopolitan Europe', referring to an 'image of a peaceful, cooperative Europe, open toward other cultures and capable of dialogue', especially if these characteristics are projected back onto Europe's long-term history.[30] Though I would be the last to deny that Europe has been shaped in interaction with other cultures, this happened in complex and often contradictory ways, including rejection and opposition. Even today, even if the EU favours international dialogue and cooperation, openness and empathy are not the features that one associates with the EU in the first place.[31]

This book discusses different plans for the organization of Europe, whether implemented or not – and most are not. Obviously, the emphasis lies on federal plans, but I do include imperial models – the boundary between the two is not always as obvious as may appear at first sight. As should be evident by now, the popular idea that Europe has since the Peace of Westphalia been dominated by nation states, whose impact has been waning since the end of WW II and the creation of supranational institutions such as the EU, is in all respects completely wrong. Nation states, I argue – though they are not the focus of this book – actually became a dominant political format only after the French Revolution, and were probably never so predominant as between the years 1945 and 2000, certainly from a global perspective: after all, all the new states created after decolonization – whose impact still is largely underestimated – followed the model of the nation state as did the new states established in Europe after 1989, as is exemplified by the Yugoslav Wars of the 1990s. And as A.S. Milward pointed out in a series of seminal publications in the 1990s, the early European institutions did not obliterate the nation state in Europe, but basically ensured its enduring success.[32]

But the nation state was not created by the Peace of Westphalia either, even if new concepts of sovereignty, particularly linked to visions of bound territoriality, emerged in the seventeenth and eighteenth centuries.[33] Actually plans for a European federation that were formulated in these times contributed to that idea of sovereignty. These ideas about a federation implied the recognition of territorial states. Nevertheless, the focus on states rather obscures the enduring and even increasing significance of empire, though what was understood by the latter certainly changed. Many, if not all Europe's states developed global empires, mainly overseas, first in the Americas, and then in Asia and Africa. As Jane Burbank and Frederick Cooper observe, what made the difference was less the modified relationship to territoriality than the huge extended spaces that European empires controlled.[34] Moreover, in the colonies the European sovereigns were able to exert more power and authority, and in more innovative ways, than they were in Europe. Empire also remained the prime political organization in Europe in the so-called age of nationalism, the nineteenth and twentieth centuries, even if major empires in and around Europe collapsed, such as the Habsburg Empire, the Ottoman Empire and the Russian Empire – the latter being replaced by the USSR, which in many ways can be considered a modern empire as well. But, as Eugen Weber already acknowledged decades ago, even a quintessential 'nation state' such as France was not unified before the end of the nineteenth century: it was indeed an empire that succeeded in homogenizing its people into a 'nation'. It has become customary recently to distinguish between different kinds of empires in nineteenth-century Europe, the most obvious distinction being between colonial and 'continental' ones, though one should perhaps rather think of a continuum, or else cling to even more complex forms of blurred and unstable 'fluctuating' concepts of nineteenth-century political entities.[35] Europe's unification was not only pursued by federalists, but also by empire-builders, from Napoleon to Bismarck to Hitler – especially, Central and Southeastern Europe were seen by many as colonial territories. Incidentally, imperialism was not only an ambition of reactionaries, but often a liberal enterprise: the main imperialists were the British, but liberal nationalists were also promoting empire-building within Europe.[36] This context should be taken into consideration when discussing European integration as well. Nevertheless, my focus is rather on the projects for a federal or 'confederal' organization of Europe, or substantial parts of what we may associate with that continent.

2
Peace in Christendom?

> Unity seems to be the root of what it is to be good, and plurality
> the root of what it is to be evil.
>
> Dante Alighieri[1]

Europe before Europe

Politicians and traditional historians usually find the starting point
for their narrative on European integration and identity in classical
antiquity.[2] Postcolonial writers such as Enrique Dussel, however, have
denounced the European practice of constructing a direct lineage to
the ancient Greeks, identifying it as 'an ideological construct (...), a
conceptual by-product of the Eurocentric "Aryan myth" '.[3]

Europeans are not alone in connecting their origins to the ancient
Greeks. The great Malay kingdoms of Melakka and Srivijaya, for example in the *Hikayat Iskandar Zulkarnain* ('stories of Alexander the Great'),
whose origins go back to the fourteenth century, relate their history
to the exploits of Alexander the Great. In fact, the Malay civilization
appears strongly influenced by the ancient Greeks, as can be seen, for
example, in (rare) representations of the Buddha (showing the influence of ancient Greek and Roman models) and, of course, in Islamic
culture, which has absorbed the Hellenistic heritage as has no other
(apart from Eastern Orthodox Christianity). It is most clearly visible
today in the architecture of mosques (with characteristic Corinthian
capitals), but the Greek influence penetrates deep into Islamic thinking. Similarly, some contemporary Indians locate the origin of their
'argumentative' tradition in Greek philosophy, as Nobel Prize winner
Amartya Sen forcefully argued in a deservedly famous essay.[4]

The modern European discourse about Europe's Ancient Greek and
Roman origins likewise follows a venerable tradition that goes back

11

to Frankish kings, Germanic emperors, Renaissance minds, Enlightenment philosophers, Romantic artists, Fascist politicians and modern
lawmakers – though obviously what they all considered 'Greek' or
'Roman', and what they claimed to have inherited, diverged quite
substantially. In any case, although the ancient Greeks considered themselves the most civilized people in the world, they would have been
most surprised by the appropriation of their culture, both by modern
Europeans and by the 'medieval' Malays and Indians – perhaps less so by
the latter than by the former, as they knew that civilizations (other than
their own) were to be found to the east of the Aegean Sea rather than
in the barely inhabited northwest, populated by illiterate wanderers and
'the home of everything that was considered barbaric' (E. Dussel). Certainly the Greeks coined the term 'Europa', but Europa was a Phoenecian
princess, with no relation to the territory that we associate with the
term today, let alone its culture and politics. That did not really change
with the Roman Empire, which, mainly through conquest, would have
a more direct impact on the civilization that would emerge in the dark
woods of the north.

However, Romans did not use the term 'Europe' in a political or cultural sense that is relevant to today either. Although they conquered a
large part of what is nowadays considered Europe, their world remained
focused on the Mediterranean. After the fall of Rome at the end of the
fifth century, the historical continuity with the empire was largely broken in the areas west of the Adriatic and north of the Alps, in contrast to
the east where the East Roman Empire revived. Neither ancient Hellas
nor Rome can be considered direct antecedents of modern Europe. The
Roman Empire, whose remnants remained visible for centuries after the
fall of Rome and which was continued in the Byzantine Empire, certainly cast its shadow over the continent, but mainly functioned as a
dream, a chimera or perhaps an ambition to recreate the grandeur of
the ancient Romans in a new empire – for the French philosopher Rémi
Brague, it is precisely in the recurrent reference to the ancient Greeks
and Romans as an *alien* culture that underpins the many 'renaissances'
that characterize Europe and may well constitute its singularity.[5]

The Merovingians and the Franks certainly tried to tie their empires
to Roman legacies – Charlemagne by adopting the title of emperor
and Otto I by referring to the doctrine of *translatio imperii* ('transfer of
rule') and the creation of the Holy Roman Empire, which was explicitly intended as the continuation of the West Roman Empire. There
certainly were some continuities, particularly in the long transition
period between the fall of Rome and the emergence of new powerful

kingdoms in what we call Europe today. The early Middle Ages, for example, saw many references to Roman cultural forms, not least in architecture, though the origin of new imitations was often Byzantine. In reality, the impact of Roman practices remained quite limited and fragmented, and later evaporated altogether. Latin, for example, was gradually eclipsed and replaced by vernacular languages, a process more or less completed by the eighth century. Although parts of Roman law were integrated within Frankish and Germanic law, including the *lex salica*, the Roman legal tradition as such almost disappeared from the western areas of the late Roman Empire. The Roman public sphere continued in some form, but dwindled away in the west between the tenth and eleventh centuries.[6] New political and social traditions emerged, such as feudalism, with a few (if any) links to Roman or Greek practices.

Christendom's offspring

While there is no solid historical connection between classical antiquity and modern Europe, there are good reasons to look for origins of Europe in the Christian heritage, even if that is not as simple as it appears. Christianity was a particularly expansionist Middle Eastern religion that spread over Central Asia and North Africa before establishing itself slowly in the western parts of the Roman Empire, rather late in Roman history. It became a significant political factor under Constantine the Great and especially so once Christianity had become the state church of both the West and East Roman Empire in 380. Still, Christianity advanced rather slowly in Europe. It was only around 700 that wandering monks engaged in a sustained effort of Christianization beyond the limits of the former Roman Empire.[7]

Through this Christianization, new political and legal concepts were also introduced. This was, for example, the case with the idea of a sacral bond between God and monarch. The association of worldly with religious power in Christianity goes back to Constantine's convention of the Council of Nicaea (325), but has far more ancient origins. It was also continued by the East Roman and Byzantine emperors of Constantinople. Though in the era of the waning Roman period in the west clerics manifested themselves as earthly authorities, gradually the secular princes regained political and religious power, acting as the defenders of faith. Hence, the Frankish king Clovis' baptism in 508 was shared by his troops. Though Charlemagne's father, Pepin the Short, had already benefited from papal support, one more step was taken with the coronation of the Frankish king Charlemagne as emperor by Pope

Leo XIII in Rome in 800. Increasingly the European monarchs acted as 'Christ's deputies', which not only meant that they somehow received their power from God and by intercession from the Pope in Rome, but also that they felt competent to organize the Church, for example, by appointing bishops.[8]

While Christian monarchs saw themselves as holding ecclesiastical authority, the popes in Rome also yielded worldly power, particularly since the 'Donation of Pepin' in 756, which had created the Papal States. In fact, it was the Holy See of Rome which argued for universal papal supremacy over the whole church, including kings and emperors.[9] This diverged from the ancient Roman and Byzantine traditions and introduced a fundamental tension between a secular and a religious authority in the Catholic world, where, especially since the late eleventh century, the Holy See had claimed to be the supreme head of the Christian lands. This claim culminated in the Investiture Contest between the popes and the princes and monarchs in Italy, the Holy Roman Empire and England, where these leaders also saw themselves as responsible for ecclesiastical affairs within their own lands.

It is this close yet separate association between religious and worldly power that established 'Christendom' in Europe, which was further forged by the struggle against the expanding Islamic empires that advanced from the Mediterranean and, later, the southeast, as well as the 'pagan' empires of Scandinavians in the north and Slavs in the east, which were gradually brought into the realm of Christianity in post-Carolingian times. With the establishment of Christendom, expansionist wars, particularly those of Charlemagne, became holy wars, and the conquered peoples were compelled to convert and their original cultures eradicated as much as possible.[10] In this way Christendom actually unified the continent, not only by imposing common cultural practices but, through its universal ambition, also by eclipsing competing ethnic and political identities.

Some place the birth of Europe in this era, and herald Charlemagne as the forefather of Europe.[11] The argument for this is quite convincing, as Charlemagne portrayed himself as a Christian emperor reigning over a large part of what is today Western Europe. Contemporary sources occasionally associate the Frankish Empire with Europe, not always as a clear geographical entity but rather when the exact boundaries were undefined, or to express some sort of 'hegemony' of the Franks over other areas, such as the British Isles or the Iberian peninsula.[12] 'Europe' hence appears as an expression of domination and superiority. Earlier sources used the term 'Europe' to refer to invading tribes, as did Pope Gregory I at the end of the sixth century.[13] An unknown Mozarab chronicler living in Umayyad Spain described the Christian forces of the Frankish leader Charles Martel during the Battle of Tours (732) as 'Europeans' – which implied that the Umayyads were not considered such.[14]

However, the Carolingian empire was only a very loose one and covered only a part of present-day Europe. Moreover, it collapsed rather quickly after Charlemagne's death. In addition, the whole region was not yet stabilized. While the old Mediterranean order had not yet completely vanished, Europe remained a place of quasi-permanent mass migration, the migrant peoples changing the basic fabric of culture and society. Only at around the end of the first millennium did the migratory domino stop, when the last of the great invaders from the Asian steppes, the Magyars, no longer set in motion a chain of other migratory waves. The locals had stood up and fought; they knew there was much at stake and had built stone castles and wore modern armour. Nonetheless, the invaders still left their mark, leaving behind a more diversified ethnic landscape in Central and Eastern Europe.[15]

In the tenth century a network of political, economic and cultural interaction and commonalities had evolved, connecting the Atlantic to the Volga and the Baltic to the Mediterranean. Moreover, in Central Europe a mighty empire emerged that was sometimes referred to as European.[16] The German king Otto III was crowned Emperor of the Holy Roman Empire in 996 by a Pope whom Otto himself had appointed to the See of Rome. By so doing, the emperor not only established his worldly power, but also affirmed his authority over the affairs of the Church. In the meantime, though, the Catholic Church established a separate legal order, based on canon law, which set the Church apart from secular society. By so doing, the Church contributed considerably to establishing a new common legal order all over Europe, based upon common Christian views and a merger of different legal traditions and practices, which would shape European thinking for centuries.[17]

In this context, Europe and the *Christianitas*, the world of the Christians, could become synonymous in the eleventh century.[18] Pope Urban II situated Christendom in 'Europe' when calling for a crusade to liberate the Holy Sepulchre in Jerusalem in 1099, allegedly referring to the threat to 'the small part of Europe which is ours' after '[the Saracens and Turks] had conquered Spain and the Balearic Islands'.[19] 'Ours' in this and similar texts incidentally included Constantinople. This appears a more fitting time in which to place the beginnings of Europe, even if the term was still not widely used and even though competing concepts, such as the land of the Franks, coexisted and the Holy Roman Empire remained a loose confederation. But perhaps the latter also illustrates the fundamental departure of this new 'Europe' from the centralized and unifying traditions of the Roman Empire. Until the late eighteenth and early nineteenth centuries, the political system of Europe was characterized by loose boundaries, overlapping authorities and flexible vertical hierarchies.

The context of this draws attention to the opposition to Islam, though one should be cautious here. Relations between Christian monarchs and Islamic empires were not always antagonistic. Jansen Enikel's chronicle of the world illustrates that 'Europe', even in the thirteenth century, still included Moors (Muslims) within its geographical concept. It also comprised Armenians, albeit Christian, living in an area considerably further to the east of Europe.[20] As Malcolm Yapp observed, the crusades may even have hindered the equation of Christendom and Europe, as the crusaders were termed 'Franks' and 'Christians' rather than Europeans.[21] Furthermore, especially in the Mediterranean, intensive trade relations persisted and Islamic motifs, particularly in architecture, continued to inspire Christian artisans and artists, even if as a general rule they did not employ Muslims in any way whatsoever.[22] Nevertheless, an anti-Islamic tone underpinning the concept of Christendom could be discerned throughout the whole of Europe, particularly in the Iberian West. It was also more or less clear that Europe was a separate region and, perhaps, also a culture or civilization, as Christianization gave the continent a relatively distinctive character. The latter also implied that it shared the exclusivity of the Roman Christian state religion.[23]

Although some emphasize that European medieval society, certainly in its later years, had a great deal of influence from other cultures,[24] medieval Christendom in reality was an exclusive club in which non-Christians were not welcome and 'heretics' of all sorts discriminated against, compelled to convert or persecuted, as Cathars, Jews and Muslims, among others, experienced.[25] From the early days of the Christianization of Europe, and particularly from the eighth century up until the wars of religion in the sixteenth century, Christendom's history was largely one of destruction and violence, eradicating anything deemed pagan or heretical. Hrabanus Maurus, Bishop of Mainz between 847 and 856 and known as the *Praeceptor Germaniae* (the teacher of Germany), knew exactly what he meant when he said: 'Christianity destroys errors.'[26] The medieval Christian identity, even if more complex, tolerant and sophisticated attitudes did exist and periods of persecution alternated with times of relative stability during which such people were tolerated, was basically totalitarian, essentialist and firmly based on the violent alterization of others.[27]

There were several reasons why this was so: Christianity had from antiquity already developed into a universal but exclusive religion for which there was no salvation beyond Christ. Hence, it was the duty of all Christians, and in the medieval mindset certainly of rulers, to promote, by all possible means, true Christianity – which certainly implied a tendency to determine the exact boundaries between the truth and that which they deemed falsehood. Incidentally, since Augustinus, peace in this respect had been associated with order and unity or 'ordered unity' (*ordinate concordia*), and, as such, with the victory over diversity – diversity, considered essentially as dissidence from God's will, was hence the cause of war and, as such, detrimental to peace. This very fundamental idea would dominate the view of peace until at least the late eighteenth and early nineteenth centuries.[28]

Certainly in the early days of Christianization, the demonization of non-Christians also expressed a fundamental uncertainty about Christian identity itself and was actually an instrument of Christianization.[29] The religious choice of the monarch had a profound political meaning: royal conversion demanded careful consideration, especially as different Christianities competed in the early days of Christendom.[30] Hence, in contrast to many other civilizations (particularly in Asia), Christian Europe became a homogenous society with little dissent. Still, there were more relaxed periods during which minorities, in particular Jews, were mostly left in peace. These alternated with periods of persecution and intolerance. As a result of internal conflicts between secular and religious elites, European Christendom in the twelfth and thirteenth centuries developed into a 'persecuting society', which targeted heretics as well as Jews, Muslims and other 'different people', such as lepers.[31] In the fifteenth century, when the fear of the approaching Apocalypse underpinned much of the religious rage, millenarian prophesies boosted eruptions of violence.[32]

Though there were periods and places of relative tolerance – such as Norman Sicily and Aragon – medieval Christian Europe always appeared anything but welcoming to outsiders. In this respect, in the absence of much contact with the external world, Jews especially functioned as the 'outsiders within', in which Europe's Christian self was mirrored. Though they were 'related', they were considered alien and increasingly isolated, particularly from the thirteenth century. The same applied to the Muslims in Christian territories, especially in the Iberian Peninsula when the *Reconquista* advanced. There, Muslims and Jews enjoyed only a limited protection from the Crown.[33] Increasingly after the *Reconquista* in 1492 – which drove the Umayyads out of the Iberian Peninsula – they were either persecuted, expelled or – the standard treatment – compelled to convert. Hence, few Muslim merchants ventured far beyond Mediterranean harbours (this is surprising, given the amount of trade with the Islamic world): the distinct opposite to the customary interaction and integration which occurred along the Silk Road and at Indian Ocean ports. 'Eurocentric' scholars emphasize the development of universities in medieval Europe, where 'other civilizations and cultures were studied' (one must assume that the author of these words refers to the study of Ancient Greek, Arabic and Jewish texts), as evidence of Europe's 'openness to the world'.[34] To be sure, European culture and scientific development benefited greatly from Ancient Greek, Jewish and Arabic translations from the twelfth century onwards.[35] However, this was by no means unique to Europe: non-European civilizations also had their inventors and explorers, such as the Persian historian of India Al-Biruni in the tenth century or the fourteenth century North-African traveller Ibn Battuda, not to speak of ancient Chinese travellers such as Zhang Qian, who opened up the Silk Road routes to the Chinese in the second century BC; Gan Ying, a Chinese envoy who reached the Persian Gulf in his quest to find Rome; or Fa-hsien, a Buddhist monk who explored Central, South and Southeast Asia in the early fifth century AD. The singularity perhaps resides rather in that – apart from some occasional Muslim mapmaker or Muslim captives employed as translators of Arabic manuscripts, or even doctors in border regions such as Sicily[36] – no foreign scholars or experts from outside Europe were to be found at European centres of learning or courts. This stands in contrast to common practices in Arabic, Persian, Indian or Chinese civilizations, which attracted scholars and experts from anywhere, irrespective of origin or creed – hence, 'European' scholars and advisors could later be found at Muslim universities, Persian courts or Chinese academies. Medieval Christian Europe was anything but the cosmopolitan region, 'open to the world', that some imagine it was.

Admittedly, the continent became connected to the great, mainly trans-Asian trade routes both overland and overseas from around the mid-thirteenth century, and major cities both in the Mediterranean and the North (Bruges and Ghent) developed into world trade centres.[37] However, even then the cultural exchange remained rather limited compared to the intensity of interaction in Asian civilizations, essentially only focusing on the commodities deemed desirable. Although it is fashionable to consider Europe 'multicultural', in medieval and early modern European times it was so only to a very limited extent (depending on the criteria used to distinguish cultures) and mainly restricted to borderlands such as Sicily – although there too possibilities were limited[38] – or the Muslim lands of either Al-Andalus, the Turkish–Mongol Cuman-Kipchak confederation (Cumania) or the Ottoman Empire in the east. There at least 'people of the book' received opportunities to develop and shine – though they were also discriminated against: Islamic lands were more tolerant compared to Christian, but less so than other civilizations more to the east.

Reorganizing Christian Europe

As Europe became Christian, Christianity gave it a distinctive and relatively homogenous identity. However, Latin and East Roman Christianities soon drifted apart, and by the mid-eleventh century the break was complete. The old East Roman Empire declined, gradually becoming essentially Greek, 'Byzantine'. It remained obviously Christian, but also Roman: it spent a great deal of energy in debating its Roman origins.[39]

One of the main differences between Eastern and Western Christendom concerned the Pope in Rome, whose authority as supreme head of the Church both in ecclesiastical and political matters was rejected by the East Romans. Orthodox Christianity, apart from divergent theological, spiritual and ecclesiastical conceptions, did not experience the same tension between secular and religious authority as Western Christendom: the patriarch and the Byzantine emperor, both residing in Constantinople, remained closely associated, with the emperor dominating the Church. Though connections with western monarchs still existed, in the eyes of the west Byzantines became alien and were increasingly seen as an enemy, as several fatal incidents during the crusades illustrate. Hence, the term 'Christendom' actually referred to 'Latin', that is Western Christendom. However, Europe and (Western) Christendom were still rarely equated.

Europe in late medieval times consisted of 'states', albeit loose ones, without clear boundaries. The idea that they constituted a fundamental unity appears largely absent. And one of the basic features of Christendom was the inability of the 'Christian kings', as well as clerical and worldly authorities, to co-operate, as the many medieval wars demonstrated.[40] Moreover, the ecclesiastical authority of the Catholic Church was also regularly challenged. Due to the intertwining of church and state, religious dissenters always threatened established order, and worldly authorities were effectively used to crush them. However, when princes and monarchs also joined the dissent, as happened with the Reformation, the whole international order was suddenly threatened.

In the thirteenth and fourteenth centuries the term 'Europe' appears with some regularity, albeit far less than *Christianitas*. It is often in a context of confrontation or comparison with other cultures, African and Asian, though predominantly Muslim, that prompts the use of the term 'Europe'. After the fall of Constantinople in 1453 and the completion of the 'Reconquista' in 1492, *Christianitas* and Europe became synonymous with one another, though the latter term was still not often used.[41] If it was, it referred to a certain territory inhabited by Christians and ruled by Christian monarchs, in contrast to the lands of pagans and Muslims. However, the term 'Christendom' became increasingly associated with internal division and conflict.[42]

Though most of them simply took sides, intellectuals often perceived this division within Christendom as a reason to plead for a European 'organization'. The French lawyer Pierre Dubois is a case in point. In his most famous pamphlet, *De Recuperatione Terrae Sanctae* (About the Recovery of the Holy Lands), in 1306, he considered peace among the Christian states as a necessary condition for a successful crusade. While Pope Boniface VIII strongly emphasized papal supremacy (*Unam Sanctam*, 1302), Dubois, though respecting the Pope's spiritual authority, relegated the leadership of such a crusade to the 'most Catholic' French king, Philip IV 'the Fair', who was to unite the Christian monarchs. Incidentally, the king and the Pope were engaged in a long-standing conflict which would survive the death of both protagonists and eventually provoke the Western Schism (1378–1417). Dubois' proposal must be viewed from this perspective, as a case in the fight for supremacy of the Christian world.

More radical thinkers than Dubois imagined a political order in which the authority of government would lie solely in the hands of the secular authorities. That was the basic argument of Dante Alighieri's *Monarchia* (Monarchy) of 1307, as well as the more developed proposals of Marsilius of Padua, formulated in his tract *Defensor pacis* (The Defendor of Peace) in 1324. In the latter, the professor at the University of Paris argued that the leaders of city-states, kingdoms or empires should be elected by the citizens and follow the policies established by a 'Christian Council', which excluded (direct) clerical interference.[43] The famous allegory of good and bad government, painted in fresco by Ambrogio Lorenzetti in Sienna in 1338–1339, by stressing the compelling nature of justice above all, actually carries a similar, profoundly republican message.[44]

In the meantime, however, a longing for unity in Christendom grew stronger, fuelled by the menace of the Ottoman Turks in the east. In the fifteenth century the association between Christendom and Europe became part of a normative discourse, in which Europe appears as a region 'privileged by God'. It was hence 'united' in a common faith. Humanist scholars such as Desiderius Erasmus and Juan Luis Vives, for example in the latter's *De Europae dissidiis et bello turcico dialogus* (On Europe's Wars and the Campaign against the Turk, 1525), lamented the division of Christendom and referred to Europe in terms of its opposition to the Turks. For the humanist scholar and papal diplomat – and later Pope Pius II – Enea Silvio Piccolomini, writing in 1551, the fall of Constantinople meant that now 'we have been hit and brought down in Europe, which is our home country, in our home and our seat'.[45] As Pope Pius II, he systematically identified the *Respublica christiana* with Europe in his appeals for a new crusade in 1459–1464. Gradually, the view that Europe had to unite first to face the Turks prevailed – previously the hope was that the division of *Christianitas* would be healed *after* Jerusalem had been liberated.[46] Still, one should not overestimate this opposition between Christians and Muslims. The rhetoric of an absolute religious division must also be viewed as a way to reinforce the political ambitions of the Habsburg monarchs. The Dutch Republic, France, Britain and several Italian city-states saw no impediment to concluding treaties of friendship with the Ottomans. France and the Ottoman Empire, for example, constituted a lasting alliance in 1536 that bound the two empires together until Napoleon's invasion of Egypt in 1798, while the British, after the excommunication of Elizabeth I in 1570, equally entertained a centuries-long relationship of cordiality with the Sublime Porte. And the very same Piccolomini, alias Pius II, wrote a letter to Suleiman the Magnificent to suggest the latter convert to Catholicism and so heal the division of Christendom and establish universal peace.[47]

Gradually the terrain was paved for more concrete (yet still quite utopian) ideas about the organization of Christendom. The King of Bohemia, George of Podiebrad, himself a Hussite and hence, in the eyes of Catholics, a heretic, proposed the creation of a federation of Christian lands in his famous *Tractatus* of 1464, declaring the need to establish an effective counterweight to the 'abominable Turk' who had conquered Constantinople in 1453 and threatened to move even further to the west. The 'four nations' which, in his rather peculiar interpretation, would take the lead in this endeavour were, in this order, the Gallicans, the Germans, the Italians and the Spanish. This federation would convene regularly in an elected legislative and judicial council, grafted on to the model of the ecumenical councils of the Christian Church. Each representative would have one vote, and the council would arrange a 'president', an executive body and proper finances of its own. As members of the same faith (not 'Church'), all would agree to resolve disputes in a peaceful way. Incidentally, the role allotted to the Holy See was marginal: the Pope would guarantee the payment of money and to impose the establishment of peace between Christian princes, while also theoretically having to persuade the Italians to build a fleet for the war against the Ottomans. There was no possibility he would play a greater role in the federation or in the war, let alone lead it, and nor would the Emperor of the Holy Roman Empire, who was not even mentioned.[48]

The Reformation and the domestic organization of Europe

The sixteenth century witnessed the emergence of a momentous event in the history of Europe: the Reformation, which shook the foundations of the medieval order and led to an age of unseen violence and war which ravaged the continent for at least 150 years. It precluded an existential crisis in which the natural order was questioned, resulting in traditional ways of settling disputes becoming obsolete and unavailable.

However, the Reformation and the ensuing wars offered opportunities, especially for monarchs to increase their power and to terminate their age-old disputes with clerical authorities. Some of them saw the chance of seizing Church property – a reason why some monarchs actually joined the Reformation. But the wars, more specifically, allowed them to tip the balance of their long-lasting contention for power with the Church in their favour. The Reformation, though unintended, therefore settled the conflict in Christendom between the Royal Crown and the papal tiara. But the perception that the world of Christendom had split implied that references to the *Christianitas* had quickly made room for a geographical term, 'Europe'. The parallel discovery of new lands across the Pacific and the wave of exploration and conquest that followed somewhat surprisingly did not modify that. 'Europe', not *Christianitas*, was the term to which 'Europeans' referred when distinguishing themselves from the rest of the world. This emerging European identity, however, did not require in any way an organization of Europe. The divisions of Christendom did.

According to the standard interpretation, the wars of religion ended more or less in the mid-seventeenth century with the signing of the Peace of Westphalia (1648). However, the Peace did not make war in Europe redundant: France and the Spanish Habsburgs continued their fight for the next 11 years, while the English Civil War (1642–1651) remained unaffected. And many more other wars were to follow. Moreover, the Peace did not organize Europe on the basis of national sovereignty, as was the standard interpretation until very recently.[49] The relationship between the Holy Roman Empire and the German lands, for example, remained virtually unchanged; that is, they remained fairly autonomous within the boundaries set by the imperial system. Neither did the treaties introduce the concept of *cuius regio, illius religio*, by which people had to follow the confession of their sovereign (the *jus reformandi*), as is still widely believed.[50] That principle was to some extent attempted in the mid-sixteenth century, most notably in the Treaty of Augsburg in 1555. However, it was a system hard to sustain when princes converted to other religions and was partially reversed in 1648, when the system was returned to its former position of 1624, thereby forbidding princes to convert. In addition, the famous *jus emigrandi*, the right to emigrate with all one's possessions in order to follow one's religious conscience, was not quite an option for the majority of the population. The Westphalian Peace did introduce rules on the toleration of different minority denominations – initially only Catholicism and Lutheranism, later extended to others – within the areas in which they were valid. Catholics and Protestants were attributed equal rights in the imperial Diet and other decision-making bodies in the Holy Roman Empire as well. Nevertheless, although one could argue that to a certain extent the bond between territoriality and confession slackened, Westphalia maintained the idea that religious diversity was essentially detrimental to peace. It cherished the principle of religious conformity, accepting some exceptions for the sake of political stability.

Even if its significance has been overestimated or misinterpreted, the Peace contributed a great deal to redrawing the European political and religious landscape. While non-territorial entities such as the Hanseatic League and monastic military orders were eclipsed, territorial states did become stronger, with much clearer boundaries, although no strong national feelings developed and no clear hierarchies between different spaces and political units (such as trade companies with extensive political powers) yet existed.[51] Although the Holy Roman Empire remained a significant political institution, some lands developed into mighty states, such as Brandenburg, Saxony and Bavaria, as well as the Archduchy of Austria. The Habsburg monarchs, while elected as Holy Roman Emperors, ruled the vast Austrian Habsburg Monarchy extending far beyond the Holy Roman Empire – this particular situation was in some ways illustrative of the complex territorial organization of Europe and hardly compatible with the notion of a modern sovereign state. Other loose political conglomerates or 'empires' became powerful nation states or 'nation empires', such as France and Great Britain. Louis XIV actually hoped to reconstitute the old empire of Charlemagne. Not only did he fail, but his references to that Christian empire further discredited the imaginary notion of a *res publica christiana* and stimulated the use of Europe as an alternative *topos*.[52] In many cases royal or princely power was extended, giving way to 'royal absolutism' (however much the term has fallen out of favour). But strong states were also created through other forms of government, such as in the Dutch Republic and even in those cases where royal power was restrained, as in the Polish–Lithuanian Commonwealth and, of course, Britain, where the Bill of Rights (1689) curtailed royal power and introduced or reinforced basic liberties and the sovereignty of Parliament. Gradually, then, but also very firmly, the concepts of territorial sovereignty and fixed borders did begin to impose themselves by the eighteenth century, although other political structures continued.

Also very important was the relationship between church and state, which changed substantially. Quite obviously the Pope had lost his authority in Protestant lands, and in the new Lutheran and Reformed states – as well as in Britain – the churches became subordinate to the state: the princes and monarchs either became heads of the churches or at least obtained important powers of control over them, even if a separation of their sphere of influence was respected. Even in Catholic states, where the Council of Trent reinforced the episcopal structures, the monarchs strongly extended their authority over the Church and emphasized loyalty and obedience to the state and its sovereign: Gallicanism became a major policy, not only in France.

The introduction of forms of religious toleration must be seen from this perspective. The religious disputes gave way to various forms of modern (European) scepticism, as with Michel de Montaigne. Scepticism could lead to toleration – as the truth, also in matters religious, cannot be known – but did not necessarily do so. Most sceptics in the sixteenth and seventeenth century actually followed Justus Lipsius' recommendation that heretics should be persecuted, as 'here is no place for clemencie, burne, sawe asunder, for it is better that one member be cast away, than that the whole body runne to ruine', as his advice read in 1594.[53] Political thinkers such as Hugo Grotius and Thomas Hobbes would continue the same line of argument, and legitimate extensive state authority over matters of religion in order to preserve peace and harmony. Only when, for whatever reason, state power was not capable of imposing one view, was it 'tolerated' to allow free expressions of faith. The main early modern thinker on the new religious and political order, John Locke, considered toleration only insofar as it was 'in keeping with the Gospel and co-extensive with reason'.[54] Actually the defence of a relatively 'positive' toleration – relatively as it only applied to Christians – was adopted by some 'evangelical' theologians in the wake of Martin Luther, along the line of reasoning that free access to the Scriptures would automatically lead to enlightenment and the acceptance of truth. The latter interpretation would eventually prevail in colonial and early republican North America.[55] But most 'dissident' churches actually opposed religious diversity. Incidentally, the laws on toleration in Europe also generated division, sectarianism and conflict in practice.[56]

The limited and conditional recognition of toleration obscures a deeper dynamic of confessionalization (Heinz Schilling), through which European states strived towards homogeneity, which was mainly conceived from a religious perspective. As confession remained the most meaningful source of identity and conflict, if possible sovereigns adopted one state church, which became subdued to and integrated within the political system. In return, the state supported the Church, in particular by suppressing dissidents. However, this also compelled churches to emphasize their theological and ecclesiastical distinctiveness and purity, as it became essential to distinguish between accepted and non-accepted religious traditions. The process was further paralleled at the level of local communities, which also underlined their distinctiveness (even sometimes at odds with the clerical directives). Notwithstanding their differences, notable exceptions and inconsistencies, European societies during the 'confessional age' all expressed a similar abhorrence of diversity, considered as the root cause of war.[57] Hence, European states, in line with the very idea of Christendom, continued to aim towards religious homogeneity in their lands or, if that was unachievable, tried to bring the different religious factions under public control and supervision. Dissenters and (religious) minorities were looked upon with suspicion as possibly disloyal subjects and traitors whose allegiances were elsewhere, other than with the ruling sovereign.

The Revocation of the Edict of Nantes by Louis XIV in 1685 serves as an ominous example of what could happen if the king deemed it possible to crush the heretics. Likewise, the Austrian Archduke and Emperor of the Holy Roman Empire, Charles VI, adopted a policy of religious orthodoxy and inquisition in the 1730s (actually he was compelled to do so as a result of the initiative of the Archbishop of Salzburg in the 1720s). He even ended the *jus emigrandi*, but introduced mass deportation of Protestants to newly conquered lands from the Ottomans in Transylvania.[58] Nevertheless, the combination of confessionalization on the one hand, in particular the subordination of churches to the demands of the state, and the gradual toleration of individual liberty in matters of religion and conscience on the other, at least insofar as they did not threaten the established order, made religious dissent less of an issue.

Paradoxically, however, confessionalization also paved the way for toleration and the recognition of religious diversity, as it actually considered the interests of the state and internal harmony and peace as the supreme values. Sometimes it would require too high a price to stick to one church, in which case toleration could be considered. Where toleration was implemented, it usually applied only to the main 'denominations' or 'confessions', rather than atheists, people of faiths other than Christianity (Jews, Muslims) or Christian groups that threatened the local political or ecclesiastical order. Hence, it excluded groups that were considered 'unreliable', such as Anabaptists or Catholics in Protestant lands. Protestant sovereigns particularly suspected Catholics of disloyalty because of their alleged obedience to the Pope (an obsession that would be further developed in the nineteenth century as a side effect of nationalism, even more beneficial to the nation state as a prime source of loyalty and identity). However, suspicions of disloyalty could actually be addressed to all dissenters.[59] Religious diversity remained, in the predominant view, contrary to God's will, but also and especially detrimental to maintaining peace and order, and, as the wars of religion had demonstrated, potentially lethal for the royal thrones.

There were some major exceptions where toleration became more widely accepted, as was the case in Brandenburg-Prussia (mainly because the monarchy lacked resources and needed all the support it could get, hence a very open immigration policy), the Polish–Lithuanian Commonwealth, the Dutch Republic and England, though confessional dynamics can be easily discerned in the latter two. After all, the Glorious Revolution which gave way to the Bill of Rights aimed at eradicating the political clout of Catholics and implied the sidelining of them. The Dutch Republic is another, less obvious example: not only were religious policies clearly discriminatory, allowing maximum privileges to the Reformed Church as the only recognized 'public Church',[60] in the Dutch overseas colonies, including, incidentally, New Amsterdam, the Reformed Church did function as an established 'state church'.[61] This did not mean, however, that no interaction existed: much research has illustrated the 'ecumenism of daily life' (Wilhelm Frijhoff) virtually everywhere in Europe. In this respect Christine Kooi, with regard to the Dutch Republic, recently introduced a very illuminating distinction between the confessional sphere of intense mutual denunciation and conflict between denominations, the civic sphere of daily interaction and tolerance, and the private sphere where distinctions were upheld, but in reality often transgressed.[62] But such transgressions were strictly secondary to the dominant order.

In the wake of European expansion and its colonization of the Americas and its forays into Africa and Asia – where European advances had remained limited – Europe to some extent also welcomed non-Europeans. Most of them were slaves, but there were also free men and (very few) women who ventured into the continent. Apart from diplomats and missions from lands as far afield as India, China and Japan, by far the majority of them were Christians, though there were also Jews. After the Catholic conquest of the Iberian Peninsula in 1492, Jews had been forced to convert, or were either persecuted or expelled from Spain. As a result, many of them had wandered throughout the rest of Europe, eventually finding refuge in such places as the great ports of Bordeaux and Amsterdam, though even there they were also often victims of persecution. In general the gates of Europe, still considered as the bastion of Christendom, remained closed to non-Christians. It is noteworthy, however, that race or ethnicity apparently mattered less in Europe itself than in the colonies.[63]

An everlasting peace through a Christian federation of Europe?

Confessionalization and the introduction of a limited degree of toleration reduced religious conflict in Early Modern Europe. Nevertheless, the continent remained a battlefield, although religion gradually became subdued to more mundane issues of power and succession. No authority existed that could function as arbiter to calm international relations and impose peace.[64]

In the context of these turbulent times, 'utopian' thinkers developed quite radical plans to generate peace through a European association of Christian monarchs – non-Christians usually remained excluded. These peace projects included deconfessionalized politics and religious freedom for Christians, on the one hand because confessional unification appeared utterly unrealistic, and on the other because individual beliefs were increasingly perceived, by some at least, as a matter of personal conscience and part of man's liberty. That was certainly the case for the 'Grand Project' which was drafted in 1603 by Maximilien de Béthune, the Duke of Sully, a Huguenot and a minister of the French king Henri IV, on whose behalf he wrote the plan. Henri IV had converted to Catholicism after being a Huguenot himself, and had promulgated the Edict of Nantes, which (provisionally, as it turned out) ended the French wars of religion, five years earlier, in 1589.

> God holds the wills and deeds of men in his hand, and still leaves such a large amount of people rambling on about religion, which educates rulers enough to leave God the realm of the spirit and to be content with bodily services for civil and temporal things, so that he only has to have declared by each of his associates the religious that he wishes to be followed.[65]

Influenced by the experiences of Italian city-states and the ideas of Niccolo Machiavelli, Sully suggested a Christian Europe – excluding both the Ottoman and the Russian Empire – that would consist of monarchies 'nearly equal in power, as to kingdoms, wealth, extent and dominion' in order to respect some sort of balance of power (implying the breaking up of the Habsburg Empire, France's main political adversary, suggesting his real aim could have been an alternative European order beneficial to France rather than perpetual peace). But in addition it would include a political body constituted by representatives of the European states – at least the most important ones, 15 in total – which would be able to produce 'an unchangeable peace and an everlasting commerce' between its members. Sully's 'federal council', incidentally, should have the right of arbitration and to levy an army for the fight against the Ottomans. Here Sully stands in the tradition of Dubois and Podiebrad and confirms the oppositional stance towards the Muslim world.

As early as the seventeenth century, European expansion gave way to affirmations of Europe's – or rather Christendom's – superiority, as the pre-eminent Renaissance Dominican Thommaso Campanella (1568–1639) argued when he not only confirmed Charles V's universalist ambitions but also proposed a plan for a European federation with a seat in Rome. The great German philosopher Gottfried Wilhelm Leibniz (1646–1716) actually shared this view of a superior Christian civilization which would expand and spread the Christian faith, emphasizing the unity of a common Christian European culture even though he argued for toleration between Christians.[66] However, there were some (rare) alternative views, such as the cosmopolitan pacifism of Émeric Crucé. This humble French monk also extended the principle of liberty of conscience to other faiths, as 'it does not belong to men to punish or correct the mistakes of faith'.[67] His roadmap for a universal perpetual peace, as can be found in his *Le Nouveau Cynée* (1623), nevertheless focused on Europe. Crucé foresaw an extended European Council which would meet in Venice on a regular basis, made up principally of the Pope, the Ottoman sultan, the German emperor, the King of France and so on, with the object of settling conflicts by arbitration. Non-interference and respect for the inviolability of borders were crucial. But above all Crucé argued for establishing an economic base for the peace, as self-interest was a better way to realize peace than noble principles. Hence he argued for the introduction of free trade a single currency, equal weights and measurements, and the protection of business and commerce, principles that could be applied everywhere.

Crucé's plan for a universal and perpetual peace, today almost forgotten, was far ahead of its time. Most peace plans, however, emphasized the respect for national sovereignty, the introduction of rules of law and above all of justice, imagined in a European or 'Western' space only. The latter was, as William Penn's famous *Essay towards the Present and Future Peace of Europe* (1693), observed in a real Augustinian way, the essential condition and means towards peace. Justice, however, results from government:

> But to return, I say, Justice is the Means of Peace, betwixt the Government and the People, and one Man and Company and another. It prevents Strife, and at last ends it: For besides Shame or Fear, to contend longer, he or they being under Government are constrained to bound their Desires and Resentment with the Satisfaction the Law gives. Thus Peace is maintain'd by Justice, which is a Fruit of Government, as Government, is from Society, and Society from Consent.[68]

For Penn the sovereign princes emanated from society and represented the nation. Therefore, to realize justice and peace they should organize at a European level an 'Imperial Diet, Parliament, or Estates' that could act as arbiter and international meeting place, recognizing the right of national sovereignty. International relations should hence obey 'rules of Justice and Prudence' rooted in the Christian faith – not quite the same as a balance of power or of Machiavellian realism, but also not universal, as the rules would not apply to non-Christians.

The illustrious Quaker proposed disarmament as a major step towards peace. Unlike Sully or Saint-Pierre later, he foresaw a representation of each state according to its size, an idea that would be developed further in the more rigorous plan of another Quaker, John Bellers, *Some Reasons for a European State* (1710). Remarkably, Penn would admit Russia and the Ottoman Empire as members of his European organization, 'as seems but fit and just' (section VIII). This does not mean, however, that he abandoned the concept of Christendom and the equation with Europe. His plan would actually benefit Christendom, as 'the Reputation of Christianity will, in some Degree, be recovered in the Sight of Infidels; which, by the many Bloody and unjust Wars of Christians, not only with them, but with one another, hath been greatly impaired' (section X). Such an alliance would also offer security against a Turkish invasion – 'The Great Security it will be to Christians against the Inroads of the Turk, in their most Prosperous Fortune' – but that was obviously not the main issue. It would nevertheless, as Penn subtly remarked, also prevent Christian princes from being able 'to oppose, or break such a Union', a barely disguised reference to the alliances of France and England with the Ottomans.[69]

The French writer Charles-Irénée Castel, known as the Abbé de Saint-Pierre, who had read and even translated Penn's essay, went even further in rejecting the principle of a balance of power in his *Projet pour rendre la paix perpétuelle en Europe* (A Project for Settling an Everlasting Peace in Europe), his alleged proposal to end the War of the Spanish Succession. In vain, as it turned out, since the idea of a balance of power underpinned the Peace of Utrecht in 1713, which settled the Spanish succession and halted, at least temporarily, French ambition for European hegemony. As he considered neither treaties nor leagues to maintain a balance of power sufficient to avoid war and maintain peace 'because it can never procure any sufficient Security for the Execution of Treaties', Saint-Pierre proposed a 'European union' of Christian sovereigns, based on the (idealized) model of the Holy Roman Empire. As in his 1717 *Projet pour rendre la paix perpétuelle entre souverains chrétiens* (A Project for Settling an Everlasting Peace between Christian Sovereigns) Saint-Pierre explicitly restricted his Europe to the Christian monarchs, including the Russian tsar. Although he initially conceived his model for the world at large, he admitted that 'even though in the following Ages most of the Sovereigns of Asia and Africa might desire to be receiv'd into the Union, yet this Prospect would seem so remote and so full of Difficulties, that it would cast an Air of Impossibility upon the whole Project'. He actually foresaw that a Christian European union 'would soon become the Arbiter of the Sovereigns' of 'the Indies'.[70] Inspired by Hobbes, he pleaded for reason and the rule of law in international relations, laid down in a European constitution. These should underpin the right of compelling arbitration. Incidentally, according to Saint-Pierre, reason would not only lead to the conclusion that peace was more beneficial than war, but would also demonstrate the superiority of Christianity. Furthermore, just as Sully and Crucé had, Saint-Pierre saw international trade as a way to peace.[71] The latter has been a powerful trope in the European discourse ever since, especially after new theories of the importance of free trade and commerce – such as Adam Smith's *An Inquiry into the Nature and Causes of the Wealth of Nations* (1776) – caught the imagination. For the French Physiocrats, free trade did indeed constitute a necessary condition for peace, and few concluded that to establish peace in Europe, the continent should gradually be federated. The latter idea, considered, for example, by Turgot, a minister of Louis XVI in the 1770s, would nevertheless gain prominence much later.[72]

The reference to non-Christian lands invites us to point to the expansion of European empires overseas: Charles V reigned over an empire that stretched over Europe, the Americas and Manila in East Asia. The Catholic Spanish and (to a lesser extent) Portuguese would actively promote the proselytization of Catholicism in the worlds they conquered, by so doing extending the notion of Christendom – making the term less and less useful to refer to the European continent. Protestant merchants and colonizers, including religious refugees, would incidentally implant their religion in distant lands as well, without, at least prior to the eighteenth century, very actively promoting their faith.

3
Enlightenment, Revolution and the Evaporating Dream of a Perpetual Peace

> If only Europe wanted to awaken again! And if only a state of states, a new political theory of science, were impending. (...) It is impossible that worldly powers come into equilibrium by themselves; only a third element, that is worldly and supernatural at the same time, can achieve this task. No peace can be concluded among the conflicting powers. All peace is only an illusion, only a temporary truce.
>
> Novalis, 1799[1]

The continuing perspective of war

Parallel to the continuing wars in Europe, nations considerably extended their power through taxation, new forms of administration and militarization. The mid-eighteenth century, especially after the Seven Years' War – a great deal of which was fought outside Europe and exhausted the treasuries of the belligerents – constituted a pivotal period which compelled states to improve their state apparatus and augment their revenues, which implied better organization, centralization and policing.[2]

This development had some remarkable consequences. One was a growing aversion to the politics of the absolutist rulers, particularly from the new merchant class that benefitted from increased economic opportunities – not the least as a result of European colonial expansion – but saw its benefits curtailed by increasing taxes. 'The stupidity of wars, both wars of religion and succession, and wars of trade and ministers' was deeply resented, and the absolutist rulers were deemed responsible.[3] This gave way to new ways of thinking about government.

Republicanism and the separation of powers were increasingly seen as means to moderate the ambitions of monarchs – for Kant, republicanism was the most rational form of government, and as the people would never prefer war over peace, the best guarantee to avoid war and generate peace. However, the impression grew that peace could no longer be conceived of as 'a state of tranquil repose', but rather as the result of a continuous process and therefore also increasingly, as Kant in particular observed – out of reach: it appears that with Christendom, the ideal of perpetual peace also vanished.[4]

The main instrument for safeguarding peace in this context was the idea of a balance of power, for which Francesco Guicciardini, David Hume and William Robertson developed the intellectual foundations. The Peace of Utrecht, which concluded the War of the Spanish Succession in 1713, was one of the first instances where the 'balance of power' theory as such was effectively used to pacify Europe. Its effect was less than had been hoped for, which certainly contributed to the idea that 'eternal peace' remained a utopia: Europe did still experience major wars after 1713, although most of the battles were fought overseas and imperial opposition gained importance. Hence, it remained, as Voltaire – often considered as a proponent of the balance of power, also by contemporaries – conceded, a difficult act.[5]

While in the seventeenth century international relations were framed in terms of Christendom, the latter concept gradually evaporated as the sovereigns gained control over the churches and international politics secularized. Europe manifested itself very strongly as a unifying concept, which transcended values and culture, but had a political significance as well. Voltaire represented a radical expression of new 'Enlightened' philosophies that challenged the role of the churches in society more than ever before and argued for a more radical separation of church and state in Catholic lands. The Enlightenment imagined a break in the history of Europe, though in many ways it continued the seminal battle of influence between the secular and the religious, legitimizing the secular assault on the Church. The 'culture wars' that ensued also would deeply divide the continent until long after the French Revolution.

This context of secularized international politics stimulated new ideas about popular sovereignty – making the people responsible for politics – and international politics, to ensure peace between nations. Gradually a new concept was imagined: that of the sovereign state or, in contemporary sources, the nation.[6] It should be stated, though, that the practical impact of this novel concept remained limited to the world of the imagination and consisted of ideas on how to organize politics and society differently from the existing situation.[7] In practice, empires dominated in Europe, while very different forms of sovereignty also existed, such as sovereign trade companies active overseas.[8] With the French Revolution, a new type of empire was born: conceived more as an extended nation than as a conglomerate of peoples and states as earlier empires had been, and many nineteenth-century empires (the Austrian Habsburg Monarchy, the Holy Roman Empire, the Ottoman Empire, the Russian Empire) remained. I call it a 'modern empire', or an 'empire-nation': the idea would be pursued by Napoleon as well as the German emperor Wilhelm II and later Adolf Hitler. This modern empire is considered here only in the European context: whether the concept can also be applied to the new colonial empires is not the issue here and would require much more discussion.[9]

Peace through the federation of European nations?

The new ways of imagining the continent's organization were gradually applied to the nation, a concept that was further developed by the nationalist thinkers of the nineteenth and twentieth centuries. The idea of the nation elaborates on the concept of sovereignty that emerged from the seventeenth century onwards, but basically refers to the identification of the people with a given territory. It gradually eclipsed other forms of organization of territoriality; at least insofar as it became the primordial expression of political power, without totally effacing others.[10] With the notion of the nation, a secular concept, the notion of a Christian community was also eclipsed. While previous authors, such as Leibniz, Sully and Saint-Pierre, considered the unity of Europe as a Christian one, the new thinkers, such as Montesquieu, Voltaire or Rousseau, believed in a European culture, even a European nation.[11]

Jean-Jacques Rousseau is most credited with developing the idea of a sovereign people, the nation, bound to the state through a 'social contract'. This, incidentally, also entails the concept of human rights and civil liberties, which in the eighteenth and nineteenth centuries came to be seen as essential components of citizenship and hence constituents, and conditions, of the formation of the nation state.[12] From this perspective, Rousseau also considered ways to bring peace to Europe. He developed his ideas in 1761 in a fascinating 'abstract', actually a dialogue with the Abbé de Saint-Pierre's *Projet pour rendre la paix perpétuelle* of 1713–1717, in which the philosopher summarized and commented on Saint-Pierre's ideas, but also in various notes in the years 1754 and

1758, as well as in his *Jugement sur la paix perpétuelle* (Judgement on the everlasting peace) later in 1782. Even if he conceded that peace should be considered more advantageous than war, Rousseau did not share the Abbé's optimistic belief in reason. Still, Rousseau thought that a federal European organization, similar to that of the Holy Roman Empire or the Swiss Confederation, might offer a solution to the continuous wars that haunted the continent and create the conditions for a lasting peace based on justice and prosperity. This federation of peoples, represented by sovereigns but bound by a political contract, should be more than a legal construction or a political and economic union, but inspired by social and moral considerations. In contrast to Sully and Saint-Pierre, Rousseau incidentally rejects trade as a means towards peace, as it leads to greed and is thus one of the root causes of war. In contrast to previous European projects, the necessity to unite against a possible external menace seems to have vanished, as 'there is no Power in the world now capable of threatening all Europe', and in the unlikely event such a power would appear, a united continent would still be better prepared to withstand it than the different countries separately.

In contrast to later ideas about a unified European empire, Rousseau's Europe is 'Ossianic' in nature, an 'order' based on natural divisions by rivers, seas and mountains, but continuously in flux – hence the quasi-perpetual state of war and the reference to the Holy Roman Empire and the Swiss Confederation as alternative forms of organization.[13] A voluntary association of nations which puts each of them in a state of interdependence might offer a way to generating a peace that is more than a mere truce. In addition, the federation should include ways to enforce its decisions and to avoid a situation where one state could ever find it advantageous to break loose – a policy, not of power balance, but of deterrence was necessary, also in order to make war 'a bad choice' (as Saint-Pierre's project also suggested). But for Rousseau the issue was mainly to avoid there being any incitement to start a war, and the only chance to achieve that was through a 'social contract' concluded between free peoples – a prospect that he deemed not very likely, though, and certainly not on such a scale.[14]

Initially Rousseau thought that a union of European peoples could work, as

> the Powers of Europe constitute a kind of whole, united by identity of religion, of moral standard, of international law; by letters, by commerce and finally by a species of balance which is the inevitable result

of all these ties and, however little any man may strive consciously to maintain it, is not to be destroyed so easily as many men imagine.[15]

Apparently Rousseau had not totally abandoned a link with Christianity, even if his Europe cannot be considered equal to Christendom, as the political order he defends is profoundly secular and republican. Rousseau nevertheless excludes the Ottomans as not sharing the same culture and (historical) connections.

The idea of a common European culture figured prominently in European Enlightened texts. The Russian Vasil F. Malinowski, for example, influenced by Saint-Pierre, observed in 1803 that

> Europe is well prepared for peace. Law, customs, science and trade unite its inhabitants and create some sort of special society. Even language, which separates one nation from another, does not constitute an important obstacle in the interaction of is inhabitants; in general the languages resemble each other, and some of them can even be used as a common language for all Europeans. Many Europeans have common ancestors, and almost all are mixed. They should be ashamed if they would consider themselves as enemies.[16]

The last comment, formulated during the first Napoleonic war and the French invasion of Russia, already anticipates a major theme in later texts, formulated against nationalists, of the mixed character of the continent, particularly in Central and Eastern Europe. In the meantime, a common organization of Europe seemed the logical conclusion of this enlightened project of European civilization, although Malinowski actually focused on an Eastern European federation (including Russia and Greece) as a first step to a continent-wide organization. Similar ideas were developed by the Polish aristocrat Prince Adam Czartoryski, a trusted advisor and from 1804 onwards (adjunct) minister of foreign affairs of the Russian tsar Alexander I, who argued for a Russian-led federation in Central Europe which would respect the autonomy of the different nations and stimulate free trade, and by so doing prevent armed conflicts. This confederation, which would allow for the re-establishment of an autonomous Poland, would eventually give way to a wider Pan-European association.[17] As Czartoryski appealed to Britain to take the leading role in such a European federation alongside Russia – at the expense not only of France but also of Prussia and the Habsburg Empire, which could jeopardize his ambitions for the reconstruction of Poland – the British had to answer his proposals. The British Prime Minister, William Pitt, however, remained cautious and rather thought along the lines of a balance of power, suggesting territorial adjustments to contain France. Instead of a European federation, he preferred an association of the main powers to guarantee the rights and territories of each supported by 'a general and comprehensive system of public law in Europe'.[18]

This idea of a common European space or civilization sounds wonderful, although in this Europe of nations some were more likely to be more important than others. For the Polish prince Czartoryski the more important nations would be Britain and Russia, but increasingly European writers and intellectuals imagined a cultural division line between east and west, the west being more advanced and 'Enlightened' than the barbaric east. For the eighteenth century diplomat Count de Ségur, for example, travelling to Poland was like having 'left Europe entirely', referring not only to the landscape but also to the enslavement, poverty and backwardness, and also the multitude of its people consisting of 'hordes of Huns, Scythians, Veneti, Slavs, and Sarmatians'.[19] This view would give the Western Europeans the noble task of 'civilizing' the east, even by conquest. The French revolutionaries would effectively universalize their 'liberating' project to the east by force. One should note, however, that Ségur actually still did consider these lands as European. That was not always the case, as the origin of the difference increasingly was sought in ethnicity and even race – although Eastern Europeans were, sometimes to the surprise of travellers, 'white' (though they would later 'darken' in the representations). For the Marquis de Custine 'There is between France and Russia a Chinese wall – the Slavonic language and character. In spite of the notions with which Peter the Great has inspired the Russians, Siberia commences on the Vistula.'[20] Also emerging were German ideas of a sense of their own superior destiny. The German historian Nicolaus Vogt, for example, (*Über die europäische Republik*, 1787–1792) initiated a new tradition in which 'Germany' would become the 'mother' and focal point of European unification.[21] Obviously, these representations of superiority would cast a long shadow over Europe's history for more than a century. The emphasis on a European community and civilization also illustrates the opposition between Europe and the rest of the world, an opposition to which Enlightenment thinkers contributed considerably.

The Enlightened peace project par excellence was, of course, Kant's famous essay, *Zum ewigen Frieden* (*Towards Perpetual Peace*, 1795).

Although Kant, writing his text while Poland was being divided up by Russia, Prussia and Austria, and the French Revolution was shaking the European traditional political order, shared Rousseau's pessimism about the possibility of 'eternal peace' – expressed in the irony by which he presented his case – he, far more than Rousseau or Malinowski, argued unambiguously for a republican Europe. This should be based on independent, free republics that should unite in a 'peaceful' federation – a republic, being mainly defined by the separation of powers, somewhat surprisingly could include monarchies, even though the monarch might require the consent of the citizens, for example to declare war. Respect for national sovereignty and the acceptance of the separation of power and universal moral laws constitute the foundation of his international order. However, universal moral laws were quite different from what classic international law in his eyes offered, namely 'legitimization' for the ambitions of aggressors, as the Partition of Poland illustrated (which, as a citizen of Königsberg near the Polish border, particularly outraged him).[22] This attitude certainly distinguishes him from Bentham and other federalists.[23] Neither did he share with many British liberal thinkers the idea that commercial ties between nations were by definition conducive to peace. However, he conceded that the extension of commerce would in the long run generate the conditions for an international state of law.

Kant shared several basic ideas with Utilitarians, such as the recognition of a common European culture and the need for a European organization, which Jeremy Bentham's 1789 'Plan for a Universal and Perpetual Peace' also considered in purely secular terms. Bentham's cosmopolitanism was more radical, though. The inventor of the 'international' concept predicted that all European nations would disband their standing armies and settle international disputes through the acceptance of international arbitration and international law. In this respect, Bentham believed that openness would compel governments to comply with reason and justice – he actually believed in the power of public opinion and hence in the development of a global critical citizenship. His vision was also broader in another respect. He identified the global ambitions of the European empires as a major cause of wars, as in the eighteenth century many colonial wars were indeed mainly extensions of European conflicts – something which would change after 1815. Hence, he called upon the Europeans to give up their colonial ambitions, as colonialism implied injustice.[24] Kant's ideas aimed at universalism, but remained somewhat tarnished because he initially considered non-western people, in particular Africans, as essentially not capable of rational thinking, although he later revised his opinion on the matter and also opposed imperialism as immoral.[25]

An empire of liberty?

The discourse on national sovereignty and the emphasis on the nation with regard to republicanism obliterate the continuing, even reinvigorated attraction of empire in the nineteenth and twentieth centuries. After all, the nineteenth and the first half of the twentieth century were dominated by large and powerful empires, and the disintegration of some of them – the Austrian Habsburg and the Ottoman empires in particular – in the late nineteenth century should not cloak the fact that new empires were formed or other ones were able to massively extend their power, albeit mainly outside Europe. The French revolutionaries, who placed national sovereignty at the centre of their revolution, soon embarked on a European war, establishing a French European empire: an empire of reason and liberty in their view, perhaps, but an empire nevertheless.

The French revolutionary European war, however, introduced not only a new vision for Europe but also a new interpretation of empire, described by the French writer Nicolas de Condorcet as the diffusion of 'the freedom, reason, and illumination of Europe'.[26] The ideologue of the French Revolution, Emmanuel-Joseph Sieyès, directly referring to Rousseau's republicanism, similarly considered peace as the natural course of history, as emerging from the will and need of the people, when no authority stands in the way.[27]

While the French General Assembly of 22 May 1790 declared that 'the French nation renounces undertaking any war in order to make conquests and will never use its forces against the will of any people' (Article 4), Robespierre did not really endorse the limitations Condorcet suggested. Provoked by the anti-revolutionary European forces which invaded the country, Robespierre would retaliate and send French troops abroad. However,

> In countries that are or will be occupied by the armies of the Republic, the generals will proclaim immediately on behalf of the French nation the sovereignty of the people, the removal of all the established rights, of the tithe, of feudalism, of manorial rights, banal rights, real and personal servitudes, privileges of hunting and fishing, chores of the nobles, ... They'll announce to the people that

they'll bring them peace, relief, fraternity, liberty and equality. They'll convene primary or municipal assemblies.[28]

Nevertheless, the revolutionary drive would be continued with the perspective of exporting the Revolution.

This republican ideal resonated positively with many intellectuals in Europe, who were literally fed up with the existing international political system. Even Kant famously hoped that republican France would change the international order for good:

> If by good fortune one powerful and enlightened nation came to form a republic (which is by its nature inclined to seek perpetual peace), this will provide a focal point for federal association among other states. These will join up with the first one, thus securing the freedom of each state in accordance with the idea of international right, and the whole will gradually spread further and further by a series of alliances of this kind.[29]

And the still young German philosopher and writer Johann Gottfried Herder hoped that republican France would end the 'mad, raging system of conquest' that characterized the early modern international political system.[30] Herder, referring to Archbishop Fénélon's *The Adventures of Telemachus* (1699) but ridiculing the Enlightened thinkers' belief in the balance of power (including Voltaire and Kant), dreamt of a 'fraternal community of peoples'. The German philosopher Johann Gottlieb Fichte also, and in very similar terms, imagined a world of mutual aid and humanity instead of a ferocious war machine. For Herder, however, this was something quite other than either Kant had proposed or the French Revolutionaries pursued. He especially opposed the republican ideal as a justification for yet again war and bloodshed. In order to establish eternal peace, it was the state itself that needed to be pacified, and this implied, more than Kant recognized, the acceptance of rights within the framework of a constitutional state.[31] That was not quite what was going to happen, however.

Napoleon Bonaparte would actually engage in an imperial conquest of the continent which, incidentally, need not be restricted to the lands between the Mediterranean and the Ural, as his troops marched to Egypt where he associated himself with the ruler of Mysore (in Southwest India), Tipu Sultan, an admirer of all things French. Napoleon paradoxically combined the republican ideals of the French Revolution with a Carolingian imperial vision of Europe as one:

it would have been possible to carry out the chimera of the beautiful ideal of civilization. In this state of things, there would have been some chance of establishing, in every country, a unity of codes, principles, opinions, sentiments, views, and interests. Then, perhaps, by the help of the universal diffusion of knowledge, one might have thought of attempting, in the great European family, the application of the American Congress, or the Amphictyons of Greece. And then what perspective of strength, size, enjoyment, prosperity [that would offer]! What a great and wonderful spectacle![32]

Napoleon's ambitions went far beyond France itself – similar rhetoric would also accompany European expansionism elsewhere for the next 200 years. It is quite clear that here a fundamentally new vision of empire is expressed – actually one that initially refused to be called imperial – quite different from such loose federations as the Holy Roman Empire or the Austrian Habsburg Monarchy. This new vision of empire actually merged ideas of the nation with 'imperial' ambitions of universalism and conquest. As the British conservative Edmund Burke argued, the Napoleonic wars were not just 'France extending a foreign empire over other nations' but an ideological campaign aimed at installing a new political and societal regime in Europe, including, incidentally, in France itself (Burke rather spoke of 'a sect aiming at universal empire, and beginning with the conquest of France').[33]

This imperial-universal vision had its supporters throughout Europe, not least in the German lands. The Archbishop of Mainz and Arch-Chancellor of the Holy Roman Empire (after 1806 Prince-Primate of the Confederation of the Rhine), Karl Theodor von Dalberg, his nephew the Grand Duke of Baden Metternich von Dalberg, and the German historians Nicolaus Vogt and Karl Ludwig von Woltmann were among those who hoped Napoleon's universal empire would bring the desired peace by uniting Europe the way Charlemagne had done – reviving the 'Carolingian' myth that also inspired Louis XIV, but interpreting it even more as a unified, universal empire. In this respect, they imagined an ecumenical council that would reunite Europe again spiritually as well. In addition, many shared the idea that the French not only waged a war of political liberation, but also an economic war, against the growing, monopolitistic, global economic grip of Great Britain's colonial empire.[34]

Reality, however, was more complex. The revolution may have refused to call itself imperial, but Napoleon soon connected with the imperial pomp – his coronation is a case in point. And his empire in practice faced the same challenges of ruling over a diverse population as any empire, past or present. Imperial rule was not identical from Paris to Warsaw: Napoleon reverted to traditional patriarchal modes of rule, relying on local elites where possible and associating allies by allotting titles and donations, creating an 'imperial nobility'. And in Saint-Domingue he aimed at restoring the colonial order, including the reintroduction of slavery.[35]

Notwithstanding his final defeat at Waterloo, Napoleon's legacy was an enduring one, as many innovations, not the least of which were his idea of empire with its taxation schemes and legal and institutional framework – the *code Napoléon* is a case in point – had a lasting impact on the lands that belonged to it. To be sure, their impact varied depending on the length, intensity and the form of government, structural preconditions, distance from Paris and degree of resistance – some see in the 'inner circle' of regions most closely associated with the imperial policies (significantly not 'countries') a prefiguration of the later core of the European communities. The historian Michael Broers does indeed distinguish between an 'inner empire' (most of France, Switzerland, the Low Countries, the Republic/Kingdom of Italy and Western Germany), an 'outer empire' (Spain, Greece and the Western Balkans, Venice, the Papal States and parts of Northern Germany) and an 'intermediate zone' which included not only the Kingdom of Naples and the Grand Duchy of Warsaw, but also some notoriously rebellious areas of Western France such as the Vendée and Brittany, where the empire ruled 'lightly', associating with local elites.[36] Recent research incidentally revealed that this Napoleonic Europe was more 'European' and, particularly in the way it was perceived, far less 'French' than is often imagined. French imperial government in large parts of the empire was connected to local elites and could count on important support from different strata of the population. Real national feelings, nevertheless, hardly existed; hence, they could not constitute the basis of grassroots revolt either. But one could argue that Napoleonic policies did contribute to awakening (or rather inciting) national feelings.

Napoleonic policies were not only about institutions, but contained a real 'civilizing mission', albeit within a European perspective (meaning that the underlying alterization was conceived only in cultural terms, not in racial ones as would be the case later in the European colonial empires in Africa and Asia).[37] One of these policies relates to the role of the Church in society, as the French pushed the age-old struggle for hegemony between the Crown and the Mitre to its extreme. The Revolution ended up persecuting the Catholic Church and eventually replacing it with the 'Cult of Reason' (or, more correctly, of the state itself). Also, after Napoleon restored relations with the Holy See, the primacy of the state over the church was clearly confirmed. Those countries that had been French, even for a short while, also inherited this state–church conflict.

This model and the Napoleonic universal 'empire of liberty' – to borrow Jefferson's words in a different context – would continue to inspire French writers in particular, long after the death of the empire.[38] But those who wrote from this perspective preferred to distance themselves from the 'totalitarian' aspects of Napoleonic imperialism and rather emphasize the idea of a voluntary European federation, while the new idea of the nation-empire would be taken on by German emperors in the nineteenth century. The federalist model was, for example, defended in Germany by the philosopher Karl Christian Friedrich Krause and in France by the utopian aristocrat Henri de Saint-Simon.

Krause argued along the lines of Herder for a federal Europe, to be constituted by a voluntary association of nations, as a necessary condition to ensure peace. However, peace was more than the absence of war: it was the result of a political system that respected the nation itself, and the condition of justice, which was the ultimate goal: 'The purpose should not be just eternal peace, but the justice of the peoples themselves. The free federation of states not only makes this peace possible, it is the only way through which a lasting peace can follow spontaneously.' This federal model was not restricted to Europe. Other world regions should follow suit and also constitute independent states and associate within federations; ultimately all would join into a world federation – a 'United Nations'.[39]

Krause's concept of Europe was not that far removed from the one advocated by Saint-Simon, who, referring to Charlemagne, aimed at recreating a unified European federation around a common ideal and religion – it was the failure of a common inspiring ideal, he argued in his *Mémoire sur la gravitation* (Essay on gravitation, 1811, published 1848), that caused the nations of Europe to oppose and fight each other.[40] In *De la réorganisation de la société européenne ou de la nécessité et des moyens de rassembler les peuples de l'Europe en un seul corps politique en conservant à chacun son indépendance nationale* (On the Reorganization of European Society or the Necessity and Means of Uniting the Peoples of Europe in a Single Body Politic, While Preserving for Each Their National Independence, 1814), published on the eve of the Congress of Vienna, Saint-Simon and his secretary, A. Thierry, proposed an elaborated federal vision of Europe (which, however, rather pointed to the British model) to be followed by the rest of Europe. They suggested the creation of a European two-chamber parliament with an elected monarch – the Napoleonic conquest freshly in mind, the Frenchmen placed their proposal in the context of national sovereignty. Great Britain and France would function as the continent's leading powers, with which other democratic nations would be associated. From that perspective, they particularly emphasized the 'German nation', as the latter comprehended almost half of the population of Europe and had a 'noble and generous character'. A precursor of socialism, Saint-Simon saw this unified Europe as the nucleus for a continent-wide 'planned' economy, in which industrial development would constitute the motor of progress and trade the cement of peace. However, 'Europe' for Saint-Simon and Thierry equalled 'civilization': 'Where civilization ends, where uncultivated rudeness begins, there must be the walls of Europe, and the only walls in Europe', Thierry wrote, which incidentally excluded not only the Ottomans but part of Russia as well: Saint-Simon and Thierry's boundaries of Europe cut right through the Russian empire.[41] From this perspective, Europe – the European Diet or Parliament – had a particular mission, 'to populate the world of the European race, which is superior to all other races of men, and make it voyageable and habitable'. It was nothing less than the legitimization of imperial conquest and exploitation.[42]

Anti-revolutionary Europe

The French Revolution and Napoleon's European campaigns were inspiring moments in European history, but raised fundamental concerns as well. Friedrich von Gentz, a pupil of Immanuel Kant and initially an admirer of the French Revolution and its 'Carolinian' or 'Frankian' vision of Europe, became deeply disillusioned within two years after the outbreak of the Revolution.[43] Gentz, who became secretary to the Congress of Vienna and of the Concert thereafter, translated Burke's *Reflections on the Revolution in France* and became one of the harshest critics of Napoleon's European ambitions. As a result of Napoleon's 'Europeanism', the word 'Europe', he wrote in 1814, 'has come to inspire me with horror'; he had 'lost all desire to be a European'.[44]

The most poignant critique of the Revolution came from the liberal Benjamin Constant, who rejected the idea that a revolutionary war (or any war) and the uniformization of laws and customs could ever produce peace and justice.[45] Likewise, his one-time lover Madame Germaine de Stael emphasized the diversity of European nations – anticipating the nationalist revival that would alter the European landscape profoundly.[46] Widespread among the Romantic artists and thinkers was nostalgic longing for the lost unity of Christendom, as epitomized by French philosopher, writer, lawyer and diplomat Joseph de Maistre and the German Romantic poet Novalis. The latter recalled in 1799 the 'beautiful, magnificent times, when Europe was a Christian land, when *one* Christianity dwelled on this civilized continent, and when *one* common interest joined the most distant provinces of this vast spiritual empire. Without great worldly possessions *one* sovereign governed and unified the great political forces.' (emphasis PP) His assessment was more subtle than these often-quoted words suggest, however, as the German poet understood the dynamics of history, including the Reformation, as essentially positive. He considered the French Revolution to be a 'second Reformation' and a turning point in history. It would culminate in a new European empire, which would be based upon an association of states and would 'resurrect' the papacy as the leading power in Europe. How that was to be realized remains unclear, though, as Novalis opposed the 'modern' idea that history could be made by man and had no trust whatsoever in the power of politics.[47]

Novalis' anti-politics was common in those days, and shared by thinkers as diverse as William Blake – who, in *Europe: A Prophecy* (1794), presented European history as the playground of superhuman forces – and Edmund Burke. The latter's assessment revealed more penetrating political insight into the French Revolution's destruction of the old order. Still, he too considered Europe as a cultural and in some ways even political unity:

> There have been periods of time in which communities, apparently in peace with each other, have been more perfectly separated than, in later times, many nations in Europe have been in the course of long and bloody wars. The cause must be sought in the similitude in Europe of religion, laws, and manners. At bottom, these are all the same.

For Burke, the ideological assault on Europe's political order actually destroyed its very essence: the unicity it had inherited from its ancient past and which had been expressed through its institutions as well as its customs and practices, and maintained and cultivated by international (intra-European) trade and commerce. This vision of the 'old' Europe, incidentally, was mainly an objection to the revolutionary, political ambitions of the Revolutionaries, which they shared with religious zealots, such as those who were responsible for the equally revolutionary wars of religion in the sixteenth century. But his idea of Europe as a commonwealth of nations did emphasize a fundamental unity, 'a similitude throughout Europe of religion, laws, and manners':

> The writers on public law have often called this aggregate of nations a Commonwealth. They had reason. It is virtually one great state having the same basis of general law; with some diversity of provincial customs and local establishments. The nations of Europe have had the very same Christian religion, agreeing in the fundamental parts, varying a little in the ceremonies and in the subordinate doctrines.[48]

Hence, the idea of diversity was actually perfectly compatible with that of a European federation, as the German Romantic writer and Austrian diplomat Friedrich Schlegel argued in a series of lectures on modern European history in 1810, in which he proposed the imperial order of Charles V as the model for Europe. At least in Schlegel's idealized view, Charles V had guaranteed peace among the Christian powers, brought peaceful negotiation to disputes, established a unified front against the Turkish menace and maintained good relations between the Holy Roman Empire and the Papacy. Hence, Schlegel suggested, 'the ideal . . . of a free association, which would encompass all nations and states of the educated and civilized world, without sacrificing the unity, the freedom and idiosyncratic national development of each individual nation'. This proclaimed liberty, incidentally, also applied to the Jews, who should be granted full civil rights.[49] Not all shared this rather optimistic idea, though.

Perhaps the most fundamental criticism of a European federation around the turn of the century was expressed by Fichte, whose humanitarian ideals we have already mentioned in connection with his initial welcome of the Revolution. In contrast to Gentz, his main intellectual opponent at the time, Fichte surprisingly (as he is mainly known for his idealism and as a theoretician of German nationalism) remained an ardent Francophile – actually, he supported French arguments that put the blame for the wars on British imperial expansion.[50] However, Fichte gradually came to realize that in order for peace to be established in Europe, the root causes of war had to be tackled and that required a reconsideration of both the state and the international system. Though he certainly acknowledged that there was some sort of European spirit, he believed that this was being annihilated by the modern state system, based on national taxation. This still very immature state system generated instability and conflict both internally and between states. To complete their transformation, Fichte argued in his fundamental treatise *Der geschlossene Handelsstaat* (The Closed Commercial State, 1800), the states first had to complete their development towards true republics. Eliminating the class conflict that resulted from the increasing inequalities implied that they had to guarantee the establishment of a fair economic and social distribution of wealth, as well as the recognition of the right to work. This required the development of a national autarkic, self-sufficient 'planned' economy, with a determining role for the administration, which would control monetary policies. In line with Kant and Rousseau, Fichte argued that 'the spirit of commerce' actually generated conflict and competition and had destroyed the unity of the continent. This, incidentally, also incited the German philosopher to a strident critique of colonial imperialism. Actually, the closed commercial state had a universal utopian ambition. Once the root cause of war was eliminated, states could again engage in some sort of state-led interchange without focus on profit. Hence, a universal perpetual peace could be realized.[51]

The *Realpolitiker* Friedrich von Gentz proved far more realistic and immediately influential than Fichte. The former 'Europeanist' first turned 'German' – seeing in the union of Austria and Prussia the salvation of the continent – [52] and Austrian nationalist thereafter. Gentz thought that Fichte's closed commercial state would restrict Europeans to a perpetual state of childhood and would halt all progress. He not only considered commerce as essential to modern states, but saw it as a means of 'enlightenment' and 'combatting the most deep-rooted prejudices'. He increasingly believed that realizing peace implied the balancing of powers and the establishment of 'countervailing powers' ('counterweights') rather than a fully fledged federation, what he called the restoration of 'the natural European federal constitution'. Here he found himself thinking along the same lines as other advocates of a 'restoration' of the European order, such as the French Catholic philosopher and diplomat Joseph de Maistre and general Charles-François Dumouriez in France, and the Prussian historian Friedrich Ancillon.[53] For the former student and friend of Immanuel Kant however, such a dynamic system would particularly protect the weaker nations from the imperialist appetite of the stronger ones – be they French, British or, for that matter, German. His ideas supported those of the Austrian foreign minister, Prince Klemenz von Metternich, who became a close friend and political partner in establishing a new political order that both confirmed and transcended the limits of the balance of power.[54]

In the meantime, the concept of peace experienced a dramatic change. If anything, the French Revolution showed that peace was not likely to emerge from the 'natural desire of the people' who needed to be liberated, or the application of 'practical reason' as the Enlightened thinkers imagined. Romantic visions of politics and society considered war as natural, sometimes just and productive – in the final stage of modern imagination, everlasting peace can only be realized in the graveyard of humanity.[55] Peace was hence a temporary state, realized through reconciliation after battle – a battle that was both natural and productive. Indeed, while Enlightened philosophers considered war as the product of the personal ambitions of absolutist rulers and peace the natural desire of the people, that idea was definitively buried after the French Revolution, and with it – at least for the next 200 years – that of the everlasting peace that was the ideal from Augustinus to Kant. In this context, the pursuit of peace became on the one hand a moral demand for politics and society, and on the other a technical issue – an evolution that had already been initiated by the reference to trade, as well as the 'balance of power' politics of the previous century. It led to the first effective European peace organization in history (albeit the most unlikely one): the Concert.[56]

4
Peace during the Concert

> Upon whatever principle the theory under consideration may
> have been at first devised (...) it is certain that it would have
> been held fatal to the success of the balancing system for any
> one power, and that one amongst the most civilised, wealthy,
> and commercial, to have refused to subscribe to its constitution.
>
> Richard Cobden, 1836[1]

The Concert as a peace-keeping organization

Napoleon contributed to the process of European integration in two
quite distinct ways. On the one hand, his conquests 'unified' large parts
of the continent, with the French revolutionary ideals exerting an influence far beyond the territories that he conquered – even if not all of
Europe was convinced and though some of his innovations were later
reversed after Waterloo. On the other hand, he provoked a common
reaction from the anti-revolutionary states and empires who, unwill-
ingly at first, joined forces in an alliance that would not only survive the
hostilities but would regulate – or at least attempt to do so – European
international relations for almost a century: the European 'Concert'.
For many, it proved a highly successful format and a precursor of the
present EU.[2]

The Concert resulted from the reaction of the major European powers against Napoleon's successful international campaigns between 1800
and 1815 and came about in steps. The Congress of Vienna, which
was held in the Austrian capital from September 1814 to June 1815
and gathered all the crowned heads of Europe, established the basic
principles and objectives of the new order, but these were further
developed and implemented during the negotiations between the main

protagonists – the Russian Empire, the Habsburg Empire, Prussia, Great Britain and Bourbon France – after the escape of Napoleon and his final defeat at Waterloo, in Paris (Treaty of Paris, 20 November 1815) and Aix-la-Chapelle, in 1818. The European monarchs engaged in a sustained common resistance against a common enemy, in a way never seen in European history before – certainly not with regard to the Ottomans in the previous two centuries: the sultans, even when directly threatening Christian lands, had always been able to count on other Christian powers, especially France, to prevent a joint action. The system of peace that the five major European powers (i.e. with Bourbon France included) invented, continued, in this new-found sense of connection, to restore the old monarchical order. Their ideological view was in many ways diametrically opposed to that of Napoleon: whereas the latter dreamed of a new European empire based on universal secular values and laws, the powers searched for a way to maintain an imperial order on the continent. Nevertheless, some of the negotiators shared some Enlightened ideas and ideals and were at least partially guided by the thinkers we discussed in the previous chapters: the main protagonists were familiar with the European views of, particularly, Sully, the Abbé de Saint-Pierre, Rousseau and Kant. Some of the advisors and negotiators, such as Friedrich von Gentz and Adam Czartoryski, had established plans of their own.[3] William Pitt's view, formulated in reaction to those of the Polish-Russian prince, also still resonated strongly in British government circles in 1815.[4]

Especially after the return of Napoleon in March 1815, the monarchs and diplomats, who explicitly considered themselves as the leaders of Europe, concluded more than a truce or peace treaty: they established the first European peace-keeping system, the European Concert, which would be backed up by the Holy Alliance of the Austrian Empire, the Russian Empire and the kingdom of Prussia – the UK initially did not join the Alliance, neither did France (the latter would join in 1818), although they did participate in the Congress. The Holy Alliance unambiguously referred back to Christendom: inspired by the Russian tsar Alexander I, who after the French Revolution came to be influenced by Orthodox mysticism and saw himself as a spiritual liberator of Europe, the monarchs made their agreement 'in the name of the Most Holy and Undivided Trinity'. These words suggest the conclusion of a moral order, but should not necessarily be interpreted as a return to confessional politics: while nobody shared Alexander's religious zeal, the three monarchs considered their faiths – Catholicism for the Austrian emperor, Protestantism for the King of Prussia and Orthodoxy for the

Russian tsar – on an equal footing. What that meant for the position of the Ottomans remains subject to debate: while the terms of the Concert excluded them, the Ottomans were nevertheless still considered essential to the European order and, hence, *European*; indeed, the Ottoman sultan would later be able to join.[5] Still, the Congress referred to common European values, in which the influence of the Enlightenment is clearly discernible. In this respect, it forbade the slave trade and introduced protective rights for Jews in the German confederation, although it lacked means to enforce these dispositions.

The Concert introduced a number of measures to contain a possible threat from France, but mainly appealed to the balance of power and a system of alliances to guarantee peace and stability, together with the restoration of the monarchical system. The five major powers – the Austrian Empire, Russia, Prussia, the UK and Bourbon France – acted as the natural leaders of the continent. But the Congress also appealed to international law and established more rules and practices for international relations. It was the Congress of Vienna, not the Peace of Westphalia nor even the Treaty of Utrecht that provided the basis for an international order based upon respect for sovereignty and national borders: these, for example, could not be altered without the consent of its eight main signatories. The 'Concert' did not have any permanent structure, though, nor a true constitutional act. It was actually a far cry from the effective federation that earlier plans had proposed, even though Metternich had presented it otherwise when, speaking about the Holy Alliance in 1817, he stated that 'This noble and great fraternity values more than all the treaties and assures for long what the good abbé de Saint-Pierre aimed at establishing for ever.'[6] In 1818 the Russian tsar in fact proposed further developing the Concert into a far more powerful anti-revolutionary federation, which would even possess a common army to impose the *pax europaea* upon all those who dared to imperil the status quo. This ambitious plan, however, was skilfully torpedoed by the British, who increasingly doubted if it were wise to embed the status quo in Europe, irrespective of politics.[7] The Concert nevertheless convened in times of crisis: eight times at the level of the monarchs and 12 at ambassador level between 1815 and 1914. It was intended to act as an international police force curtailing liberal uprisings, but largely failed in this respect and actually stopped doing so as early as 1823, when France and the UK quarrelled over an intervention in the Spanish constitutional revolution and the colonial war which followed in Mexico. Nevertheless, it did continue as a loose European association.[8]

The question of whether the Concert was effective as a peace-keeping organization or not will continue to divide historians and political scientists; it is not the issue here. What is certain, nonetheless, is that contemporaries valued it highly: witness the godfather of the historical profession, Leopold von Ranke who, in 1854, believed that 'The separation of nationalities against one another is no longer possible [because] they all belong to the great European concert.'[9] That idea was not universally shared, though, and would be rebutted on more than one occasion. And it was especially advocates of the new ideologies of liberalism and nationalism, at odds with the principles of the Concert, who would come up with new blueprints for Europe.

European perspectives on peace and trade

Liberals such as Benjamin Constant and Richard Cobden especially opposed the new order introduced by the Concert. They embodied a vision of a dynamic policy of free trade and democracy that responded to the tremendous technological, economic and social transformations that were altering the fundamentals of society. Peace would not be realized by power balancing and clinging to a traditional order as the Concert imagined, as these were inherently unstable and would only lead to hegemonic and imperial ambitions, while at the same time hampering the development of trade and commerce. It would only be realized by doing the opposite: creating a democratic, free and open Europe where people were not divided, but *united* by race, religion or language. In particular, free trade would forge relations of brotherhood among nations, generating peace and civilization both in Europe and overseas, making war utterly unrealistic and obsolete. Reality, however, would very quickly prove otherwise.

It is quite obvious in hindsight that, in contrast to the anti-imperialist conviction of Cobden, free trade (in the nineteenth century at least) actually led to plunder, ruthless exploitation and conquest in Asia and Africa, with the Opium Wars as an early illustration of the pernicious effects of British free trade discourse. In Europe itself, that was perhaps less obvious, although Bentham, Rousseau, Fichte and even Constant had already argued that commercial interaction and transnational private connections did not automatically result in peace.[10] They could actually lead to national rivalries and international conflict. Hence, British arguments for free trade were also interpreted as unfair, partisan and hypocritical, seeking only to benefit British imperial interests. The Navigation Acts, for example, which were only repealed in 1849, gave British ships the monopoly on trade with British colonies. Fichte's *Closed Commercial State* can actually be read as a stunning criticism of British imperialism as the root cause of the late eighteenth–early nineteenth-century revolutionary wars, an argument made most explicitly by the count of Hauterive in defence of Napoleon earlier in 1800.[11] The German liberal nationalist Friedrich List virulently opposed free trade liberalism, pointing precisely at the protectionist policies that had brought Great Britain to the vanguard of the world economy. But List realized that the fragmented nature of Central Europe seriously hampered its development, particularly since industry was highly dependent on effective postal and transport systems, such as steamboats and railways. Hence, in 1819 and 1820, List, comparing the fragmented German lands with a centralized France, urged both the German Diet and the Austrian emperor to abolish these many customs and to create a large Central European free trade zone, eventually connecting the Levant and the Adriatic.[12]

List further developed his ideas on how continental Europe could compete with the expansionist British from 1825 onwards in his chosen exile in the US.[13] An economically united 'Mitteleuropa',[14] based upon the association of 'state-nations', would not only be able to successfully compete with Great Britain, but also to organize international trade with Asia and 'the South', where climate compelled nations to remain forever the producer of agricultural commodities for the industrial products exported to the temperate 'North'. List, incidentally, was not always consistent: he regularly changed his views on who should be part of Mitteleuropa and who should not, as well as on whether there should be equality between all or only some nations, and the necessity for one, in particular 'Germany', which would take the lead. Germany, in his view, included smaller states such as Belgium, the Netherlands, Denmark and Switzerland; Mitteleuropa hence covered a large part of Northwestern as well as Eastern and Central Europe. Other figures, such as Friedrich Engels and German imperial nationalists, would later share this idea, though in contrast to the latter, List had no imperialist intentions: he considered these states as economically unsustainable and his 'greater Germany' was meant to be based upon free and independent constitutional states which recognized the rights of all, including Catholics and Jews.

List's main competitor for Central Europe was Great Britain, but the US also emerged as a possible threat. It was the American menace which was central to the work of Konrad von Schmidt-Phiseldeck. In a widely distributed essay on the economic relations between Europe and

America, the former director of the Danish National Bank observed that the loss of the European colonies in the Americas had deprived Europe of valuable resources and markets, while the fledgling US was fast becoming the leading political, economic, social and intellectual power of the world. The political and economic union of the early republic, however, pointed towards Europe's redemption: a European federation, as the continent shared a common culture and religion, while intensive trade relations existed and rivers and roads could offer easy ways of communication. Moreover, the Concert had already developed something akin to a joint political structure, albeit minimalistic in its present state. Hence, the next step should not be that difficult: a real federation of sovereign states (he used the strong term *Bund*, though its concrete meaning is not always that clear), with a common Parliament, court of law, currency and army. Remarkably, he believed in a European citizenship, giving a European court jurisdiction to protect citizens from states. In addition, he thought a European federation would contribute to strengthening the common spirit. The current situation was quite different: the diverse states competed against one another and, by doing so, ruined each other, as in reality their economies were closely intertwined. In a global rivalry, Schmidt-Phiseldeck predicted astutely, they stood no chance. Hence, they should develop their economies jointly.[15]

While the economy figured prominently in Schmidt-Phiseldeck's European vision, his view was much broader than this, looking not only at the US but at the world as a whole. Here he emphasized obvious European superiority as a civilization, with the right and the duty to impose its will upon those lesser civilizations. However, that position of superiority, it seems, rested upon a strong economic base.

List's and Schmidt-Phiseldeck's ideas did inspire politics. Prussia initiated an important customs reform as early as 1818, creating a free internal market within the kingdom's scattered territories, stimulating exports but with high protective custom duties. As a result, other German states were compelled to unite, which they did so reluctantly only when their treasures had been exhausted. This policy led to the foundation of the German Customs Union or *Zollverein* in 1833, which supported the gradual unification – or 'Prussification' – of the German lands. This included a unified commercial code, harmonized mining laws, a common Bill of Exchange Law, a single weight system, common railway tariffs and a single judicial system, as well as fixed exchange rates, which eventually resulted in the acceptance of a common currency in 1857. The *Zollverein* was administered by a Congress (and from 1867 onwards, a Federal Council), in which each member state would have one vote. It was entitled to conclude commercial treaties, as it did with the Netherlands (1839), Belgium (1844), France (1862) and the UK (1865). This regional integration policy served the economic interests of its members well, albeit probably less well than is sometimes believed. It was nevertheless an instrument in Prussia's economic and fiscal policy, and provided – intentionally or not – the basis of German unification.[16]

Austria developed similar plans. The most perspicuous came from the minister of commerce, Karl Ludwig von Bruck, who in October 1849 suggested constituting a customs union between the German Confederation and the Austrian Empire, including its non-German lands. This was to be complemented by a Swiss and an Italian federation, thereby forging a huge Central European economic bloc. Prussia, however, interpreted it as a hostile move and torpedoed it, as it did with other similar initiatives.

A united Europe of nation states?

Liberal nationalism and European federalism

Though things may (or may not) look different today, from a political as well as an economical perspective, liberalism and nationalism were not opposed in the nineteenth century. Nationalists, indeed, aimed at liberating peoples from tyranny and oppression by archaic royal sovereigns, as represented by the Concert and defended by the Holy Alliance. At first glance, nationalists seemed to defend 'plurality' and diversity in Europe. In reality, though, by rendering the nation absolute, nationalism became even more exclusive. Moreover, nationalists easily – though not always – developed feelings of superiority and contempt for other nations, which can be discerned in the denigrating attitude towards small states – *Kleinstaaten* – characteristic of 'Mazzinean' nationalism. Conservatives such as Burke, in contrast, explicitly endorsed the plurality of Europe and its traditions, at least insofar as they did not undermine the sacred order of Christendom.

The Concert was presented as embodying this conservative idea of diversity, but it did not: it accepted the political plurality of states, but cherished the existing order and opposed everything that could disrupt the stability of the continent. The divisions the Concert rejected related to nations and social classes, but also still included religion – though irreligion and atheism were on the rise and governments further extended their 'secular' powers within society. Religion, incidentally, made an important comeback: the idea of the nineteenth and twentieth centuries as a secular age is largely a misinterpretation of the changing place of religion in society. Also, nationalism was not, as is often contended, some sort of 'secular religion'. Certainly in the early nineteenth century, nationalism did present itself as secular, as it strived towards liberation from the Church which was, at the time, also seen as an oppressive institution. Often, however, though not always, they later reinforced each other as nations recognized the power of religion or associated themselves with one religion, striving towards homogenization.[17]

It is a widespread prejudice that nationalism and Europeanization are opposed. The reality, however, is different. Major nationalist thinkers, in fact, also actively promoted a European federation, though of course conceived quite differently from the one the Concert defended. As a volunteer in the Polish uprising of 1830 – crushed by the troops of the Holy Alliance – the Polish scientist Wojciech Jastrzębowski, for example, published a remarkable, albeit quite utopian 'constitution' for a Europe without borders and without armies, with a unified judicial system and institutions consisting of representatives of all nations, in which the latter would be subordinated to European laws voted by a European parliament.[18] Jastrzębowski represented a relatively wide political current around 1830 which associated nationalism with an outspoken European federalist conviction. These 'Euro-nationalists', incidentally, did not necessarily reject the Christian heritage: quite a lot, though by no means all, could be considered 'Liberal-Christians'. They accepted the separation of church and state but still emphasized the Christian character of Europe. The poet and Polish activist Adam Mickiewicz even proposed a Europe-wide revolution, after which a new order would emerge, a true Kingdom of God, a republic of independent nations, based on a division of power. An important element in this respect was Polish messianism (somewhat similar to that of Alexander I, though the latter saw Russia as the centre of Christian redemption), which considered the Polish people as 'redeemers' of Europe. It is very present in the European federal visions of Polish authors such as the scientist Józef Maria Hoene-Wroński, the philosopher and political activist Karol Libelt, and even the socialist Stanisław Gabriel Worcell.[19] Their Europeanist convictions, incidentally, appear to be conceived as a way of restoring the Polish–Lithuanian Commonwealth; their federalist conceptions and, in particular, their views on church and state express this legacy as well.

In the Italian peninsula, more famous revolutionaries shared similar convictions to those of their counterparts in Poland, albeit without the same Christian messianic dimension. Guiseppe Mazzini, for example, the ideologue behind the Italian unification and no doubt the most illustrious and influential revolutionary of the times, saw Italian unification as one step in a Europe-wide struggle for liberation which would eventually lead to a European federation of free, sovereign nations. His universalism recognized the diversity of nations: 'the nation should embody the universal language of humanity, spoken in the tongue of each specific people', Stefano Recchia and Nadia Urbinati summarize his thoughts on the matter.[20] Hence, Mazzini argued for a 'holy alliance of the peoples', a 'cosmopolitanism of nations', certainly not for a Napoleonic empire.

The essence of Mazzini's plea for a liberal federation of Europe was that it had to be based upon free and democratic constitutional nation states, as these would not be so prone to going to war, though he was not so naïve as to think that war was no longer possible. But an alliance of democratic nations would be a powerful argument against others. In addition, trade relations could contribute towards establishing peaceful relations. The main issue then was, and has remained ever since: what is a nation? For Mazzini, following German nationalist thinkers, only peoples with a long-standing history and common culture, living in larger territories and capable of sustaining a modern economy, could claim to be a nation – he identified 12 of them in Europe, excluding the Irish, the Scots and the Belgians (no question yet of the Flemish), for example.[21] Smaller 'nations' would have to curb themselves for the benefit of the greater ones. Also other causes, such as the class struggle or religious diversity, in Mazzini's perspective should not interfere with the sacred cause of national unity – a view which made him the laughing stock of Marx.[22] And like Saint-Simon, whose writings he was familiar with, he saw for Europe a task as 'civilizer' of the world, explicitly legitimizing colonial conquest.

The question of what would become of those 'people without history', without the right to a proper state of their own, tended to be overlooked, and certainly nationalists such as Mazzini remained rather silent on this issue, which would come to the fore in the latter part of the nineteenth century. The question was particularly acute, though, in the Hungarian revolt of 1848, when the leading nationalist Lajos Kossuth argued that only Hungarians would be recognized. As revolutionary Regent-President in 1848–1849, he rejected any kind of regional administration within Hungary based on the nationality principle. Nevertheless, some other *peoples* (in contrast to *nations*) could benefit from certain rights. Hence, Kossuth in 1851 proposed the first legislation on the recognition of minority rights in Europe, referring mainly to the use of their mother tongue in local administrations, education and law. However, these did not apply to all minorities: the Romanians and the Croats found a more understanding ear with Kossuth than the Slovaks, for example.[23]

Central European federalism

Associations of nations did not necessarily encompass all of Europe. Especially in Central Europe, there were people who suggested a more limited scale, largely based on ethnicity. We have already referred to Friedrich List's idea of a unified 'Germanic' Mitteleuropa. List's economic and political views were based upon a deep conviction in German lands that Mitteleuropa was a distinct political and cultural sphere in Europe, with little in common with, particularly, British politics and culture, but also different from the Balkans.[24] Although List did not emphasize ethnicity, Mitteleuropa in his eyes should constitute an intermediate zone, perhaps even a buffer between Slavonic and Romanic peoples. Eventually, though, Germany would have to dominate the Balkans and Central Europe after the anticipated disintegration of the Ottoman Empire. This implied some sort of economic union between the Habsburg Empire and a 'greater Germany' as well – just as Austrian Minister of Commerce von Bruck proposed in 1848. However, for List this federation would imply the gradual 'Germanification' of Hungary – given the increasing Magyar awakening, which would lead to the transformation of the Habsburg Empire into the Austro-Hungarian Double Monarchy in 1867 (the *Ausgleich*), not a very perceptive perspective. It also required an understanding with the UK, which List hoped to realize by suggesting that the German confederation would constitute an alliance with the British Empire, by means of which the Germans would protect the latter's expansion in the east in return for a free hand in Central and Southeastern Europe.

Along with Pan-Germanism, there were also Pan-Slavic ideals, the latter divided into Russo-Slavic and Austro-Slavic versions (the latter of these emphasizing a republican federation excluding Russia). Particularly in Poland, a strong current existed that aimed at resurrecting the Polish–Lithuanian Commonwealth as a federation that, initially at least, would also include Russia, as a way of avoiding Poland becoming completely absorbed by its neighbours. Increasingly, however, Polish Pan-Slavism would turn its back on Russia. Even Adam Czartoryski reacted against Russian centralizing politics and strived towards a federation of Poles – including those living in East Prussia –, Czechs, Slovaks, Hungarians, Romanians and South Slavs, excluding Russia from 1827 onwards. Twice there appeared an opportunity to realize this – during the revolt of 1830, when he became the president of the Polish National Government, and in 1848–1849. However, the first opportunity slipped by when the revolt was crushed, and the second because of a lack of international support and the resistance of other nationalists. Czartoryski continued with his efforts to create a Pan-Slavic federation with Poland, Romania, Bohemia, Hungary, Croatia and Serbia which would respect different nationalities, including Hungary, after his second exile in Paris. Some Polish nationalists still left the door open for Russia, such as the painter and revolutionary writer Zygmunt E. Gordaszewski, who imagined a two-level federation in 1848, with at its base three federations for Latin, Germanic and Slavic nations, competent to stimulate trade. Together, these would constitute a continental European federation that would include Russia but not the UK.[25]

Polish projects were often inspired by a particular form of Pan-Slavic messianism, imagining the Slavs as a chosen people. This messianistic dimension, however, was not shared by other Slavs, who did nevertheless envisage similar plans. In the Hungarian lands, which had been gradually reconquered from the Ottomans in the eighteenth century, the main issue was the integration of the many people who spoke a different tongue and who belonged to different faiths, though intellectuals were also preoccupied with forging an alliance against Russia. The Hungarian Baron Miklós Wesselényi, for example, foresaw a confederation of independent Slavic nations, with which new nations that had liberated themselves from Russian or Turkish occupation (such as Moldavia and Wallachia) could associate. Though Wesselényi recognized Italian, Polish and Czech nations as equal to Germans and Hungarians, he did not recognize other people as 'sustainable nations', while also considering the traditional Hungarian lands as mono-ethnic.[26] Likewise, the aforementioned Kossuth proposed the association of different Central European nations, in particular Hungarians, Poles, Czechs, Croats and also Serbs, in an economic and political 'Danubian federation', respecting the rights of 'minorities', so as to constitute a bulwark against Russian Pan-Slavism.[27] Others preferred to follow the line of Schlegel, such as the Czech nationalist František Palacký, who aimed to revive the Habsburg Empire as a federation of eight 'Lands' that would act as the protector of 'small nations', including Czechs, Slovaks, Poles and Jews.[28] Such regional associations did not preclude a wider European association, however. Indeed, many Central and East Europeans imagined a Europe composed of different regions – mostly Latin, Germanic and Slavic – that could somehow federate into a Pan-European federation.

1848, birth of the 'United States of Europe'

The year 1848, sometimes considered the year when the 'nation' was invented, was also the year when the idea of a United States of Europe, in the image of the United States of America, first broke through. Arguably the first to formulate the concept of a United States of Europe was Carlo Cattaneo, one of the fighters of the revolution in Milan in 1848 and a major precursor of the Italian *Risorgimento*. Its most famous proponent was the French writer Victor Hugo, who in a classic speech at the Paris Peace conference of 1848 proclaimed his vision of a peaceful United States of Europe on equal terms with the United States of America: a European union in which the different nations would maintain their own identity, but melt into a superior unit and constitute a 'European brotherhood, just as Normandy, Brittany, Burgundy, Lorraine, Alsace, all our provinces are merged together in France' – the last-mentioned illustrating the fundamentally modern imperial vision of the Frenchman.[29] The reference to the US is important in this respect, but should not be interpreted anachronistically: in the mid-nineteenth century, the US was not much more than a loose federation of states (not nations), but one which was able to organize a common market, a common political representation (the senate, to which Hugo referred explicitly) and a common defence. This federation constituted an American empire – empire referring to the North American territory that belonged to the federation – and not (yet) a nation state that could count on a federal sense of loyalty and connection. Nevertheless, the US increasingly figured as an alternative to the European order: even before the Civil War (1861–1865), the advantages of the American model had already became apparent. Not all believed something similar would be possible in Europe, though, as the old continent was divided into nations that were based upon language and culture. Increasingly, these nations were imagined as having ancient roots, even if nationalists also widely acknowledged some common European cultural basis.

However, the idea of equality among nations constituted an important aspect, as particularly emphasized at a congress of Slavic nations in Prague.[30] It even figured prominently in 1848 in the argument of Julius Fröbel, leader of the German democrats. Fröbel imagined a Great German federation of German lands, together with Austria and the Slavic nations, for whom 'the free association of nations

(*Bundesgenossenschaft*) should be the principle according to which a new Europe would take shape', regardless of the degree of kinship.[31]

It was not always obvious, however, who belonged to this European culture and who was to be excluded. Insofar as Europe was equated with modernity and progress, some certainly believed that Austria and, to a greater extent, Slavs were virtual outsiders. Many Slavs even considered themselves to be outside the realm of modernity, even if they felt strongly attracted by it.[32] Still another issue was if it included other peoples, such as Jews, who for a variety of reasons did not fit into the ideal of a homogenous nation-state.

5
Between Empire, Market and Nation

Free Trade! What is it? Why, breaking down the barriers that separate nations; those barriers, behind which nestle the feelings of pride, revenge, hatred, and jealousy, which every now and then burst their bounds, and deluge whole countries with blood; those feelings which nourish the poison of war and conquest (...)

Richard Cobden, 28 September 1843[1]

For precluding war it is not sufficient that the power of justice should be a little greater than the power of the disputing parties. Justice must be so overwhelmingly superior that resistance may be out of the question.

John Robert Seeley, 1871[2]

The revolutionary wave of 1848 is usually interpreted as a turning point in Europe's long nineteenth century. Liberal, democratic dynamics gave way to more conservative, even reactionary political realities, as an imperialist state nationalism took over from liberal nationalism, and nationalism became more exclusive at the end of the century.

Around the same time, Northwestern Europe in particular entered a phase of unprecedented population growth. This was the result of industrial and agricultural innovation, productivity increase and an acceleration of economic development, even though the latter was uneven and fluctuating and went through a sizeable depression in the 1870s. Hence, Europe witnessed intense competition and rivalry which resulted in economic divergences and political tension, leading to major wars even within its heartland. Moreover, this tension spilled over beyond the geographical boundaries of the continent, leading to a new wave of imperial and colonial conquest in Africa and Asia in the last quarter of the century. Although European powers were by now in possession of unrivalled machinery and military power, Europe's dominance was already being disputed both from outside and from within, by countercultural movements such as Theosophists and anti-colonial idealists. Even at the high end of European colonialism, doubts about the sustainability of that position of superiority existed, all the more so as the US became a major international competitor, particularly in economic terms. Japan was also a potential threat on two fronts. Firstly, militarily it had gone from strength to strength by the end of the century, having inflicted defeat upon both China and Russia in, respectively, 1895 and 1904–1905. But it had also successfully competed with western companies in China and, to a lesser extent, even in Europe and the US, well before 1800. Nevertheless, whatever credentials it may have had as a possible threat to European dominance, it was not Japan but Russia and the US who were perceived as potentially the most threatening, and as a motive to unite Europe.

In the 1860s and 1870s, several strategies were developed that aimed at liberating trade and politics, suggesting a fundamental reform of the continent. The economics of free trade, the law of international relations and political reconsiderations of the relationship between nation and state offered different possibilities for a new and quite different organization and pacification of Europe. Especially between the 1840s and the 1860s, the Saint-Simonian confidence in the pacifying power of industry, trade and communications ran high – not for the first, nor for the last time the prophets announced that war in Europe had become anachronistic and counterproductive and was therefore unlikely to happen again. International lawyers, adding their own slice of utopianism, stepped in when those optimists' dreams dissolved after the confrontation with reality – paradoxically, at a time when the interconnectedness of networks of trade and communications was increasing at an unprecedented speed. The peace that the Concert had finally produced remained very relative indeed: it was at most 'a work of diplomacy and authority, not a work of justice and diplomacy', commented a most prominent French lawyer in 1864.[3] It was German lawyers who particularly emphasized the need for a judicial backbone of a European federation, including a European court of justice.[4] Notwithstanding the high expectations, neither trade nor law was able to pacify the continent, perhaps because they did not sufficiently address the root causes of its political instability.

The crumbling European order

After 1848, the international order installed by the Concert began to crumble. Napoleon III, who ruled France from 1848 to 1870 – from 1852 onwards as emperor – felt restricted by the limitations of the Concert and sought expansion both in Europe and in the Far East. Likewise, Prussia manifested itself more and more as the leading power in Central Europe, extending its influence over the German lands and striving towards the establishment of a new German empire. Russia also embarked upon a perilous journey of modernization (the abolition of serfdom in 1861) and expansion in the Far East (Manchuria), in the Middle East (Persia) and in the southwest towards the Mediterranean. The Crimean War (1853–1856) demonstrated that the Concert was no longer up to its task as peace-keeper. Though the Ottoman Empire would become an integral part of the European Concert at the Paris Peace Conference of 1856, and despite the Concert being able to conclude a series of multilateral agreements stretching into the Balkans, Morocco and Central Africa, none of this could prevent its demise.[5] New alliances created a new, yet very uncertain, balance of power.

Prussia emerged as the dominant European force, eclipsing the Habsburg Empire and eventually even France, upon which it afflicted a crushing defeat in 1870 – the King of Prussia, Wilhelm I, was crowned emperor of the new German Empire at the former palace of Louis XIV in Versailles. This humiliation would ultimately haunt France for more than a century, motivating much of French international politics in the country's thirst for revenge and its efforts to forever avoid a similar humiliation again. The Austrian Empire also suffered defeat, this time in 1866, after which Hungary imposed a Compromise (*Ausgleich*) resulting in the creation of the Austro-Hungarian 'Double Monarchy' in which Austria and Hungary (and in the subsequent year Croatia-Slavonia) became largely autonomous. The most immediate victims of Prussian expansionism, however, were the different German principalities, remnants of the former Holy Roman Empire that constituted the German Confederation. They completely lost their independence and were integrated into the new German Empire, which by its size alone would constitute a permanent factor of political instability on the continent; the same was true, for different reasons, of the weakening Ottoman Empire in the Southeast, where national movements and the imperial ambitions of both Russians and Austrians clashed. Nevertheless, after 1870, Prussia and the German Empire developed into the key ingredient which would eventually mould future European integration, dominating the continent's destiny and, particularly, the way its future was imagined. The 'German problem', as it later became known, was caused by those dynamics specific to a vast region where elites and masses shared a common language. Though many competing visions of *Deutschtum* existed, gradually nationalist-imperialist visions prevailed, aimed at uniting the lands where large numbers of people spoke German; a great many of these were living in Central Europe outside German lands. In addition, some core German lands experienced an economic and industrial boom which propelled them to economic as well as political and military might. The Prussian chancellor Otto von Bismarck proved remarkably apt at steering these processes towards Prussian expansion.

In many ways, Bismarck is a most unlikely candidate to figure in an overview of the history of European integration, as he was a notorious anti-European – he considered the concept of a federated Europe detrimental to his ideal of a unified 'Germany' under Prussian control and opposed it vehemently[6] – and his expansionist policy allegedly made a 'United States of Europe' less probable than ever. His ambitious policies by far exceeded the territorial boundaries of Prussia – indeed, his objective was to include all German lands except Austria (*Kleindeutschland*). Hence, he introduced measures that would prove important in the history of European integration, such as the creation of a European institution to regulate the traffic on the river Danube, which traverses many European countries. These were actually part of a more extensive development, certainly not restricted to German lands, of increased transnational connections through trade as well as transnational associations and international institutions. However, these economic ties did not prevent some of the Southern states siding with Austria during the Austro-Prussian War of 1866. The actual unification of Germany was achieved by diplomatic and military means and was concluded after the Franco-Prussian War of 1870 and the establishment of the German Empire.[7]

Occasionally Bismarck did express the idea that there was a common European culture, which in his eyes excluded the Ottomans, but his interest remained mainly in the 'German' people. From that perspective he opposed the Slavs, whom he viewed as 'non-European', though he did continue to cherish his links with Russia. After Prussia's decisive victory over France, however, Bismarck attempted to organize a new European order that would curtail France's power. Although the League of the Three Emperors that went into operation in 1873, allying Germany, Russia and Austria, was perhaps not what he initially imagined, he did present it as an effective peace force:

> We have witnessed a novel sight to-day: it is the first time in history that three Emperors have sat down to dinner together for the promotion of peace. My object is fully attained, and I think your Government will approve of my work and praise me for it. I wanted these Emperors to form a loving group like Canova's three Graces, that Europe might see a living symbol of peace and have faith in it.[8]

As a British diplomat observed, the League not only aimed at appeasing German fears of a French revenge for 1870 but also strived towards the maintaining of the (newly established) status quo, respecting *une France forte et sage* ('a strong and wise France') as well as a stable Ottoman Empire. The League intended to suppress dissident intra-European movements such as the First International – though apparently the danger of nationalism was largely underestimated.

As an organization advocating peace, the League of the Three Emperors was not particularly successful, lasting only until 1875. The system of alliances continued, though, even if it was more a game of geopolitical strategy and 'power balancing' than a real peace-promoting alliance. The British in particular made attempts to establish a stable order through the system of alliances – after the disappearance of Bismarck they entered the power game in Europe to countervail the expansionist policies of the German emperor, Wilhelm II. Lord Salisbury, who dominated British international politics from 1878 up to 1902, was an ardent believer in the 'legislative' order that the Concert had brought to Europe – 'the only authority competent to create law for Europe'. He effectively considered it 'the embryo of the only possible structure of Europe which can save civilization from the desolating effects of a disastrous war'.[9]

The European order was challenged not only by imperialist ambitions but also by nationalism. Ethno-national feelings were fuelled by emerging ideas of social Darwinism, regeneration and racism, developed in the first place by the fear of degeneration and which sustained the drive towards *Lebensraum* ('living space') for the population. They also inspired a new wave of colonial expansion in which the new German Empire would fully participate after 1885, directed both overseas and at Eastern Europe. The foremost ideologue of this development was the Orientalist Paul de Lagarde. Lagarde, whose interpretation of the distinction between Indo-Germanic and Semitic languages was grounded in a virulent anti-Semitism, pleaded for a huge Pan-Germanic Mitteleuropa, implying the 'colonization' of non-German lands in the East. Lagarde became notorious as one of the founders of modern anti-Semitism, but he stands for a more general trend of emphasizing the idea that land belonged to one people and that the interests of one prevailed over others.[10]

National and religious divisions and the longing for homogeneity

The new nationalism

While Prussia's rise resulted in the creation of the German Empire in 1870, the Ottomans had more and more difficulties in maintaining their grip on their far reaching empire. Their demise left room for Austrian, Russian and Pan-Slavic imperialist policies and emerging nationalism in the Balkans. The resulting instability would lead to a series of 'Balkan wars' and eventually to WW I. Also, elsewhere in Europe, nationalism and imperialism – sometimes hardly distinguishable – provoked major changes in the political landscape, such as in Italy, where the many principalities, including the Papal States, were 'unified' under the banner of 'Italy'. However, none of these European states were fully fledged 'homogenous' nation states, even if their populations shared a common language (albeit mainly spoken by the elite). Hence, the new and old European (nation) states as well as the 'modern nation-empires' strove towards internal unity and homogeneity, first of all by focusing not only on language but also on religion, and by trying to generate feelings of belonging and connectivity created by national education, politics of memory and the imagining of common traditions.

Though scholars distinguish between inclusive 'civic' and exclusive 'ethnic' nationalism, the trend was one of growing exclusivism, both on the continent and outside.[11] The many wars, especially those since the French Revolution, required a discourse of alterization and nationalization: the enemy was no longer solely other empires, but the people themselves. Hence, 'the French' were supposed to fight 'Germans', while Poles opposed not only Hohenzollerns but also Germans (though in actuality this only began to be the case in the latter part of the nineteenth century, not earlier, unless perhaps during revolutions). The very essence of nationalism, either of large or small nations, implies homogenization: the only questions are by which means – exclusion or assimilation – this is to be achieved, and which space is, as a result, provided for outsiders (as 'others' are per definition outsiders). In most of Western Europe, the process of 'nationalization' largely succeeded: French peasants ultimately turned French when they accepted Voltaire's tongue as their own.[12] The same happened in Italy and Germany after their 'unification' of 1865 and 1870, where one language offered a relatively solid base for forging a national identity. In this age of alphabetization and reading culture, language appeared a stronger source of identity than religion, though it did not totally obliterate it: religion often constituted an important source of 'national' identification as well. Language and ethnicity became strongly connected, though the identification remained far from absolute: people continued to identify 'ethnic' diversities even among those who shared the same language, as Jews often experienced, while language can divide nations as well.

Nationalism also meant that ever more people discovered their 'national' past and identity and strove towards autonomy and recognition, while the larger 'nations' tried to impose their language and culture upon others: as the peasants in France were turned into 'Frenchmen', the Austrians and the Hungarians (after the Compromise in 1867) tried to do the same in their multi-ethnic empires, though largely in vain. In Central and Eastern Europe, the claim for homogeneity made no sense at all. As a result of its complex history, the population was both more heterogeneous and more mixed than in Western Europe.[13] In the lands that were or had been part of the Ottoman Empire, the people had experienced different ways of dealing with diversity. Speaking different languages and practising different religions had been far less of a problem, as Islamic empires recognized people of different faiths, even if they did not provide them with the same rights. In the eastern and southeastern parts of Europe, people lived side by side, intermarried and mixed, with many (particularly, but not solely, Jews) wandering around between Vienna and Prague, Saint Petersburg and Istanbul.[14] However, the emergence of western nationalism and the disintegration of the Ottoman Empire (which, as part of its attempts to modernize, increasingly adopted national policies of exclusion in the latter part of the nineteenth century) put an end to this world of plurality: westernization and modernization turned the Balkans into the infamous 'adder's nest' it became.[15]

As the new nation states created rules of citizenship, introduced passports and failed to recognize double nationality, many 'minorities' were cast as outsiders. They were forced to completely assimilate, giving up their religion and ethnic and cultural traditions, or to leave the countries that they found themselves trapped in, or face an even worse fate, as the Poles and Jews did in Posen (Prussia) in 1885–1886, when 32,000 of them were deported to Russian Poland. In the mid-nineteenth century, Jews especially constituted the litmus test for the way Europe dealt with this new situation, as they appeared to have 'no country'. Within the German Empire, Bismarck initially followed a policy of inclusion and considered Jews (potential) Germans, but he changed policy after 1885. Increasingly, many believed that considering Jews as potentially 'good Germans' was detrimental to racial and ethnic purity. Especially in the vacated Ottoman Empire, ethnic and religious antagonists emerged with dramatic consequences for millions of people, especially Jews and Muslims.[16]

This situation did provoke a reaction, though. The Congress of Berlin in 1878 introduced minority rights, which offered minorities some protection in the Balkans, though in practice, Muslims hardly benefitted from them.[17] In the core lands of Greece and Serbia, virtually all Muslims vanished; elsewhere in former Ottoman territories, they were systematically excluded and discriminated against. The expropriation of Muslim landowners destabilized the existing social order and forced many to flee. The nationalist process followed a fixed pattern: first different ethnic and religious groups were counted and mapped – anything but an easy task and one which forced people to choose – and later these data were used to isolate the minorities or to motivate claims for territorial expansion.

In the Ottoman Empire, similar dynamics accompanied the modernization – that is, westernization or Europeanization – of the empire. Although the Tanzimat reforms (1839–1867), which abolished the Millet system granting self-rule to religious communities, had attempted to integrate religious and ethnic minorities in the empire, Christians and Jews faced increased discrimination and hatred in the second half of the nineteenth century. The fate of the Armenians became especially emblematic, as they were the subject of persecution and mass murder from the late nineteenth century, culminating in the 'Armenian genocide' of 1915.[18]

With the Balkan Wars in 1912–1913, a huge wave of ethnic cleansing swept over Southeastern Europe. Religious as well as ethnic-national minorities were systematically slaughtered or driven out of the new countries, creating massive migration and resettlement. The latter were not only motivated by push factors, though: states also appealed to their 'compatriots' living elsewhere to join their alleged 'motherlands' and populate newly conquered territories. Greece in particular, though also Serbia, Romania and the Ottoman Empire, deliberately referred to this strategy in order to reinforce their national population. In this they were, incidentally, stimulated by the UK, which emphasized the link between nationality and territoriality in its international politics. Nevertheless, before 1914, the aim appears not yet to have been complete ethnic and religious homogenization by all available means. Hence, important minorities remained in the many new states in Southeast Europe.[19]

Both in Europe and in Africa and Asia, social Darwinism and the fear of degeneration underpinned colonial expansion and racial politics of exclusion, which legitimized extreme, sometimes genocidal violence – hence, they are often seen as a prelude to the Holocaust, though the association is also heavily disputed.[20] Although direct links cannot be sustained, there can hardly be any question that the hierarchization and 'racialization' of society were necessary steps in this fateful development. They were part of a form of 'purification' similar to that of confessionalization.

The resurgence of religion as a factor of division

Confessionalization is mainly associated with the sixteenth, seventeenth and eighteenth centuries (see above). However, in contrast to a still prevailing secularist interpretation of modern history, religion remained an important factor in Europe, also in politics, even if the space for the churches in much of Europe, in Protestant as well Catholic and even Orthodox lands, shrank as governments and state apparatus increased and some parts of the population – large sections of the industrial workers, intellectuals, bourgeois – stopped practising religion, sometimes embracing freemasonry, spiritism or other spiritualities.[21]

In Southeastern Europe, religious and confessional allegiances infused with emerging nationalism, mainly opposing different Christian churches – Catholics, Protestants and Orthodox – and Muslims. Religious antagonism fuelled the Greek independence movement in the early nineteenth century, as it also did in the many territorial disputes in the Balkans at the end of the nineteenth and in the early twentieth century (and again in the 1990s).[22] However, a new conflict had arisen since the late eighteenth century, between the Catholic and, perhaps to a lesser extent, the Reformed churches and the new secularists (known as 'anti-clericals') – liberals and, certainly on the continent, socialists – who increasingly defined the public sphere as 'secular'.[23] This opposition gave way to the 'Culture Wars' of the late nineteenth century in continental Europe. In comparison with the early modern wars of religion, colonial violence or the ethnic and nationalist cleansings during the

Balkan Wars, these appeared largely as wars of words only. This was most likely the result of the force of domestic policing, which also contained the social struggles of the emerging working classes. Still, occasionally physical violence did happen, and the depiction of the enemy, often referring to age-old wars, could certainly be particularly violent.[24]

The churches, in particular the Catholic Church, vehemently reacted against the secularist attacks and reinforced their transnational ties from this perspective. Ultramontane Catholics even constituted a secret 'Black International' with close links to the Vatican to co-ordinate the resistance and to inform Catholics within Europe and beyond of what was going on.[25] These transnational contacts would, in the long run, become important for European integration as well. Nonetheless, the churches, including those in Germany, continued to be 'nationalized' and focused on their national integration.[26] Only when that proved impossible would they associate with regional nationalist movements.

The European culture wars resulted in bringing the Church back as a main political actor. Catholics in particular, but also Reformed churches in Switzerland and the Netherlands, organized political mass movements to protect their interests.[27] Their activities gave a new impulse to those dreaming of restoring Christendom, also at a European level: the influential Austrian ultramontane aristocrat Gustav von Blome, for example, the driving force behind the 'Black International', pleaded for the return of Christendom as a necessary condition for a European rebirth in a widely distributed essay in 1872.[28]

But the reawakening of political Christendom revived the rivalry not only between sword and mitre but also between the confessions.[29] Churches and chapels continued, with new vigour, to combat each other.[30] The dynamics of purification provoked new schisms, not unlike that which happened in North America, although to a lesser extent (for reasons that would take me far too long to elaborate; this will be a major subject in my next book). Hence, intolerance increased, especially in mixed states. Those especially victimized were the Jews, as Catholics and Protestants used latent anti-Semitic sentiments in their propaganda and made Christian communities profoundly anti-Semitic.[31]

The longing for purity certainly characterized not only modern empires and nation states but also the churches and denominations. But in this, the latter were not really different from secular political movements: the fratricide divisions among the socialists constitute notorious examples of the phenomenon. But they all pale in comparison to the nationalist ambitions, aimed at the identification of territory and nation.

Peace by trade?

The second half of the nineteenth century certainly saw mounting nationalism and imperialism from different sides. Nevertheless, at the same time, Europe became more and more integrated through economic and technological interconnections. According to liberal free trade thinkers such as Cobden and Smith, this would eventually lead to peace. Their view was not to remain a theoretical construct, but was actively pursued in practice as well.

A commercial peace project

In 1859–1860, in reaction to the increasingly aggressive international politics of Napoleon III, both in Europe and overseas, the British liberal MPs John Bright and Richard Cobden suggested the British government initiate a reduction of tariffs on wine and textiles in order to appease France. This initiative received a warm welcome across the Channel from the liberal politician and economist Michel Chevalier, who convinced Napoleon III to conclude a free trade treaty in 1860, afterwards dubbed the Cobden–Chevalier Treaty. It constituted the start of a series of similar treaties: in a period of six years, France concluded 11 more treaties and the UK four. Others, among which Belgium was a particularly eager participant, followed suit. By 1865, the network included Prussia and the German *Zollverein,* as well as the Austrian Empire, and reached from Portugal to Norway. Overall, tariff duties plummeted to an average of 8–15 per cent, with 25 per cent as an absolute maximum.

Physical barriers on the main waterways – the Rhine, the Scheldt, the Danube – were also dismantled, but it was the rapidly expanding railways which particularly removed the many obstacles to European commerce. Trans- and international economic and technologic cooperation projects further stimulated European connectivity. A pioneer in this respect was the Telegraphic Union, which emerged from bilateral treaties dating back to the mid-nineteenth century to regulate communications traffic; the Union was set up between 1865 and 1875. It was followed, not without tension and debate, by similar associations for radio and post, as well as transport over railways, roads and waterways. Such organizations imposed rules of uniformity, also as regards the use of machinery, counting and uses of land.[32] The increased infrastructure facilitated the movement of people: the American historian Carl Strikwerda demonstrated how mobile the workforce actually was, resulting even in European transnational bargaining.[33] Moreover, different industries became closely connected, which gave way to the first multinational companies in Europe. The iron and steel indus-tries in France, Belgium, the Netherlands, Luxemburg and Germany became connected, while food, oil and chemical enterprises also oper-ated throughout Europe.[34] Trade skyrocketed, though it always remains difficult to assess what part of this increase was due to tariff reduc-tions, technological innovation, new infrastructure or other factors. In this respect, it is worth remembering that while inner-European trade increased, that was also the case globally, and Europe actually became part of a global network of intense trade relations, partly – though not completely – colonial. Regardless, the European countries became less and less autarkic and relied on imports of agricultural products from all over Europe as well as overseas – their dependence on American grain, however, cost them dearly and led to the crisis of the 1870s (after 1873).

In some ways, a European 'common market' was constituted with the UK and France as its kingpin. In addition, European monetary integra-tion was well underway, based upon an extension of the French 'franc zone' that had existed between Belgium and France since 1830 and which was extended to Switzerland in 1848 and Italy in 1861. These four nations concluded a Latin Monetary Union (LMU) in 1865, adopting a common fixed exchange rate for silver (until 1874) and gold and allow-ing currencies to circulate freely within the union. Spain and Greece joined the LMU in 1868, and Romania, Bulgaria, Venezuela, Serbia and San Marino followed in 1889.[35] Other countries and regions also connected their currencies to it, while Sweden, Norway and Denmark concluded a similar Scandinavian Monetary Union in 1873. Hence, we may conclude that an economic space was developing that could effec-tively rival the US – if there had not been political rivalries that would eventually lead to its disintegration.[36]

Disappointing results

Initially, the increasing commercial relations incited hope for more. The French liberal politician Michel Chevalier, co-architect of the Cobden–Chevalier Act, for example, grasped the opportunity to plead for a new European order in 1866 – a new 'Westphalian Treaty' – based upon a republican union of nations and citizens, largely in the image of the US. He was not only concerned with peace in Europe but also wor-ried that only a united Europe would be able to successfully compete with the emerging New World in the long run. But the political antago-nisms proved too strong, and after the Franco-Prussian War, he changed his mind. Apparently Rousseau and Fichte had been right in doubting the peace-making character of international trade, and it dawned on

Chevalier that growing economic interconnectedness and interaction were not necessarily conducive to peace.[37] In contrast, the increasing economic integration actually coincided with a mounting spiral of nationalistic effervescence.

After 1870, Southeast Europe in particular would experience waves of wars, though Western Europe, remarkably, appeared to have been spared. Nevertheless, instead of moving closer to each other, states used trade policies to enhance their power and to dominate others. That was obviously the case for Napoleon III, who hoped to extend his political influence through commercial ties, but even more so for Prussia, which pursued a commercial policy that would strengthen its authority and influence over those with whom it traded. Obviously the liberation of trade since 1848 benefitted the British enormously, but it caused increased rivalries in Asia. Hence, commerce did nothing to obliterate political oppositions, quite the contrary. It certainly did not prevent wars either. Surprisingly, however, these rivalries and wars did not disrupt trade, in fact just the opposite, and economic growth apparently continued. Nevertheless the wars, particularly the outcome of the Franco-Prussian war, sowed the seeds of the demise of the network, even if Bismarck – partly also *because* Bismarck – imposed upon France a guarantee to grant the German Empire a 'most favoured nation' status, while at the same time demanding huge indemnities. The economic depression of the 1870s (after 1873) and the move towards protectionism of Germany undermined its effectiveness: tariffs increased again, and in 1878, Germany moved out of the network.

Relations between France and the UK stalled as well, partly because of not only domestic policies but also conflicting colonial interests. Still, notwithstanding the failure to maintain the treaties and the protectionist policies of continental Europe, intra-European trade remained important. While France gave up the treaties, the successor of Bismarck as chancellor of the German Empire, Count Leo von Caprivi, in 1891–1892, negotiated a European Commercial Treaty System as an economic counterpart of the Triple Alliance between Prussia, the Austro-Hungarian Empire and Italy, which also included Belgium and Switzerland. While the Treaty System officially aimed at maintaining peace, it also explicitly strengthened its political partners at the expense of others, in this case France and Russia, which had imposed upon them substantially higher duties.[38] By 1892, a new Europe-wide network was again in place, extending from Portugal deep into Central Europe, this time with Germany as the main centre. France, and to some extent also the UK, went into a self-inflicted isolation. The UK mainly looked for markets overseas, in its colonies.[39]

The American spectre

The growth of Russia and the US increasingly incited fears that Europe would not be able to compete with these giant empires. The British historian and federalist Sir John R. Seeley – who had already suggested creating a European federation in the 1870s – warned in 1897 that 'If the United States and Russia hold together for another half century, they will at the end of that time completely dwarf such old European states such as France and Germany and depress them into a second class.' Also, the UK risked the same fate if it did not federate its empire.[40] In particular, the McKinley Tariff Act (1890), which used customs and tariffs as a means to protect American economic interests and to stimulate its exports, raised concern in Europe. Jules Huret, a journalist for the French conservative newspaper *Le Figaro*, in 1907, spoke about a 'gigantic struggle between the old Europe and the new America, which is no longer a fight, but a massacre'.[41]

The American protectionist policies threatened the European economies, but they also provoked Europeans into thinking about answers to these threats, and these were sought in unification. The Austro-Hungarian Minister of Foreign Affairs Count Agenor Gołuchowski put things sharply into perspective when he compared American policies to economic warfare in a widely published speech in 1897: 'The nations of Europe must unite in order to defend their very means of existence.' Likewise, the French diplomat Paul d'Estournelles de Constant saw the Atlantic Ocean as 'one large invasion field against Europe', which incited him to argue for a German–French rapprochement and to stimulate a 'European consciousness' as first steps towards European unity. The failure of the European Commercial Treaty System illustrated the difficulty of such grandiose ideas, however. The most realistic approach seemed to be that of a customs union comprising Germany, Austria-Hungary and France, that others could join.[42] The industrialist Walther Rathenau, for example, who would play a major role in the early Weimar Republic, formulated a visionary plea for such a continental European customs union from a German perspective in December 1913:

> There remains one last option: to strive towards a Central European Customs Union, that the Western states would join sooner or later, whether they like it or not. (...) The goal would be to create an economic unity that would be equal, perhaps even superior, to the American. Within this union there would be no backward, stagnant and unproductive regions anymore. (...) At the same time the

sharpest sting would be taken out of the nationalist hatred of nations.
(...) What prevents the nations from trusting each other, to lean on
each other, (...) are only indirectly questions of power, of imperialism and expansion: fundamentally they are economic questions.
If the European economy merges into a Community, and that will
happen sooner than we think, so will politics as well...[43]

The interdependence of European economies incited some to imagine
that war was no longer possible, or at least – the difference is essential –
illusionary. In one of the great bestsellers of the early twentieth century, *The Great Illusion*, the British correspondent of *The Daily Mail* in
Paris, Norman Angell, contended that, economically speaking, war was
counterproductive.[44] The Great War that broke out a few years later
actually did not refute his conclusion, as the war only produced losers.

Civilizing and uniting Europe

Initially, the context of economic and technological co-operation in
the 1860s stimulated the formation of international, mainly European
associations – the distinction between 'international' and 'European'
often remained blurred, although 'internationalists' explicitly included
a view on international relations with other parts of the world, including not only the US but overseas colonies and independent nations in
Latin America and Asia as well, particularly Japan and Russia.

The pacifist voice
International peace movements have a particular interest from our perspective. Even if they were concerned with what happened in the Far
East between Russia, China and Japan in the late nineteenth century
(the colonial conquests, incidentally, raised much less concern), their
main interest actually remained with the European continent. In particular, Prussia and the French Second Empire were perceived as potentially
dangerous for European peace. The interest in peace was able to generate more support for European federalism: it is in this context that
Europeanism became a political movement supported by organizations
and journals, more than had been the case with the 'European nationalists' of the preceding decades. These had been able to launch a Pan-
European debate but did not really constitute a European movement.
That started to change after 1848 and particularly from the mid-1860s,
when Prussian expansion and Italian 'unification' jeopardized peace in
Europe.

The Society for the Promotion of Permanent and Universal Peace, for example, which had already been founded in London in 1816, offered a platform for debates on European unity in the 1860s. The aforementioned British historian Seeley delivered a famous speech to the Peace Society in 1871, in which he exhorted the European nations to unite. Constituting a European union was a necessary condition for creating an effective international law court to be able to intervene in case of international disputes, as the existing system was obviously inadequate. An international law court could effectively intervene but only within the framework of a state, as 'the law-court is not only historically found invariably within the State, but also [...] it takes all its character and efficiency from the State'. In that respect, however, he emphasized that 'a slight but effectual federation' – 'which it is so natural to conceive' never worked in practice, and that only a strong federal state possessed sufficient power resources:

> In order to be really vigorous and effectual, such a system absolutely requires a federation of the closer kind; that is, a federation not after the model of the late German Bund, but after the model of the United States, – a federation with a complete apparatus of powers, legislative, executive and judicial, and raised above all dependence upon the State governments. (...) The indispensable condition of success in such a system is that the power of levying troops be assigned to the federation only, and be absolutely denied to the individual States.

This implied no less than an entirely new citizenship, a 'real union of peoples', implying a common constitution, legislative and 'an executive force greater than that of any of its component States' and a common federal army. That the chances of such a federation's succeeding were slim, and infinitely slimmer than when the US was constituted, was obvious. Nevertheless, European history demonstrated that 'differences of language, of institutions, of economical condition, of religions' could be overcome, and the possibility was all the greater as the forces of religion and politics were both strongly united in their outrage against war and could be mobilized in this respect: the possibility of doing so had never been greater.[45]

Also, the *Ligue internationale de la paix* (International League of Peace), which focused on international arbitration – it changed into the *Société française pour l'arbitrage entre les Nations* (French Society for Arbitration), in 1870, after the Franco-Prussian war – was almost exclusively concerned with Europe and explicitly demanded the conclusion of a federal organization of Europe at its Universal Peace Congress of 1889, 1891 and 1892.[46] Its main inspiration and founder, the French economist and pacifist Frédéric Passy, was, together with Henri Dunant (founder of the Red Cross), awarded the first Nobel Peace Prize in 1901 – hence, 'European peace' actually motivated not three, but four Nobel Peace Prizes.

The main peace association that defended European unification, however, was the League of Peace and Freedom, set up during a large international conference in Geneva in 1865. Believing that 'If you want peace, prepare for freedom and justice', the League brought together many of the most prominent intellectuals and political activists of the time, from the English philosopher John Stuart Mill to the French liberal novelist Victor Hugo, as well as the leader of the Italian Risorgimento Guiseppe Garibaldi and the anarchist Mikhail Bakounin, although the latter fell into disgrace soon after. Marxists too had been invited to its founding congress, as the International Workingmen's Association was also perceived as a peace organization, but Marx finally declined the invitation. The League would elaborate on Victor Hugo's idea of a United States of Europe as a condition and means to achieve peace; significantly, the League's journal was called *États-Unis d'Europe* (United States of Europe). For its main architect, the follower of Saint-Simon, philosopher and lawyer Charles Lemonnier, the introduction of international law and arbitration were essential conditions to pacify international relations. Real peace, however, required more, and in particular co-operation between European nations in a federation which was to be organized by combining elements from Switzerland and the US. Though Lemonnier's proposals remained more prudent and, strictly speaking, 'confederal' (respecting the autonomy of each state), Victor Hugo had an even more radical dream when he predicted the coming of a new European 'nation', characterized by 'Unity of language, unity of currency, unity of measurement'. Though he – of course – foresaw Paris as its capital, 'this nation will be not be called France, but Europe. She will be called Europe in the twentieth century and, in the following centuries, even more transformed, she will be called Humanity.'[47]

His dream did not outlive the Franco-Prussian war of 1870, after which Hugo became a French nationalist, though the League survived.[48] It gave the floor to quite divergent views on Europe, the boundaries of which remained porous: according to Joseph Hauke-Bousak, representative of Polish exiles, Europe included Russia, if the latter were able to respect the liberty of the Polish nation. Hauke-Bousak, incidentally, was a rather unusual peace activist: a former colonel in the Russian army, revolutionary 'general' in the Polish insurrection of 1863–1864 and a commander in the French forces opposing Prussia in 1870 (which caused his death), he was also a sympathizer of Bakounin.[49]

The voice of law

Lemonnier's views were widely shared by international lawyers and jurists, even if they were not necessarily pacifists by principle. Pacifists and jurists shared the idea that Europe needed instruments to settle international disputes, and these could be set up within the framework of a European (con)federation, on the scope of which opinions diverged widely.

Most famous among these is undoubtedly James Lorimer, a Scottish professor of public law at the University of Edinburgh, who applied the 'domestic analogy' – according to which the international should mirror national state buildings – to advocate a close European federation, adopting a transnational bi-cameral legislative parliament competent for international affairs, an executive as well as a European tribunal, European taxes and some sort of 'rapid deployment force' to ensure the execution of decisions.[50] However, his Swiss colleague at the University of Heidelberg, Johann Caspar Bluntschli, who is most known today for his contribution to the late nineteenth-century codification of the law in times of war, was puzzled by the paradox of increased interconnectivity and rising nationalism, and concluded that Lorimer's pursuit of a European federation would be counterproductive and actually provoke more conflicts. Many liberal legal specialists around the *Institut de droit international* (Institute of International Law) established in Ghent in 1873 considered nationhood a constituent part of the international order. While they saw no contradiction between individual rights and the demands of the nation, they accepted that conflicts could arise between different legal systems and that international regulation of national legislations could be beneficial. Actually, as Francis Lieber conceded in a short but remarkable essay on nationalism and internationalism in 1868, some sort of 'community' had arisen between 'independent yet increasingly interdependent' civilized nations.[51] Hence, Bluntschli proposed the formation of a loose European confederation or *Staatenbund*, which would incidentally include the Ottoman Empire. This confederation would possess a lower chamber, composed of representatives of the nations, but actually be directed by a federal council in which the governments would determine the policy to follow. If necessary, the leading nations would compel the smaller nations to follow their lead, even by force. Even so, Bluntschli still also foresaw a court of justice, a tribunal and a court of arbitration.[52]

The question of peace remained the prime issue in all of this thinking about Europe – the decades between 1885 and 1905 proved particularly bloody all over the world, although Western Europe remained remarkably unscathed. James Sheehan even comments that at least in Western Europe, societies were increasingly pacified: not only had there been no major war since 1871, but also domestic life had become far more peaceful and pacified, partly as a consequence of increased policing.[53] But even if the latter was the case, Sheehan tends to take little heed of the mounting conflicts in the Balkans, the continuing tensions between Germany and France – which had not forgotten the humiliation of 1870 – and the imperial expansion which kept European societies in a quasi-permanent state of war, even though the major battlefields were situated far afield on non-European soil. Also, social conflicts as well as clashes between secularists and Catholics often turned nasty – not to speak of the violence Europeans practiced in their overseas colonies. The least one can say is that Sheehan's conclusions are somewhat overstated.

Jurists such as Bluntschli and Lorimer focused on international law and arbitration to regulate international relations. The law, in their eyes, reflected history and reason; hence, they saw themselves, in the words of Martti Koskenniemi, as 'gentle civilizers of nations'. However, while older legal views rooted in natural law considered the whole world bound by the same basic legal principles, their new understanding of law and civilization, deeply influenced by Spencer and Darwin, implied that the law was only relevant for nations sharing the same civilization. Hence, European legal principles did not apply to 'savage' or 'barbaric' peoples, that is, anybody in the south or the east. Hence, lawyers behaved according to Kant's cynical predictions and went on legitimizing almost anything, up to the quasi-genocidal colonial policies of Belgians and Germans in Africa, as became clear at the Congress of Berlin in 1885.[54]

A sense of racist superiority also underpinned claims for European unity, which were phrased in terms of Europe's unique and superior civilization. Jean-Baptiste-André Godin, for example, a follower of the social philosopher Charles Fourier – he founded the co-operative industrial community the *Familistère* – and a successful entrepreneur, in 1883 saw a (con)federated Europe, with full freedom of movement of goods, not only as a means to generate peace, but also as a peaceful 'civilizing force'.[55] These three concepts – peaceful, civilizing and force – do not match, though. Although he opposed brutal repression, the French politician and diplomat Paul d'Estournelles de Constant, for example, noted with satisfaction that European forces had fought together during the Boxer rebellion in China in 1900, constituting some sort of a 'European' army (actually the eight-nation alliance included Austria-Hungary, France, Germany, Italy, Russia and the British Empire, as well as the US and Japan). Somewhat surprisingly, at least from a contemporary (and thus anachronistic) perspective, the future Nobel Peace Prize winner (in 1907) connected this observation with the role of Europe as the civilizer of China:

> So if Europe wants to remain at the head of civilization, if she still wants to be Europe, she must unite not only in order to repress, but also for the organization of China, and it is here that its mission emerges and the dreams of solidarity are realized, predictions that yesterday seemed unreasonable.[56]

Occasionally Africa came into the picture as an extension of Europe and the most 'natural' continent to develop as well. Victor Hugo, for example, exhorted Europeans to 'unite' and 'go south' and to conquer and civilize Africa, a continent without civilization, without history: 'In the nineteenth century the white has made the black into a man; in the twentieth century Europe will make a world out of Africa. To remake a new Africa, to render the old Africa amenable to civilisation, this is the problem. Europe will solve it.'[57] The Berlin conference of 1885 to some extent adopted this ambition.

Even if peace proposals did not particularly focus on Europe, it proved hard to imagine them outside the European space – internationalism and Europeanism tended to be equated or confused. The leading voice of the Second International, Jean Jaurès, for example, campaigned for peace in the world, but inevitably in this respect spoke of the creation of a 'European party' or 'European League of Peace', which would include, together with the socialists, 'all people of sound mind who are aware of the constantly growing threat to humanity from militarism'. Though in hindsight a somewhat surprising appreciation, Jaurès, as many others of his time did, considered the developing European alliances – the Triple Alliance, the Franco-Italian rapprochement of 1902, the conclusion of the *Alliance cordiale* between France and the UK in 1904 – as steps towards a more general peace. Although he did not advocate the organization of a European federation, he did suggest a federation of 'small nations' (*petites patries*) and actually anticipated the idea of a proletarian Europe which would defend Leon Trotsky after WW I.[58]

Many campaigners for European integration in these pre-war years considered peace in Europe to be a prerequisite for world peace, and a European association anticipated an association of all nations of the world.[59] The German left-liberal jurist Walther Schücking, for example, considered the constitution of a European confederation as a first step towards a world state, which would be attained through the gradual Europeanization of the world. The Hague Conventions of 1899 and 1907, by establishing international laws of war and war crimes, illustrated his case, as they initiated some sort of global governance based upon the European experience.[60] Like Schücking, most jurists only considered a loose confederation a viable option for Europe. Many could include Russia, the Ottoman Empire, and the UK in such a European association.[61] Those who pleaded for a more federal formula, such as the French historian Gaston Isambert, opted for a more limited Europe. Isambert considered the Ottoman Empire 'European' only in geographical terms, but forcefully argued for the inclusion of the UK, which was in his eyes undoubtedly part of Europe's heritage. His opponents expressed fears about the possibly despotic character of such a strong federation and for the position of Europe in the world – it would make no sense to realize peace in Europe if that would provoke 'a war of the continents'.

The main issue, to which the peace planners actually appear not to have been that sensitive, remained that of the relationship between peoples or nations and the state or empire. These issues would ultimately lead to the Great War of 1914–1918.

Rethinking the relationship between empire, state and nation

Regional federations and Mitteleuropa

While many thinkers oscillated between internationalism and Europeanism, some continued to envisage smaller federations. The French anarchist Pierre-Joseph Proudhon, for example, in a classic text on federalism, considered Europe ungovernable, but nevertheless believed in the necessity of smaller regional associations – Scandinavia, the Mediterranean, the Low Countries (*Batave*); the Danube states of Mitteleuropa – which perhaps could one day unite into a European federation, but maintain their national sovereignty.[62]

In fact, similar ideas circulated more widely. Opposed to Russian and German imperialism whilst showing moderate sympathy for the position of the Ottomans, the League of Peace and Freedom of Charles Lemonnier suggested the constitution of at least three federal states in the Balkan areas after the disintegration of the Ottoman Empire: a Slavic state around Serbia, a 'Danubian' state around Romania, and a

Greater Greece, including Albania, which would join forces together in a Danubian–Balkanic confederation, with a 'neutral' Constantinople as its capital. Also, the free nations of the Austro-Hungarian Empire could be partly integrated or be transformed into a similar confederation. The idea of liberty for the nations was central to these remarkable proposals, but what constituted a nation remained unclear: not exclusively based on ethnicity, language or religion, the League distanced itself clearly from nationalist excesses.[63]

In contrast to such pacifist visions of Europe, German imperial views emphasized the idea of a common community of Central European nations – whose concrete boundaries shifted – under German leadership, with little if any consideration for the aspirations of the different nations, particularly those 'without history', in Lenin's denigrating term. We earlier referred to the German imperial view on Central Europe of Bismarck and Paul de Lagarde. There were other conceptions of Mitteleuropa, though. The influential Prussian historian and constitutional lawyer Constantin Frantz mainly turned to Friedrich List to formulate an alternative to Bismarck's ambition to create a large, Prussian-dominated German empire. Rejecting both *kleindeutsche* and *grossdeutsche* ideas about German unification (*Von der deutschen Föderation*, Berlin, 1851), Frantz proposed a confederative political system, recalling the old Holy Roman Empire, with which most European lands would associate – eventually including Switzerland, Belgium, the Netherlands, the Scandinavian countries and even Great Britain. Invoking political and historical arguments, he suggested that the German lands in the west should constitute a German federation, while Prussia should sever its historical links with Poland and Austria and integrate further with the Slavic peoples in the Southeast. Such a flexible confederal system, completely opposite to Lagarde's imperial Mitteleuropa, would respect the historical diversities of Central Europe and constitute a powerful alternative to the threatening Russian Empire in the east, as well as the mighty colonial empires of France and the UK in the west and the overseas competition of the US. For the anti-liberal Frantz, the historical essence of Europe resided in Christianity; hence, he radically argued for a return to Christendom. Not the least of his concerns in this respect was that a German federation would prevent Jews from Eastern Europe, in particular from Poland, migrating to Germany and undermining the latter's religious and racial purity. Hence, Frantz strongly opposed Bismarck's policy to grant Jews Prussian citizenship in the Polish Grand Duchy of Posen, which since 1815 had belonged to Prussia. As people without land, Jews in the eyes of Frantz could never be true and loyal citizens, certainly not in a Christian Europe – hence, they should be relegated to the status of second-class citizens (but their basic human rights, other than political, should be respected nevertheless). Such a 'pure' *abendländischen Völkergemeinschaft* (literally 'western federation of nations') would constitute a stabilizing factor in Europe.[64]

Bismarck obviously did not agree, let alone the German emperor Wilhelm II, though they at least shared one idea with Frantz, that of the German 'colonization' of the European east. The latter would become one of the cornerstones of German foreign policy in the late nineteenth and twentieth century. During the war, it was an imperialist version of Mitteleuropa that underpinned German policy,[65] though the author most associated with the concept, Friedrich Naumann, actually imagined a confederal Mitteleuropa that respected the autonomy of the different nations (see below).

The Austrian model

In the meantime, the Austrian Empire had been following a completely different path from as early as the mid-eighteenth century, recognizing its ethnic and religious minorities. Instead of the early modern 'one empire – one faith' principle, the empire had moved towards something like 'unity of empire in the diversity of denominations' (Martin Schulze Wessel). Especially after the Crimean War (1853–1856) and the Habsburg Compromise (1867), citizenship became dissociated from religion as well as ethnicity.[66] The formula of a multi-ethnic and multi-confessional Austrian Empire became a model for Slavic nationalists. Since 1848, Poles had formulated several plans for a Polish-Austrian-Hungarian federation, which certainly aimed at restoring a Polish nation in an international framework, but also at establishing a strong power against Russian and Prussian/German imperial ambitions. One of these, by the political scientist Stefan Buszczyński in 1869, suggested that the Habsburg rulers should concentrate on their Slavic lands and transform them into a Slavic federation of nation states, with Krakow as its capital (!), while the German-speaking areas (except Vienna) would be integrated in the German Empire. His very particular version of federalism – widely appreciated throughout intellectual Europe – distinguished between *ethnopoleis* (nation states) and *cenopoleis*, free associations of ethnopoleis (*Upadek Europy*, *The Demise of Europe*, 1867).[67] Others in Vienna or Budapest, following the ideas of Lajos Kossuth, suggested the constitution of a Danubian federation, an idea supported by the League of Peace and Freedom.

Such ideas were not entirely devoid of realism. In 1906, at the instigation of Archduke Franz Ferdinand, heir presumptive to the imperial throne, the Romanian jurist Aurel Popovici came up with the radical proposal of dissolving the empire, replacing it with a federation of 16 provinces, which he called the United States of Greater Austria. Inspired by the American and the Swiss constitutions, he grounded his federation in different nationalities (instead of using historical-political criteria, which would give the Hungarians a much larger share of the empire). He respected the diversity of cultures and languages of each nation – Popovici had vehemently opposed the Hungarization of Cisleithania since 1866 – but nevertheless suggested using German as a common language in the empire.[68]

As is generally well known, the Hungarians adopted a different, 'modern' nationalist policy of exclusion based upon the Hungarization of their territories after the Compromise of 1867. They implemented a national policy of Hungarization upon the diverse population, and by the end of the century imagined the reinforcement and extension of the Austro-Hungarian Empire as counterweight to the Russian and German empires. The Hungarian philosopher of religion – a graduate from Oxford and Harvard – János Györgi, for example, proposed a Danubian Empire, with Hungary as the leading power, that would extend from the Carpathian Mountains to the Mediterranean, and from the Sudetes to the Black Sea, including Greece – at first sight it resembled the plan for a Danubian federation of Kossuth, but Guörgi's project did not envisage respecting the autonomy and cultural identity of the constituent nations at all, such as the right to use one's own mother tongue when dealing with the empire.[69]

Marxist alternatives

Socialists and communists also provided different perspectives on the relationship between nation, state and empire. As far as he expressed himself on the subject – and he did so only occasionally and not in a very consistent way – Karl Marx opposed nationalism as well as Europeanism, as he saw both as instruments of the bourgeoisie to oppress the working class. Hence, Marxists believed that peace would only result from the class struggle, and neither of these was essentially constrained by national boundaries. Lenin would reiterate that position in 1915, arguing that a United States of Europe was either 'impossible or reactionary'. Marxists did share the view of Europe as a cultural area, though: reminding one of the 'national threshold' of Mazzini, they distinguished between those people 'with' and 'without' history – with, at least for Marx, the Jews as complete outsiders. But these national and ethnic differences were all subordinate to class (for Mazzini, of course, it was the opposite: nation overshadowed all other divisions).[70]

In reality, this position was hard to uphold. Polish and Austrian socialists held very different views on the place of the nation and the opportunities for a regional federation. In Poland, the founder of the Polish Socialist Party (PPS), Bolesław Limanowski, incidentally supported by Friedrich Engels, argued for an independent Poland that would then constitute a federation with Ukraine, Belarus and Lithuania (to be expanded with other free nations). Rosa Luxemburg, in contrast, opposed national independence, emphasizing the international character of the class struggle and pleading for class solidarity, in particular with Russia. Other Polish socialists also looked at the Austro-Hungarian Double Monarchy in order to establish another geo-political order with nations within either the Russian or the Austro-Hungarian Empire. But there were also many Polish liberal and socialist intellectuals who defended a future in a federalized Russian Empire.[71]

Some major socialist politicians and intellectuals in Austria imagined an entirely different relationship between state and nation, which also constituted a major departure from orthodox Marxism. Austro-Marxists considered the nation as the product of a common historical destiny but appreciated its contribution to the liberation of the workers. Moreover, they distinguished between the nation and the state, and from that perspective supported the loose, multicultural political structure that was realized in the Austro-Hungarian Empire. Hence, they could also perfectly imagine Europe as a federation modelled on that of the empire. Accordingly, the secretary of the Austrian Social Democratic Party, Otto Bauer, was able to conclude that a United States of Europe was 'not an empty dream' but the 'inevitable end of the road on which the nations set foot long ago'.[72] The view of the Austro-Marxists on the diverse ethnicities within the empire differed, though. The politician Karl Renner, who would become the first chancellor of Austria after the war, considered all nations, races and ethnicities, including Jews and Blacks, as equal and fit to become full citizens. Moreover, following a suggestion by the German historian Friedrich Meinecke (a surprising source, as Meinecke is known for his blatant anti-Slavism and anti-Semitism), he found a solution to the problem of conflicting nationalisms, an analogue of that which, in his eyes, pacified Europe after Westphalia: just as (in his interpretation) after Westphalia the bond between religion and territoriality had been released, he disconnected ethnicity, nation and territoriality, opposing the *cuius regio, illius lingua* ('whose country, his tongue') principle of ethnic nationalists. He therefore suggested introducing two passports, one referring to the state and one (cultural) to the nation – which also allowed Jews to be recognized as constituting a nation. Bauer, in contrast, emphatically supported the superiority of German culture, though he did embrace the different nationalities and their separate cultures and languages. However, he did not consider the Jews a different nation and demanded their full assimilation.

Still, both Bauer and Renner respected the diversity of the empire, though not all Austro-Marxists were quite so forthcoming; many held a different view such as the scientist Otto Neurath who pleaded for the universalization of language and culture in a stateless society.[73] As a rule, these national-universalist ideas did not go down well with the different nationalities within the empire, and also the Austrian Socialist Party imploded when different national groups disaffiliated. Nevertheless, before the war, Bauer and Renner's concept of uniting several peoples under a federative umbrella did have a profound impact beyond the Austrian borders, right up to the Baltic States and even in their relationship with Russia.[74]

All of these plans for some sort of regional federation somewhat obscure – but also constitute a reaction as an alternative to – the dominant trend of European nationalism towards homogenization at the expense of so-called minorities.

The place of minorities

The question of how to integrate diverse nationalities and minorities to some extent also preoccupied the people that we have discussed in the previous paragraph, but more research is definitely needed. Of particular interest are the Jews, the 'people without land' but also, from a contemporary perspective, the most transnational Europeans. That was certainly not the prevalent perception at the time, as Jews were increasingly considered as unreliable citizens, people without land, and persecuted and discriminated against.

Some, though, did indeed take up the defence of the Jews from a European perspective. The journal of the League of Peace and Freedom, the *États-Unis d'Europe*, for example, condemned the persecution of the Jews in Russia in the 1880s, challenged French anti-Semitism in the Dreyfus Affair and denounced the anti-Semitism of Karl Lueger in Austria in the 1890s. It did not offer very profound analyses of anti-Semitism, though, nor of the evolving position of Jews in Europe. Remarkably, its perception shifted from assessing 'the Jewish question' from a phrasing in terms of race in the 1860s – although in ambivalent terms, as in Ernest Renan's perception of Jews as race and nation[75] – to one of nation, whereby in the 1890s, Jewish 'integration' was compared to that of other minorities, particularly Poles in Russia and Prussia. In any case, anti-Semitism was viewed as an indicator of rising violence and a threat to stability and peace. By the 1910s, on the occasion of the First Universal Congress of Races of 1911, the journal painted the Jews in a particularly positive light, portraying them as dynamic citizens who were very well integrated and could function as perfect mediators of culture.[76]

Unfortunately, these ideas were not widely shared and Jews often faced violence and discrimination. The combination of nationalist 'awakening' and the contrast in imperial policy resulted in a multitude of ferocious conflicts in the southeast of Europe, where the weakening Ottoman Empire was losing its grip on the Balkans, and Pan-German imperialism came up against Slavic nationalism and Serbian and Russian Pan-Slavic imperial ambitions, eventually leading to WW I.[77]

In response, the idea that Europe should unite as 'the only resort' for peace, as the Dutch publisher Nico van Schendelen stated upon the eve of the war, peaked again – van Schendelen himself had, with a number of famous Dutch intellectuals, attempted to create a committee to defend the idea of a European association of states.[78] Many indeed believed that only a European federation, either in the image of the US or with an even more global association, could generate a lasting peace in Europe, with moral and legal provisions to regulate international relations. As the Polish Marxist historian Boleslaw Limanowski emphasized in his 1906 dissertation, all European nations should become free and equal, and if they did so, they would likely associate in a European federation like the Swiss one.[79] The German-British entrepreneur Sir Max Waechter, who created a 'European Unity League' in 1913, appealed to many a political or military leader, and in 1909 apparently even convinced King Edward VII of the necessity of a United States of Europe, in the image of the US.[80] It was, however, to no avail.

6
The Long War

The greatest and most obvious present need of Europe, for the salvation of its civilisation, is unity and co-operation. Yet the predominant forces of its politics push to conflict and disunity.

Norman Angell, 1921[1]

Europe's doom

WW I changed the shape of Europe in more ways than one. To the astonishment of many, it turned out to be a lengthy and devastating experience, which virtually ruined the continent. Officially it ended in Europe on 11 November 1918, but in Russia the civil war after the Bolshevik Revolution continued until 1922. The newly constituted Poland, aiming at securing its position amid two mighty and dangerous neighbours – Germany and a weakened Russia – and dreaming of re-establishing the Polish–Lithuanian kingdom as an 'intermare' (literally 'between the seas') federation between the Baltic and the Black Sea, grasped the opportunity to further expand through the military annexation of large parts of Ukraine and Belarus – the remaining parts incorporated into the USSR – as well as Lithuania. The Turkish War of Independence, which included a bloody conflict between Greeks and Turks, lasted until 1923. In the west, the UK faced the Irish War of Independence until 1921–1922. The occupation of the Ruhr by Belgian and French troops in 1922–1925 can be seen as an extension of the Great War itself. The war had exhausted the European economies, and in the meantime 'Uncle Sam' manifested itself as the new superpower which eclipsed all others.

The war shook the worldviews of Europeans deeply. The sense of decay was widespread, best exemplified in the two volumes of the *Untergang*

89

des Abendlandes (The Decline of the Occident, 1918 and 1923) by the German historian Oswald Spengler. Such feelings were expressed all over Europe, including France, where Spengler's work was either not well received or appropriated by the extreme nationalist Catholic *Action française*.[2] The old continent seemed overpowered by the US, while the USSR appeared an even more profound menace. Many also saw forces emerging in Asia that would end Europe's imperial domination. What was deplored was not just the loss of power and prestige, but especially of 'spiritual strength' – hence the call for a 'rebirth' which was sometimes found in pleas for of a European union. Some turned to religion for redemption – the interwar period witnessed a religious revival, especially among Catholics – but many embraced despair and nihilism.

Eventually, though, Europeans were able to recover their economies and their way of life, and continued to rule the world as if nothing had ever happened – the British Empire actually grew to truly become 'the greatest empire the world had ever seen'. Although at one time it looked as if the ancient Asian powers, even China, might finally rise again, that moment soon evaporated: eventually only Japan could impose itself as a major non-western contender in world politics and the world economy in the 1920s and 1930s. In contrast, the Republic of China, which was constituted after the fall of the last Qing emperor, fell victim to fragmentation and civil war, while most of South and Southeast Asia again found itself in the firm grip of the European colonial powers and Africa became ever more integrated, though with different statuses, into European colonial empires. However, this apparent success obscures the political and economic breakthrough of the US, which actually became the only real superpower in the new world order, and to which both winners and losers of the war became heavily indebted, either directly or indirectly. The US not only overshadowed the European powers, but also followed entirely different politics overseas, rejecting colonial imperialism.[3]

In the meantime, prudent steps were taken to increase the participation of non-Europeans in colonial government. White racism, however, prevented any serious change in the way Europe saw its role in the world, which mainly generated anti-colonial resentment and protest, particularly in South and East Asia. Europeans continued to consider themselves as superior, and believed that their moral and political superiority gave them the right to rule and exploit, but also motivated their self-assigned 'civilizing mission' by bringing 'civilization' and development to these 'backward' nations. Nevertheless, the fear of an 'awakening', particularly by ancient Asian empires, as well as a reversal of fortune, always loomed large. In addition, stressing the fundamental differences between Europe and the rest of the world incited those critical of the west to look east for inspiration, something – though I will not explore it in this book – which Asian reformers especially picked up on and used to their advantage, turning the colonial power relationships upside down.[4]

Not everything appeared so grim. In most European countries, the population was able to grasp political power as democracy broke through as the main political system, giving every single man – though often not yet women – an equal vote. However, this did not prevent democracy from remaining extremely fragile, particularly in Central and Southern Europe.

Planning 'peace' in wartime

Many, including scholars, seem to imagine that war offers favourable conditions for collaboration and brotherhood afterwards. War, however, is not usually very conducive to peace, and WW I is no exception. This is, of course, already the case with the politics of war itself, although these actually intend a new 'post-war' order of peace as well, imagined, of course, as the 'victor's peace'. Hence, imagining peace actually begins with the politics of war.

Wartime Mitteleuropa

The German Empire pursued two different yet interwoven policies of expansion during the war. On the one hand, it aimed at securing its borders using military force and turning its neighbours – in particular Belgium, Poland and the Baltic states – into vassals. On the other hand, it continued on the path of economic, political and military co-operation between Central European countries, which would eventually include France and Russia, creating a large integrated European community around a dominating Germany. A commission set up by the German chancellor Theobald von Bethmann Hollweg at the beginning of the war, in September 1914, was quite explicit as regards the overall objective, though at that time the perspective was still one of formally respecting the sovereignty of each nation:

> We must create a central European economic association through common custom treaties, to include France, Belgium, Holland, Denmark, Austria-Hungary, Poland and perhaps Italy, Sweden, and Norway. This association will not have any common constitutional

authority and all its members will be formally equal, but in practice will be under German leadership and must stabilize Germany's economic dominance over *Mitteleuropa*.

But there should be no doubt that the Reich's arch-enemy, France, should be made 'economically dependent on Germany'.[5]

The way to achieve this included bi- and multilateral negotiations as well as military conquest, though the latter was contested within the German administration, and while the war advanced, so did the geographical scope as well as the sophistication of the future European international relations envisaged, particularly with regard to Poland – at one point it was suggested integrating the country into the Austro-Hungarian Empire, which would be controlled by Berlin. Not only the Poles, who were not even consulted on the matter, but also Vienna reacted in a less than lukewarm manner. Distrusting each other's political and economic ambitions, neither of the two empires were willing to engage too far in an economic alliance that might jeopardize their own sovereignty, so the idea of a customs union was never really considered, as both allies still competed against each other. Gradually the German war goals shifted to the northeast of the continent, referred to as the *Ostimperium* (literally 'empire of the east'), where the Germans attempted to establish their power following the historical legacy of the Hanseatic League and the Teutonic Knights.[6]

Friedrich Naumann's widely distributed *Mitteleuropa* (1915) – soon translated into English and French (1916) – proposed a more moderate model for a confederal structure, competent only for economic planning and defence. Though it intended Germany to dominate Central Europe and admitted that in order to succeed, war appeared inevitable, Naumann's vision guaranteed considerable sovereignty to the member states and, significantly, foresaw friendly relations with the different peoples (Poles, Slavs, Magyars and so on) living in these areas. Though Naumann accepted German as the common language, he opposed cultural Germanification and anti-Semitism.[7] Other representations of Mitteleuropa went much further. The renowned historian Karl Lamprecht, for example, spoke of a 'Holy Roman Empire of the German nation', imagining the new 'national' content of empire as an 'empire-nation' as we described earlier, largely disregarding the fate of smaller nations.[8] However, its boundaries were anything but evident. The influential German liberal publicist Ernst Jäckh imagined a union between the three Central empires, which would thus include Bulgaria as well as Turkey, laying the foundation for a new German empire from Berlin to Constantinople and even further to Baghdad (*Das*

Größere Mitteleuropa, 1916). In contrast, Paul Rohrbach, his co-publisher of the journal for German Politics *Deutsche Politik* in contrast saw in Mitteleuropa a concept for reinforcing the German position against the Slavic peoples and particularly Russia, his main enemy.[9]

German Catholics enthusiastically welcomed the concept of Mitteleuropa, connecting it to the historical idea of a Holy Roman Empire, but interpreting it quite differently from the Prussian imperialists. Especially in southern Germany, Mitteleuropa was often represented as a way to counter Prussian centralization and to restore German diversity: their Holy German Empire rather resembled the medieval one.[10]

The zone of small states

Hungarians very much followed Naumann's logic and understood *Mitteleuropa* as an alternative to Prussian imperialism. The democrat Oscar Jászi initially adopted it to develop a view of different regions under leading nations – in particular Germany and Hungary. Jászi, however, changed his view during the war and, as Minister of Nationalities in the liberal-democratic Károlyi government in 1918, developed an extensive plan for a confederal and democratic Danube monarchy to replace the former Austro-Hungarian Empire. The new multinational state would be constituted by five major regions: Austria, Bohemia, Poland, Hungary and South Slavic Illyria. While it foresaw maximum autonomy for different nations, quite a number of minorities were not given a place within this federal model, which left the Hungarian territory intact. The post-war order imposed upon the empire, however, tore up the empire and left both Hungary and Austria mutilated, hence resentful, rump states. The Treaty of Trianon motivated mainly imperial plans for a revision of the treaty and an extension of Hungary's presence in Central and Eastern Europe. Jászi, however, who after a few months in office stepped down as minister because of Trianon and who then migrated to the US to escape the overpowering Soviet-inspired regime of Béla Kun, continued to promote his ideas as a new model for a United Nations of Europe.[11]

There were others who emphasized the value of small states and who rejected the concept of a regional union on that basis. This was, to some extent at least, the case for the Slovak-Czech nationalist intellectual Tomáš G. Masaryk. Masaryk, who had represented the democratic Czech Realist Party in the Austrian parliament until 1914 and who had been exiled since then, becoming a Professor of Slavic Studies at King's College in London, radically opposed German-Prussian imperial views on Mitteleuropa. From an almost Mazzinian perspective, he presented the war essentially as 'the liberation and freedom of the small states and nations' and saw in their association the nucleus of a new Europe.[12] However, for the Czech nationalist, not every ethnic group constituted a nation. In contrast to those authors who represented the Habsburg empire as a model of an organic unity that respected national diversities (especially František Palacký and Hugo von Hofmannsthal), Masaryk came to view the Empire as an oppressive force and an instrument of Pan-Germanic imperialism during the war. Hence, he called for its destruction and aimed at replacing it with a Central European Democratic Union of Nations around the river Danube – 'the zone of small nations' – which would respect the sovereignty and freedom of all affiliated members and their minorities, as for him 'a real federation of nations will be accomplished only when the nations are free to unite of their own accord'.[13] Increasingly, however, his perspective narrowed down to a blueprint for a new Bohemian state limited to an association of Czechs and Slovaks, based on mutual understanding and the shared political interest of both nations. The new state would inevitably also contain other minorities, including the Germans living in the Sudetenland. Masaryk proposed local self-government, proportional representation and cultural institutions, including primary and secondary school education in minority languages. He also pleaded for knowledge of the different languages throughout the new state.[14] Speaking of Europe, he recognized a distinct common European/western culture that excluded Turkey, which was to him an 'alien culture and barbaric'.

Representatives of smaller Central and Eastern European ethnic groups or minorities, including Ukrainians from Poland, Croatians living in Hungary and Jews in general, viewed the Habsburg Empire and, in particular, the emperor Franz Josef in a far more positive light than Masaryk and were wary of Czech nationalism, especially in 1919. Masaryk, however, had a great deal of influence upon the American president Woodrow Wilson. He suggested the Austro-Hungarian Empire be dismantled after the war, giving way to a multitude of small and medium-sized states that, in the event, satisfied few. One of the larger new states was Czechoslovakia, of which Masaryk became the first president.[15]

French containment policy

In response to the German imperial views on Mitteleuropa and in an effort to reinforce its political and economic position after the war, France focused on strengthening its ties with its allies. Initially, France hoped to create an allied tariff bloc in 1916, but the idea was not popular, in part due to opposition from the UK against protectionism. But the French and the British agreed that they should make the allied countries more economically independent from the Central Powers after the war. By 1917 plans for a customs union or a free trade zone between Belgium, France and Britain were formulated to strengthen the mutual economies. France seriously feared being deprived of food and raw materials. But the French also imagined ways to prevent Germany from posing a menace again. Obviously, Alsace should be returned to France – and 'purified' of unreliable Germans. The French also looked covetously at the industrial Saarland across the River Rhine, which for centuries had appeared a means of expanding France's eastern borders and could prove invaluable in bringing raw materials to its economy, while also weakening the German Empire. In this context, the idea of a demilitarized Rhineland arose. The French objective was not mainly the creation of a proper economic union, let alone an integrated Europe, but was first and foremost to find a means of gaining access to German industrial capacity while preventing the Germans from obtaining food and raw materials. Hence, at an international conference in Paris in June 1916, France proposed constituting a Western European intergovernmental economic alliance involving France, Britain, Italy, Belgium and possibly Spain and Portugal in order to co-ordinate inter-Allied industrial production and stabilize exchange rates. The Central Powers would be denied the status of most privileged nation. Apart from France and the UK, the other Allied nations, including Italy, refrained from such radical commitment: they preferred to keep all options open.[16]

As Georges-Henri Soutou argues, this implied a rather radical departure from the pre-war system of bilateral commercial treaties and initiated a new way of thinking with regard to the organization of Europe, which required new institutions and forms of intergovernmental consultation. This new way of thinking had broadened further by 1918. A large allied bloc would not only realize the containment of Germany, but also make France a major international political power again. The French government also wanted to bring the US into a common Western European – American alliance. At the same time though, they also tried to dissociate the Rhineland from Germany, creating a separate, demilitarized state under Allied control, along an autonomous Saarland region under full French control. These regions would be compelled to unite in a far-reaching customs union with France, Belgium and Luxemburg. The Grand Duchy played a key role in these plans, with its leading industrialist, Emile Mayerisch, fully supporting the suggestion of an intense social, economic and monetary union with France and Belgium which would, nevertheless, safeguard Luxemburg's independence – Luxemburg, a former member of the German *Zollverein*, understandably feared the territorial appetite of all its neighbours, including France and Belgium. In the background, the French Minister of Industrial Reconstruction, Louis Loucheur, was already striving towards co-operation between iron-and-steel consortia in the three countries and the Rhineland. Some in Germany supported the idea of an independent Rhineland: the Mayor of Cologne, Konrad Adenauer, for example, believed it would lessen the Allied demands on the German people; Adenauer also blamed Prussian ambitions for the debacle of the war.[17] Not all industrial and political leaders of these countries followed the French plans, however, as the economic advantages were not always obvious. After the war few of these plans were effectively realized, apart from a military alliance between France and Luxemburg and the Belgium–Luxembourg Economic Union (BLEU) in 1921.

In the meantime, the collapse of the Russian Empire modified the power balance in Europe considerably. France in particular feared the possibilities that this vacuum had opened up for Germany in the long term and, especially as the US continued to remain deaf to its concerns, it prioritized the constitution of strong Eastern European buffer states against a German–Austrian Mitteleuropa. It supported a powerful and independent Poland or 'a German Catholic confederation to oppose the Protestant bloc in the north', as the French army suggested in March 1917.[18] It is from this perspective that France endorsed Czechoslovak, Romanian and Bulgarian claims for national independence. French interest in Central and Eastern Europe became a lasting element of its international politics over the subsequent decades.

A new European order?

Some results of the peace treaties

By 1918 the European continent had been completely transformed. The Russian, Ottoman and Habsburg empires had collapsed and disintegrated and given way to a multitude of new smaller states in Central and Southeastern Europe. A new international framework around the League of Nations was to ensure peace in the future.

Notwithstanding continued European colonialism, new international institutions were created after the war, including those with universal ambitions, to enable the certainty of peace and to stimulate social progress. That was the principal task of the League of Nations, established in 1919, which set up different institutions to promote particular aims, such as the International Labour Organization (ILO) and, in 1922, the Permanent Court of International Justice, as had been suggested so often in the late 1890s and particularly requested by the First Hague Peace Conference in 1899. The League presented itself as the world parliament, but since the US and USSR had not become members from the very beginning, and much of the world was kept in a colonial state, it was largely a European club – it would effectively become important mainly as a platform for discussions about European issues. In contrast, the Permanent Court of International Justice certainly acted as a world body, but lacked power to effectively intervene in and settle major international disputes.

The League's objectives were ambiguous right from the start but were interpreted by many in quite contrasting ways. Many in Europe considered it to be a more extended version of the old Concert, balancing and reframing power in order to establish 'peaceful coexistence', although more democratic and internationalist aspirations did exist within Europe also. Americans and in particular French legal specialists believed in an institution of international law and arbitration, while according to Mark Mazower, the British prime minister Lloyd George preferred to see it as an extension of the British Empire, a way of generating an international order dominated by a British–American alliance.[19]

The Paris peace treaties which ended the war – there were actually five separate treaties signed in different places near Paris in 1919 and 1920, with Germany (Versailles), Austria (Saint-Germain), Bulgaria (Neuilly); Hungary (Trianon) and the Ottoman Empire (Sèvres) – were certainly unlikely to bring everlasting peace, notwithstanding the high hopes raised by Wilson's great ideals and pleas for a 'just peace'. If anything, the treaties became infamous for bringing about a 'victor's peace'.[20] Germany got the full blame for the war (through Article 231, the so-called 'war guilt clause'), was stripped of its colonies, lost important territories and was confronted with an enormous amount of reparations and indemnities to pay. The Austro-Hungarian Empire was completely divided by the Treaty of Trianon. An Austria which saw itself reduced from a world empire to a small Central European rump state caused many to resent the outcome. Rather than dreaming of a restoration of the ancient Habsburg Empire, a strong current would develop in Austria that strove towards unification with Germany. Hungary would particularly aim at revising the treaty in order to regain its former status and to expand again within Eastern Europe. Italy, although a victor, also felt frustrated, as its territorial ambitions were not granted. The Ottoman Empire was dismantled and its Asian territories partitioned between France, Great Britain and Italy – as Turkish nationalists defeated the sultanate as well as Greek invaders, a new treaty was negotiated in Lausanne (1923), by which the Turkish republic gave up its empire in return for the respect of its sovereignty. Mention should perhaps also be made of the Treaty of Brest–Litovsk (3 March 1918), by which the Bolshevik government of Russia ended the war with the Central Powers and gave up its claims on the Baltic states, Poland and Ukraine (part of which was ceded to the Ottoman Empire).

While Austria, Hungary, Germany and Italy opposed the territorial arrangements, especially in Central and Southeastern Europe many new states endorsed the new European map. As they feared that Germany would claim territories with important German minorities (or majorities, as in the Sudetenland) and Austria and Hungary would aim towards a restoration of the Austro-Hungarian 'Habsburg' Empire and question the settlement, they were usually eager to create alliances in an effort to defend their own interests and to maintain the new post-war order, an endeavour which was, however, jeopardized because some of these countries had international political ambitions of their own. In Poland, for example, which in 1918 had just regained its independence, the memory of the Polish Lithuanian Commonwealth was still vivid, which led to plans for a Polish-dominated 'intermare' federation or empire stretching from the Baltic to the Black Sea.[21] The idea of a strong federation or empire between Russia and Germany strongly appealed to all Poles, who saw in it a way of containing their mighty neighbours, and hence a condition for a stable order and peace in the whole of Europe. However, as this grand ambition motivated Polish expansion during the Polish–Soviet War (1919–1921) as well as the Polish–Lithuanian War (1919–1920), with Poland annexing large parts of present-day Belarus and Ukraine as well as Lithuania, such a vision became widely perceived as imperialist, particularly in the Baltic and in Czechoslovakia (which actually followed a similar policy).

Czechoslovakia, Romania and Yugoslavia constituted a 'Little Entente' as a military defence association in 1920 and 1921, especially to prevent Hungarian revanchist imperialism and to increase the international position of the signatories. The treaty was not backed up by economic agreements, nor were there more ongoing political engagements due to the different international political interests and orientations of the signatories. Hence, it remained rather redundant – though one could have imagined it as the basis of a more powerful association of nations.

France, incidentally, engaged in friendly relations with each of these countries and supported the regional associations as a means to contain Germany from the east.[22]

Self-determination and the issue of minorities

The new international order contained some important changes vis-à-vis the pre-war system, but in some ways was ill-adapted to the challenges of the time. The promotion of democratic and liberal values by the main protagonists was undoubtedly important, even if their interpretation of these values diverged and issues of security easily overshadowed these genuine concerns, particularly in the countries, such as France, that had suffered most from the war and which were most concerned about containing or eliminating the German menace.[23] The issue of minorities was tackled through the Minority Rights Treaties, which were imposed upon states as a condition for membership of the League of Nations – that is, the newly established states, not the old ones, which seriously undermined the League's validity, as its application was restricted to Central and Eastern Europe in practice. The treaties conferred basic rights on all nationals of the country 'without distinction of birth, nationality, language, race or religion', and declared that racial, religious or linguistic minorities would enjoy the same rights as other citizens. But they did not recognize collective rights, only those of individual citizens, which actually made it more difficult to protect minorities. In addition, the League hardly possessed any means to effectively enforce minority protection. Moreover, apart from the particular issue of imposing Minority Rights Treaties, the League no longer accepted the interference of the great powers in the 'domestic' affairs of others (principle of territorial integrity). It did offer humanitarian aid to refugees, though.[24]

In this context the idea of self-determination could hardly be considered a pacifying political concept, even if it was meant to be liberating and democratic. The principle of the self-determination of nations appeared explicitly legitimized by the American president Woodrow Wilson in 1918. Also, the leader of the fledgling Russian Soviet Federative Socialist Republic, Vladimir Lenin, and the new Turkish leader, Mustafa Kemal Atatürk, publicly endorsed the idea of self-determination. Lenin formally gave up Russian claims on the Ukraine, Belarus, Poland, Finland and the Baltic states, which gained independence, Estonia, Latvia and Lithuania becoming satellites of the German Empire. However, Lenin and Atatürk, in contrast to Wilson, did not limit the principle of self-determination to Europeans alone. Hence, they apparently had stronger moral claims than the Americans (let alone the Europeans): indeed, the American president never intended the principle to apply also to non-European nations, which provoked worldwide deep disillusionment and bitterness in Africa and Asia when they realized that they were excluded. That the Bolshevik interpretation of self-determination, as it soon turned out with regard to the Ukraine, did not imply respect for the democratic will of the people, was somehow less noticed. A similar observation can be made with regard to Atatürk's assimilation policies towards minorities in Turkey.[25]

In any case, in Europe self-determination proved impossible to implement: the main issues remained those of the definition of a nation, the sustainability of independent nation states and, last but not least, the heterogeneity and multicultural nature of Eastern and Southeastern Europe. Incidentally, the American president actually never fully endorsed self-determination himself: his ideal was self-government in a new international order under the umbrella of a League of Nations. But in the meantime the damage was done: as self-determination became the norm, the idea that nation states needed to be homogenous gained further legitimacy. However, homogeneity was an impossible chimera anywhere in the modern world, even in Western Europe, and certainly in (South-)Eastern and Central Europe. Moreover, as most strategists acknowledged, stability as well as the containment of the belligerents required larger states, not smaller ones.

While the new international system recognized a multitude of new states, few, if any, were homogenous. Some did to some extent endorse the principle of associating different nations, such as Yugoslavia and Czechoslovakia. Most, however, did so only reluctantly, such as Poland, which was compelled to accept the Minority Rights Treaty as a condition for being recognized as a major state in Central Europe, as were many other states in Europe. Hence, minorities were discriminated against and persecuted virtually everywhere, including in Yugoslavia and Czechoslovakia, provoking mass migration.

Ethnic homogenization

Many ethnic groups or 'nations' strived towards their own state; they mostly imagined it as homogenous and pursued policies of exclusion or assimilation. The pre-war policies of ethnic and religious homogenization were continued during and after the war by small and large states alike, among them the Soviet Union, Poland and Turkey. Especially, the USSR pursued harsh policies of purging and oppression of Polish, Ukrainian and Belarussian minorities, especially after the Polish–Soviet War, while Poland alienated its minorities through strongly promoting

Polish identity, culture and language. The successor of the disintegrated Ottoman Empire under Atatürk followed an accelerated and enforced 'catch-up' policy of national modernization and westernization. Striving towards national homogeneity in Turkish nationalist eyes ranked high from that perspective, as the Kurds in particular experienced. Still, they faced less hardship than the minorities in many Central and Eastern European lands, among them Jews. Many people were driven away from their homes by war and civil war (the Bolshevik Revolution), as well as by the policies of ethnic cleansing and homogenization afterwards.

For example, Greeks fled to Greece from Turkey in huge numbers after Greece had invaded Asia Minor, officially to 'protect' Greek minorities there, though in reality to expand its own territory. The Treaty of Lausanne in 1923 foresaw the forced 'exchange' of Greek and Turkish populations in the respective countries, a policy suggested by the chairman of the Lausanne conference, the British Foreign Secretary Lord Curzon, who earlier as Viceroy of India had split Bengal into a Hindu and a Muslim province and thus had some experience of – and an ideological inclination towards – separating people of different faiths in order to control them. The Bengal experience, however, should have been a warning that separation did not necessarily bring with it harmony, quite the contrary. While intended to generate a 'true pacification', the Lausanne Treaty sowed hatred and resentment. Approximately 700,000 people were compelled to leave their homes and possessions and were subject to horrific mistreatment. Nevertheless, international relations between Turkey and Greece stabilized and both entertained friendly relations until at least 1940. Hence, the lesson politicians and diplomats learned from these events was that homogenization and ethnic separation did pay off. The long-term result is less clear, though, as ethnicity and religion continue to be seen as causes of division and conflict in the region, and whether it is fundamentally pacified remains doubtful.

In the meantime, Greek refugees from Turkey drove the Bulgarian minority in Greece out into their supposed Bulgarian homeland, where the same pattern was repeated with Bulgarian Greeks in the position of the minority on the run. Similar tragedies were repeated several times in different places, as in the new borderlands between Germany and Poland. In general a policy of 'minorities exchange' developed, which looked nice at the negotiators' table – politicians, diplomats and political scientists considered it a positive contribution to a lasting peace – though the populations concerned rarely shared their enthusiasm and seldom left their *Heimat* (literally 'homeland') voluntarily. Such politics of separation were not restricted to Eastern Europe. In Alsace, which according to the Versailles Peace Treaty was returned to France after having been incorporated into the German Empire since 1870, the French government divided the population according to nationality, then introduced discriminatory measures towards those who were not considered pure French, and consequently started to incarcerate and expel the 'Germans'.[26]

In the Baltic, Poland and Czechoslovakia, a significant minority were Germans, the result of the post-war peace arrangements at Versailles. Their situation allowed Germany to take up a remarkable role as the advocate of minorities in the 1920s and 1930s.[27]

A European federation as guarantee of peace

To some, European federalism appeared a logical answer to the nationalism that they blamed for the war. For the young Italian economist and future president of the Italian Republic Luigi Enaudi, writing under his pen name Junius, the very concept of state power and national sovereignty inevitably led nations on a path towards self-reliance and political and economic expansionism. Hence, Enaudi forcefully pleaded for a reorganization of European economic and political space based upon the association of three separate unions: a Latin economic union, which would also include France, a Germanic and a Slavic Union.[28] Such ideas were developed in more depth by his friend and fellow economist Attilio Cabiati and the founder of Fiat, Giovanni Agnelli, who in their book *Federazione Europea o Lega delle Nazioni* (European Federation or League of Nations, 1918), mainly referring to British liberal federalism, concluded in favour of a European federation with a legislative parliament and executive council, and a federal court to ensure the rule of law, which they considered of paramount importance.[29]

Pacifists, particularly numerous in neutral countries such as the Netherlands and Switzerland but also very evident in France, Belgium and indeed Germany, emphasized European federalism as a means of realizing peace. The pre-war peace associations that had stimulated the idea of a European federation, however, including the League of Peace and Freedom, the International League of Peace and the Universal Peace Congresses, had a hard time, in part because many militants of the 'first hour' had died, but also because the war had set up early pacifists against each other. The League of Peace and Freedom, for example, hardly survived, as the French – who had dominated the movement since its conception – were deeply disillusioned and angered at the alleged 'silence' of their German companions during the war. Although the publication of their review *Les Etats Unis d'Europe* resumed, it never regained the significance as it had previously enjoyed and was eclipsed by movements that argued for a Europeanist 'revolution' rather than a series of laws and institutional arrangements.[30] Moreover, many initially believed that the importance of Europe was over, and that the future lay in a new world order, in an association of all nations. In 1917, the Belgian pacifist Paul Otlet expressed what many believed, that 'just wanting to create a United States of Europe was to discard the true character of international (world) relations at the present stage of their evolution'.[31] French 'internationalists', who constituted an important current in the political spectre, actually thought the same.[32]

Imagining a European rebirth

Lost soul

The concrete plans discussed in the paragraph above mainly focused on strategies for the future designed by administrators, economists and politicians preoccupied with the war itself and the power relations afterwards. However, there was a general belief that the war was only one expression of a far deeper crisis, though it certainly contributed to the general decay of the *Abendland* – mostly not used in the broad sense as the 'west' or occident, but referring in a more narrow sense to 'European' civilization.

This sense of crisis and decay was widespread and cut across the political spectre, lasting throughout the interwar period. Authors such as Oswald Spengler, Paul Valéry and Ortega y Gasset lamented the decline of European civilization, but the solutions imagined to redress the situation ranged widely. Once again intellectuals turned to Europe's history for inspiration and comfort: they looked for the origin of Europe's culture and identity, which distinguished it from the USSR and even more from the US, which was associated with materialism, individualism and modernism, and which moreover also threatened Europe from within (H.G. Wells, Christopher Dawson, Arnold Toynbee, Hilaire Belloc and so on).[33] Quickly realizing the problematic nature of such a search for a European identity, some (Edmund Husserl, Ortega y Gasset, Benedetto Croce) emphasized the historicity itself as a main feature of European civilization: in contrast to the US and the USSR, it had a profound history, which also distinguished it from other, 'stagnant' civilizations.[34] Some, such as the German Catholic philosopher Max Scheler in 1915, considered that only continental Europe shared a similar culture, distinguishing it from Russia and the Far East as well as the British-American 'spiritual' civilization.[35] As division remained a sign of weakness, many, though by no means all, believed that Europe could only redeem itself by uniting – the main questions remained, though: On what basis this unity could be imagined and what space was there for the nation state? The latter was seen both as already obsolete and as the core from which a new Europe should arise. Another issue was whether Europe should unite to resist and develop in order to remain the dominating world civilization, with the outside world mainly seen as a menace, or, on the contrary, embrace the cultural richness and spirituality of other, mainly Asian cultures in order to find again its 'lost soul'. The authors taking the latter view remained less pessimistic and more hopeful than their more Eurocentric equivalents. This was, for example, the perspective of many intellectuals fascinated by the spirituality of the 'mystic East' around the international literary revue *Europe,* founded by the literary cosmopolitan Romain Rolland, who published on Rabindranath Tagore and Ghandhi, or René Guénon, who emphasized the complementarity of western philosophy and 'Eastern' mysticism.[36]

A true 'European revolution'

Faced with an existential crisis, many believed that a true revolution was needed, and while for once division and diversity were not necessarily seen as the prime root causes of the situation of despair, views on the nature of that revolution diverged widely. The French philosopher and writer Jules Romains (Louis Farigoule), for example, imagined a true 'European revolution', leading to a European civil society with European political parties, and economic and monetary institutions.[37] Such ideas were also defended from 1919 onwards by the Radical politician and finance expert, former French prime minister and Minister of Finance Joseph Caillaux, who argued for the introduction of a continent-wide exchange system, even a single currency, as well as industrial consultation as steps towards a United States of Europe, 'the only grave in which one can bury the always threatening imperialism, for the great peace of peoples: In one word, radical-socialist democracy must take the lead'.[38]

Romains and Caillaux illustrate a strong current among the European political left, particularly significant in France, in favour of European federalism as an alternative to nationalism and the political and economic fragmentation that characterized Europe. In this respect they built upon a strong 'solidaristic' tradition in French legal thinking and philosophy, which considered only the individual as the real subject of the law, but at the same time emphasized – in quite distinct ways – the relationship between the individual and the different communities, of which the state was just one. This 'solidaristic' thinking allowed for imagining international federal institutions at European and global level. The League of Nations hence found much support in France, though these intellectuals combined their international thinking with a distinct French perspective, considering, in an almost Napoleonic fashion, the French model as universally valid, while at the same time sustaining French imperialism and colonialism overseas.[39]

The radical-socialist 'Europeanists' distanced themselves from both the Austro-Marxist position and, particularly, from orthodox Marxism as represented by Lenin. Though at the beginning of the war Lenin perceived a possibility of Europe becoming the stage of a Bolshevik Revolution – that would not happen in industrial Europe, but in the agrarian-feudal Russia – orthodox Marxists would soon return to the position that European federalism actually served the interests of the bourgeois capitalists and aimed at oppressing the working classes in Europe as well as beyond, by maintaining a colonial order of oppression. Trotsky, however, in 1923 revived the option of a proletarian revolution in the core of Europe's urban and industrial basins, directed by the communist workers' avant-garde as the first phase of the international class struggle, which would bring about a 'proletarian' United States of Europe – which would include the USSR – to save the continent from destruction and enslavement to American capitalism.[40]

A very particular attempt at creating a socialist-national (not 'national-socialist') 'European revolution' was planned in Rijeka (Italian: Fiume), on the Croatian coast in front of Italy. There, the revolutionary Italian poet and war hero Gabriele D'Annunzio and the Belgian poet Leon Kochnitzky harked back to the ideas of Mazzini when they created the *Lega di Fiume* as an 'Anti-League of Nations' in 1920. This organization saw in the association of oppressed and liberated peoples, in Europe or elsewhere, a necessary condition for a new world order.[41]

A conservative revolution

The idea of a deep spiritual and existential crisis and the fundamental weakness of Europe also animated very different pleas for European unification during and after the war, which mainly aimed at restoring Europe's 'superior' place in the world. Illustrative is the comment of the renowned conservative Belgian medievalist Godefroid Kurth, author of a celebrated history of the origins of modern (European) civilization *Les Origines de la civilisation moderne* (The Origins of Modern Civilization, 1886). Much concerned about the future of his devastated continent, Kurth compared Europe's state of decline with the dynamic development of the US and Japan, and even foresaw the imminent independence of 'Hindustan' and the other European colonies in South and Southeast Asia. Hence, he wrote shortly before his death in 1916,

> In order to avoid if not the annihilation of Europe then at least its humiliation, [Europe] should close ranks and organize itself as the United States of Europe. Hence we will have the number and we would be able to maintain the prestige of Europe and of Christianity in front of the yellow [races].[42]

Such cultural pessimism also underpinned the ideas of conservative Catholics, such as the young lawyer Carl Schmitt (before his break with the Catholic Church), the energetic prince Karl Anton Rohan, and the so-called *Abendland* movement, a broad spectre of Catholic personalities and circles that cherished the idea of European Occident as an alternative to both Bolshevism and liberalism. It combined Germanic ideas on Mitteleuropa with the need for French–German reconciliation and rapprochement.

Karl Anton Rohan in particular was a typical representative of a 'movement' of like-minded noblemen (including Hugo von Hofmannsthal, Prince Löwenstein, Count Hermann Keyserling and Otto von Habsburg) who regretted the demise of their old world, where the nobility ruled and wandered freely throughout the continent, unhindered by passports and bureaucrats.[43] Rohan dreamed of restoring a hierarchical Christian social and political order, particularly stressing the importance of a leading cultural 'elite'. Already by the early 1920s, he had committed himself to fascism and the German 'conservative revolution', and considered cleansing Europe of 'democratic corruption' one of the main objectives of a new Europe.[44] His ideas were particularly close to those of the young Italian war hero Curzio Malaparte, one of Italy's most gifted essayists, who dreamt about a 'new order' that he found in fascism. In 1923, Malaparte wrote a notorious essay which represented fascism as a Catholic restoration movement and portrayed Catholic and fascist Italy (actually 'national syndicalism') as the nucleus of *L'Europa vivente*, 'Living Europe', opposed to the despised Europe of the 'moderns', in particular international socialism and liberalism.[45] Both for Malaparte and, more explicitly, for Rohan, Europe needed to pull itself together against external threats, rejuvenate and constitute itself as a 'Third Way' (or 'third force'). Rohan in particular feared not only the USSR and the 'Anglo-Saxon' domination – the reason why he opposed the League of Nations – but also the looming 'awakening' of the Islamic and East Asian empires. Most of these advocates of a Christian Europe, incidentally, limited the concept of the *Abendländische* Europe to the old Carolingian empire, with the river Rhine as a unifying artery.

Besides the stabilizing role of the monarchy, Rohan emphasized the importance of the nation, as for him Europe could 'only be organically built as a domed building that rests on the columns of national powers. Europe's unity presupposes the unity of its nation states.'[46] Interestingly, though, he praised the value of German as a unifying language, not to impose a common German identity but as a means of communication in courts, in the military and in education. In contrast to Masaryk and other nationalists, Rohan contended that the different peoples in the Habsburg Empire lived together in perfect harmony in a real *Vielvölkerstaat*, which would also be a model for Europe to follow. He believed that the unification of Europe, however, could not be achieved as the result of political and economic decisions and convergences: a political Europe should be built upon a common European consciousness or culture. Nevertheless, and notwithstanding his fascist sympathies, Rohan rejected the idea of establishing 'national or racist divisions' (*völkische oder Rassengrenzen*). Hence, the intellectual movement that he started – the *Europäische Kulturbund* ('European Cultural Association') established in Vienna in 1922 and Paris in 1923 as the *Fédération internationale des Unions intellectuelles* ('International Federation of Intellectual Circles' – note the different terminology), which published the illustrious *Europäische Revue/Revue européenne* – united people from across the political spectrum.[47] Especially, scientific, cultural, economic and financial elites of the time attended its congresses – politicians and diplomats far less so, notwithstanding the support of the liberal diplomat Wilhelm Heinrich Solf (German ambassador to Japan) who propagated the *Revue européenne* among diplomatic circles.

Similar ideas about the rejuvenation of Europe could be found all over Europe. It is clear that they were not incompatible with that of the nation – actually most of the reactionary thinkers considered the nation as the core of Europe. That was the case not only for Rohan and Schmitt in Germany but also for Malaparte in Italy – it is no coincidence that all were close to fascism. Perhaps the most idiosyncratic of these thinkers was the French veteran of WW I and novelist, involved with Dada and surrealism, Pierre Drieu La Rochelle, who, while denouncing the decadence and decay of the 'old Europe', on the one hand admired the nationalist awakenings of the 'young Europe' in the East but on the other hand saw in a European union the only way to make Europe strong enough against other powers such as the US, the USSR and, in the future, China and India. His ideas already made him an outspoken fascist in the 1920s (notwithstanding his membership of anti-fascist associations) as well as a nationalist Europeanist, as in his main political work *L'Europe contre les parties* (1931).[48]

A similar movement developed around the journal *Abendland*. The *Abendland* movement was actually never really delineated but was rather a collective noun for a variety of militant Catholic individuals and groups, closely connected to the Catholic liturgical renewal movement and the Benedictine Abbey of Maria Laach in the Rhineland. The movement's followers basically argued for a Europe recalling an imaginary medieval sacred order that had been lost since the Reformation and the Enlightenment and cherished the idea of a 'universal' connection between Christian nations, in opposition to 'narrow nationalism and boundless internationalism'. In the 1920s, they particularly emphasized the bonds of brotherhood and religion that linked Christian Germany with France and Poland.[49] The young Carl Schmitt, for example, a lawyer who would later become one of the principal ideologues of the Nazi Party and also one of the most influential political theoreticians after 1945, pleaded for some sort of 'neo-Christendom' in the early 1920s, in which the Catholics should engage in political battle to defend humanity against the 'Antichrist', which he found particularly in Russian ideas of opposition to authority and order, shared by the Orthodox as well as by Anarchists and Leninists. In addition, he considered 'national homogeneity' – which replaces the religious homogeneity of the Ancient Regime and follows the introduction of religious tolerance – one of the defining characteristics of the new, as well as old order.[50]

A spiritual revolution

Not all who dreamt of a European renaissance strived towards a new Christendom, however. A particular spiritual alternative view is offered by the German writer and philosopher Rudolf Pannwitz, author of *Die Krisis der europäischen Kultur* in 1917, as well as several other political texts on Europe, among which is a 'visionary' essay on the state of Europe in 1920. Like his Christian brethren, Pannwitz called on Europe – limited to continental Europe, excluding Turkey as well as Russia – to spiritually 'revive'. From his Nietzschean perspective, the continent needed a new spiritual base that would join Christian heritage with the great Asian spiritualities of the Buddha, Lao-Tze and Confucius. He pleaded for a new Christian and European 'patriotism' to replace nationalism and for an *Imperium Europaeum* (European empire) which would bridge the gap between the Germans and the Slavs, who he believed constituted the future and true soul of Europe. Pannwitz's ideas were quite radical: he argued for the abolition of the nation state as well as for the breaking up of Germany into three areas: West, South and Central Germany, the latter including Austria but without the internationalized city of Vienna. This would allow Germany to take on its historical role as mediator of Europe, particularly between East and West. He still considered Germany, together with France, as the core of Christian Europe, to be organized as an 'empire of federations' respecting the diversity of Europe's cultures. Although he blended visions of empire, spirituality and race, he also saw bridges to be built with the Islamic world, which, with its historical and cultural links with Europe, was a possible ally against the rise of Japan, 'the America of the East but incomparably more dangerous'.[51]

Pannwitz illustrates the cultural pessimism and the longing for a spiritual rebirth that reigned among intellectuals in Europe and in Germanic lands in particular, and which were propagated in elitist journals all over Europe – imagining Europe as a unity was an endeavour that mainly preoccupied the elites of the time, never the masses. In addition, reactionary cultural elites especially cultivated mistrust and contempt for politicians, though the latter sometimes shared their basic ideas.

From Versailles to Locarno

After Versailles

That the peace signed at Versailles was unlikely to offer lasting solutions should have been obvious right from the beginning. Nevertheless, in the months after the conclusion of the peace treaty, Germany still played the card of European solutions. As Peter Jackson recently argued, Versailles did leave space for interpretation and negotiation.[52]

The economic blockade of Germany by the Allies, the French and Belgian claims for reparation and an indemnity for all war costs, and the enduring French–British alliance confronted the Germans with a dilemma with regard to the future course of the country in a new post-war order: should they focus on becoming more independent and autarkic, and thus maintain a strong agrarian basis, or on the contrary, continue on the road of industrial specialization and modernization, and opt for further integration within the European and world economy? The Weimar Republic chose the latter, and during the peace negotiations in Versailles the Germans 'tried to act as champions of political and economic understanding'.[53] It was in vain, as the Allies imposed a humiliating and potentially devastating peace upon the vanquished Central Powers and Germany in particular. Nevertheless, the government persevered.

The message was ambiguous, though. On the one hand, the German government emphasized that European recovery depended on the reconstruction of the German economy, so its recovery had to be ensured – also in view of the huge spoils and war debts for which not only Germany but also the European allies had to cough up. On the other hand, they argued that only together would Europe be able to fully retake its place in the world. This implied a joint organization, a true 'United States of Europe'. Common arrangements on exchange of goods and capital, all experts agreed, were desperately needed. In particular, the liberal politician and industrialist Walter Rathenau, minister of reconstruction (from May 1921) and from January 1922 minister of foreign affairs, manifested himself as an ardent proponent of such ideas. But in the short term he insisted upon the joint management of raw materials and heavy industries in Western Europe. The latter was supported by Hugo Stinnes, the leading German entrepreneur and conservative politician, who – while heavily criticizing the Versailles Treaty – advocated a customs union with France and tried to bring together the different heavy industries of Westphalia, the Rhineland, Luxembourg, Belgium and France in some sort of transnational industrial cartel.

Rather surprisingly, perhaps, they did find a listening ear in France. In particular, Jacques Seydoux, a high-ranking and influential civil servant in the French Ministry of Foreign Affairs, had become convinced that the re-establishment of French economic power depended on a broader European recovery, which in turn required the development of Germany and a 'realistic' settlement of the war debts.[54] In the meantime also Louis Loucheur, French businessman and one of the leading politicians of the republican left in France (several times minister), although tough on the reparations and war debts issue, was engaged in initiatives to establish co-operation between the heavy industries of France, Belgium, Luxemburg and the Rhineland/Germany, which offered another point of contact. The British were also thinking along these lines. Prime Minister Lloyd George hoped to solve the problems of Europe by associating all major European powers, including the USSR, to a European initiative. In this context, he proposed the formation of a Central International Corporation Limited to co-ordinate and finance European reconstruction efforts through national corporations, on which an agreement was reached with Germany on 25 February 1922.[55]

In the run-up to the World Economic Conference of Genoa in April 1922, Rathenau suggested the creation of a European Customs Union, to be realized stepwise: first by a reduction of customs tariffs and trade barriers, then gradually to be extended into customs communities and a real customs union. But the negotiations dragged on, which made the Germans doubt the sincerity of the Allies and particularly of the British. The latter were actually more concerned with their empire than with Europe – and an imperial perspective regarded European nations as rivals – which largely explains the slowness of the British response.[56]

The World Economic Conference held in Genoa from 10 April to 19 May 1922 revealed the weakness of the post-war political and economic order, and the need for European, not global, structures and agreements. The League of Nations obviously did not live up to expectations – it became clear that the Europeans should find solutions to their problems by themselves, if only because Germany was not allowed to join the League. But mounting frustration and nationalism largely aborted the momentum. Under pressure from the US insisting on the payment of European war debts, France, Belgium and the UK imposed 'an impossible schedule' with regard to the German payment of indemnities and reparations. It drove Germany right into the arms of the Soviets. The Treaty of Rapallo (16 April 1922), by which Germany recognized the USSR and its borders in return for the cancellation of its war debts, however, infuriated the British and the French. Moderates lost the argument both sides of the river Rhine: Walter Rathenau was assassinated by German ultra-nationalists on 13 June 1922, and in January 1923 Belgian and French troops marched into the demilitarized Ruhr region. They stayed for three years, facing tough, though mainly passive, resistance from the population.[57] It was as if the war had never ended.

Hope rises from the ashes

The Ruhr crisis incited much diplomatic activity, and eventually European politicians, with considerable help from the Americans, did find a way through. The early 1920s, however, also stimulated much intellectual activity. The apparent failure of the League of Nations cast the spotlight on Europe: peace in Europe should be sought in Europe, it seemed.

Non-state actors also began to involve themselves in the debate, such as the cultural movements discussed in the previous paragraph. In this respect, the tension between universalism and Europeanism surfaced again, but again a few saw the two as opposite to one another, and when the League of Nations proved incapable of guaranteeing peace and stability and solving the post-war political and economic problems, attention quickly shifted towards proper European frames of action and organization. The most remarkable among the pacifists was arguably the cosmopolitan Louise Weiss, daughter of a Jewish mother and a Protestant engineer from Alsace. She was the driving force behind the weekly *L'Europe nouvelle*, published between 1918 and 1940, which reported on the activities of the League of Nations, international politics and culture, and from the very beginning pleaded for a French–German rapprochement, in a political and economic as well as a cultural respect. The magazine published articles by politicians and intellectuals of different political orientations and backgrounds, from all over Europe, and emphasized the value of cultural and national diversity but argued for collaboration in a spirit of peace and reconciliation. *L'Europe nouvelle* mainly addressed the political, economic and cultural elites; it was very influential in this respect. In particular, the French socialist-republican politician Aristide Briand, several times Prime Minister and Minister of Foreign Affairs, was deeply influenced by it. He and Louise Weiss became close friends.[58] Other cultural milieus and magazines took on the cause. In Germany, journals and magazines such as *Germania* (the press organ of the Catholic *Zentrum* party), the *Kölnischen Volkszeitung* and the leftist literary review *Neue Rundschau*, for example, followed a very similar course.[59]

Pacifism, economic despair and the hope for a rebirth of civilization all convened in a new wave of Europeanism. Illustrative of this is a series of essays that the foremost German intellectual Heinrich Mann published in 1923, demonstrating a curious mixture of fear of the impact of conservative 'big business' in Germany and hope for a spiritual and intellectual European union.[60]

Richard N. Coudenhove-Kalergi's Paneuropa

The most vocal and arguably influential of the intellectuals urging a European renaissance, however, was undoubtedly Count Richard N. Coudenhove-Kalergi, son of an Austro-Hungarian diplomat with ancestral roots all over Europe, and of Mitsuko Aoyama, the daughter of a Japanese businessman.[61]

The polyglot aristocrat, who became acquainted with Hindus, Buddhists and Muslims in his youth, was, as a child, at home with cultural, political and economic elites all over Europe, which served him well when he engaged in a crusade for a united 'Paneuropean union'. This crusade primarily engaged the elites: notwithstanding attempts to reach out to a broader public and the publication of an international journal and several books, 'Paneuropa' never truly became a mass movement. It did bring the issue of Europeanism onto the international political table, though. Coudenhove-Kalergi's view was far more pragmatic and political than that of most other post-war intellectuals, be they pacifists, nationalists or dreamers of a rebirth of the *Abendland*, who all to some extent considered him superficial, technical and overly pragmatic, if not purely Machiavellian (which does not take away from the fact that businessmen and politicians, in particular, also considered Paneuropa utopian). Nevertheless, whatever views were held of him, Coudenhove-Kalergi's vision was undoubtedly broader and more concrete than most.

Uniting and pacifying Europe constituted the first and necessary step towards peace in the world, but was also needed to return Europe its former grandeur and prestige. 'Once feared, Europe is now pitied', he observed. And the menace was not only internal, but also lurked outside. To deal with both internal and external threats required unification: 'Can Europe in its political and economic disunion maintain its peace and independence in the face of growing non-European world powers – or is it compelled to organize itself into a confederation of states in order to save its existence?'[62] However, he did not view Europe from a simple imperialist perspective: along with Nietzsche and in particular Schopenhauer, he believed the root cause of Europe's crisis to be spiritual, and the cure was to be found in a revival of Greek aesthetics, in the Christian heritage and in eastern spirituality. However, he viewed Europe above all as a political concept: it did not, as such, exist either geographically – he shared Valéry's idea of a 'cape of Asia' – or culturally: the borders of the continent depended on political choices, not culture. Hence, the question of whether or not Turkey or the UK should be considered European and included in a Paneuropean union could be subject to debate, even if he actually excluded both.

Initially after the war he sought support from political leaders in creating a European organization, but the reactions, including from the new Italian leader Giuseppe Mussolini, were less than lukewarm. Backed by the Austrian chancellor Ignaz Seipel as well as by the Czechoslovakian president Thomas Masaryk, however, he finally launched his Paneuropa movement in Vienna with a 120-page booklet called *Pan-Europa* in 1923, in the midst of the Ruhr crisis. It would be the start of an important movement, with its own journal, *Paneuropa*, and regular congresses, attracting a large share of the political, economic and cultural elites, among whom, apart from Seipel and Masaryk, Aristide Briand – several times French prime minister and foreign affairs minister between 1909 and 1932 – should be especially noted.

Coudenhove-Kalergi saw the world as divided into five spheres, each of which should unite separately: Paneuropa (excluding the British Empire, the Soviet Union and Turkey but including the French colonial possessions in Africa and Asia); the British Empire and 'Commonwealth'; a Pan-American Union of North and South America; Eurasia around the USSR; and a Pan-Asian Union with Japan and China that would control East Asia and most of the Pacific. These regional associations should constitute the basis of a new world order and bring both the US and the USSR into the world political system. The idea of Paneuropa was actually a suggestion of the eminent Austrian Jewish pacifist Alfred Hermann Fried, winner of the 1911 Nobel Peace Prize, to organize a Paneuropean organization in the image of the Pan American Union established in 1889 between the North and Latin American states.[63] In its concrete interpretation, Coudenhove-Kalergi further built upon the federalist ideas of Aurel Popovici on Greater Austria. The count understood nations in cultural terms and dissociated the nation from the state. Hence, the Paneuropean Union should be constituted as an association of democratic states rather than nations: the latter were too small to offer a solid basis for an international order.

His ideal Europe, moreover, was one of ethnic and cultural *métissage*, quite incompatible with nationalist ideals of national purity – eventually the peoples of the world would merge with other races into a 'Eurasian-Negroid race'. Jews incidentally constituted 'a new race of nobility by the Grace of Spirit' (*'eine neue Adelsrasse von Geistes Gnaden'*).[64] All official languages in Paneuropa should be treated equally, but, pragmatic as he was, the count considered English – not French or German – as a 'natural Esperanto' and lingua franca for Europe, which should be taught in primary and secondary schools in all European countries along with the national tongue. This inclusive perspective would become an important feature of European federalism, but one mostly not shared by those who dreamt of Europe as the lost *Abendland*.

Coudenhove-Kalergi proposed a neat scheme for realizing a Paneuropean union: first, the organization of a Paneuropean Conference which would convene regularly and organize an executive committee; next, the conclusion of a series of international agreements between the European countries with regard to borders and the installation of compulsory arbitration in case of conflict; then, the establishment of a European Customs Union, the acceptance of a European constitution and the formation, following the model of the US, of a European political confederation, which would include a Chamber of Nations and a Chamber of State. As the whole endeavour rested upon the reconciliation of France and Germany, he offered a solution as perspicacious as it was fundamental to pacify their antagonism: bringing German coal and French mineral ores under the control of a supranational Coal and Steel Community.

Beyond Versailles

Coudenhove-Kalergi's initial goal was to find a way to create peace in Europe, and he formulated his ideas partly because of his belief in Wilson's international order and because the League of Nations had waned considerably. Others continued to see opportunities in the League of Nations; among these were the Jewish pacifist and Zionist Alfred Nossig, who proposed the League of Nations constitute a European Peace Association in 1923, composed of Germany, France, the UK and Poland, to guarantee the European borders, include an absolute prohibition on waging war, compulsory arbitration – a very popular idea at the end of the nineteenth century – and a military executive, as a means of imposing peace in Europe. It did not materialize, mainly because the German chancellor Gustav Stresemann feared that it actually might jeopardize the League of Nations.

Nossig continued his endeavours through the so-called 'Committees for the common interests of Europe' that were constituted in France, the UK, Germany and Poland.[65] Under the leadership of the German 'left-liberal' politician Wilhelm Heile, who initially engaged in the Paneuropa-movement but soon developed into a sharp critic of the latter's leader Coudenhove-Kalergi, they particularly opposed the latter's view on 'little Europe'.[66]

Remarkable in this respect is that in contrast to a general perception of deep ideological opposition, in reality with regard to European collaboration there was a clear interaction, transcending the political cleavages. Some nevertheless perceived European 'federalism' as mainly a liberal-socialist endeavour and argued that this did not include Catholics. That was perhaps so to some extent in Francophone Europe, where the main protagonists of Franco-German rapprochement were to be found among either liberal entrepreneurs or socialist politicians. Reactionary Catholics considered European unity as directed against Catholic views of Europe as a neo-Christendom. Most notoriously, the French reactionary Catholic movement *Action française* explicitly opposed European collaboration. However, the activities of the conservative Catholic thinkers mentioned in the previous paragraph indicate that that the perception of Catholics being generally against European unity in the 1920s is wrong.[67]

The overall picture, indeed, looks quite different. The Holy See favoured the rapprochement of France and Germany and opposed nationalism in its politics to promote peace in Europe, associating nationalism with liberalism as well as opposing its basic principles for an orderly society. Hence, the Vatican increasingly supported plans for European unity in the 1920s.[68] In Germany and Austria, Catholics were in the vanguard of European thinking. The Austrian chancellor, Ignaz Seipel, a Catholic priest and leader of the Christian Social Party, was among the first to patronize Coudenhove-Kalergi's Paneuropa movement, of which he became chairman of the Austrian section. The idea of European unity did appeal especially to the Catholic aristocratic circles around Karl Anton Rohan and the *Abendland* movement. There were like-minded figures in France as well, such as the Catholic poet and diplomat Paul Claudel, who from an outspoken Eurocentric perspective pleaded for European unity and reconciliation with Germany, and the conservative Catholic essayist Wladimir d'Ormesson and the journals he was involved in, such as the *Revue de Paris* and *Le Temps*. They explicitly denounced the narrowness of nationalism. Others saw no contradiction. Richard Kreuzer, for example, the conservative Catholic publisher of the journal *Germania*, pleaded for German–French understanding in a broader Christian Mitteleuropa, but considered 'patriotism' (*nationaler Instinkt*) one of the most profound human qualities and opposed cosmopolitan 'mixing': Catholics should proselytize Christianity and promote Christian values.[69]

Other Catholics distanced themselves from such reactionary views. In particular, the French democratic Catholic thinker Marc Sangnier, founder of the republican movement *Le Sillon*, mobilized in support of reconciliation – an international youth peace conference in Bierville (France) in the summer of 1926 gathered thousands of militants.[70] Especially in the Rhineland, Catholics, including the Mayor of Cologne and post-WW II chancellor Konrad Adenauer, favoured German–French reconciliation and European unity, mainly for economic and pacifist reasons. The International Confederation of Christian Trade Unions (CISC), constructed on a (difficult) German-French base, also supported European federalism quite explicitly: its Secretary General, the Dutchman P.J.S. Serrarens, was an active member of different pro-European associations and a convenor of an international conference on Europe in October 1923.[71]

The trade union movement in particular revealed itself as profoundly pro-European, even if it viewed Europe from a more global perspective as well.[72] Somewhat surprisingly, perhaps, the International Confederation of Trade Unions (IFTU) from an early Keynesian perspective advocated an open world economy (as did the CISC). It rejected 'economic nationalism' or protectionism, including protective tariffs and state subsidies towards 'doomed' industries, and the policy of 'raising impassable barriers around each country'. Although it argued for a fundamental reform of worldwide political organization, focusing on the international distribution of raw materials and the solution of the financial problems, in reality it sought a solution mainly in Europe. On the eve of the international conference of Genoa, for example, the IFTU pleaded for the stabilization of the currency exchange rates and the organization and control of the distribution of raw materials, and demanded the cancellation of war debts, general disarmament and the redistribution of the burden of the reparations from the working class to the moneyed classes exclusively in a European space.[73] The Dutch trade union leader Edo Fimmen pointed mainly to the need for a truly European response in his widely read *Labour's alternative*, published in 1924, because of the concentration of capital in Europe.[74]

Even if not all phrased their ideas in terms of a Trotskyist 'proletarian United States of Europe', and important national differences persisted, the left had become convinced that the post-war order was fundamentally fragile and unjust and adopted the idea of a United States of Europe more explicitly than any other political movement. This thinking was particularly strong in the moderate left Radical Party in France, to which Joseph Caillaux and the later prime minister Éduard Herriot belonged, as well as the Republican-Socialist Party of Aristide Briand, who favoured reconciliation with Germany for pacifist as well as economic reasons. Also, the German Social Democratic Party (SPD) committed itself to the 'United States of Europe' in 1925 because it offered opportunities for a socialist policy that would break with the stalemate imposed by the Versailles settlement, although its leftist Heidelberg programme in this respect was also exceptionally vague – significantly, in this programme Europe's geographical borders stretched from the UK to the USSR.[75] Similar ideas were found in other countries as well. The prominent Walloon socialist Jules Destrée, for example, systematically referred to the ideals of the Paneuropean Union.[76]

Locarno

In 1924, the French voted out the Conservative Government of Raymond Poincaré, which gave way to the *Cartel des gauches*, an unseen coalition government of republican and socialist parties led by Édouard Herriot. Both by conviction and compelled by the economic situation, especially given the increasing vulnerability and imminent collapse of the French franc, Herriot opted for an internationalist course, focused on the League of Nations and the establishment of peace through international law, and from that perspective was eager to end the Ruhr crisis. Foreign Minister Aristide Briand became convinced that an economic association with Germany was, in the long run, more beneficial to France in economic and monetary terms than further dismantling of the former German empire, and that it could, moreover, stabilize and pacify the continent.

The crisis was finally solved by the Dawes Plan of August 1924, which revised the reparations scheme in favour of Germany, and the Locarno Treaties (December 1925), which secured the western European countries' borders. It resulted from American involvement as well as from a change of tack by the French, forced into moderation by their deteriorating financial situation and the belief of the new leftist government in internationalism and arbitration. As a result, Germany was allowed to take its place as a full member of the League of Nations.[77] Locarno was widely perceived as ending the post-war stalemate – in a way, one could consider that Locarno, rather than Versailles, actually ended WW I in Western Europe.[78]

7
Hope and Deception

> The war has taught us one thing, namely, that a common fate
> binds us together. If we go under, we go under together. If we
> wish to recover, we cannot do so in conflict with each other,
> but only by working together.
>
> Gustav Stresemann, 1925[1]

The Ruhr crisis confronted Europe with its continuing fragmentation
and weakness; moreover, while after the war democracy seemed to break
through everywhere in Europe, it also appeared endangered, particularly in Italy, where Mussolini's fascists installed a totalitarian state. The
spectre of war once again haunted the continent. But a lesson seemed
learned, which gave way to 'the spirit of Locarno', the hope for a better future through European co-operation, as expressed by the German
Chancellor Gustav Stresemann in 1925.

Even if a solution to the Ruhr crisis had been found, the underlying antagonisms had not entirely disappeared, and particularly in the
east, uncertainty over the security of the eastern borders of Germany
remained. In fact, some sort of division manifested itself between a more
industrial West and a largely agricultural 'East', which was increasingly
considered not only economically but also politically and culturally
backward.[2] Nevertheless, the German and the French realized that
European collaboration offered a way to pacify their mutual antagonisms by pursuing a 'policy of détente' and wrapping both nations in
a web of interaction.[3] A new European organization, a 'United States
of Europe' would, it was widely hoped, be able to bring the necessary
peace and stability to the old continent and to successfully compete,
both economically and in international politics, with the other United
States across the Atlantic. France also looked east and tried to establish

strong ties with the new states in Central and Southeast Europe, mainly for political and strategic reasons.

But the idea of European integration also divided, and there were strong opponents both on the left and right, ranging from (economic) nationalists, arguing for national protectionism, to the most internationalist free traders. Internationalism and Europeanism did not always mesh well; in the League of Nations they were not always considered compatible. Incidentally, although nationalism – in contrast to the view held in the nineteenth century – was increasingly perceived as opposite to Europeanism, 'patriotic' considerations could apparently motivate European politics as well, as is illustrated by the view of the German *Abendlanders*, who saw the essence of Europe in its nations: the restoration of the European *Abendland* actually entailed the restoration of these nations.[4] But national interests were never far away in economic and political plans for Europe either. Nevertheless, a European spirit unmistakably animated the debate, on both the left and the right of the political spectrum.

The spirit of Locarno

Although he is notorious for being a difficult and authoritarian character and not all European movements were willing to collaborate with him, it is Coudenhove-Kalergi who emerges as the most prominent figure in the interwar Europeanist scene, and whose movement became closest to a political movement. Paneuropa, though never a mass movement, was successful in attracting political and economic leaders. It also emphasized the importance of the economy and supported the suggestion of creating a European Customs Union and an Economic Committee that would conclude an agreement on trade and tariffs with the USSR.[5]

Similar reasoning to that of Coudenhove-Kalergi preoccupied Dr. Christian Frederick Heerfordt, a world-famous Danish ophthalmologist with a passion for Europe. Heerfordt, however, believed that a European federation had no chance of being realized without the UK. Moreover, he was convinced that the latter would not join a European federation without its empire and Commonwealth, which also implied North America. Hence, he proposed a federation of 'European nations' instead of 'nations of Europe', emphasizing the common 'European' culture that the British and Americans shared – an emphasis which excluded the participation of the 'non-European' colonies, even if these remained controlled by European colonial empires. This would constitute the base of an Anglo-European (Occidental) community, in which all decisions would be taken jointly by a council with representatives of all nations. Although less famous than the flamboyant count, Heerfordt also proved to be a restless campaigner for his cause: he published his ideas widely, addressing in particular the foreign embassies with a short manifesto in 1927; he made several visits to intellectual and political leaders in Scandinavia – hence his ideas became known as the 'Scandinavian Initiative' – and toured through Europe, visiting universities as well as political centres and other Europeanist movements, looking for support and collaboration, though largely in vain. Gradually, his emphasis shifted and his proposals became more concrete, adopting a step-by-step model leading towards a European confederation, first political and military, then economic. By 1930 he had focused on the constitution of a political and military union, as he saw the danger of a new European war re-emerging.[6]

The political left seemed especially taken by the European mood. The political orientation of the *Cartel des gauches* was, on the one hand, deeply grounded in French solidaristic legal and political tradition, but, on the other hand, was also shared by the ideological orientation of the political left in Europe in the 1920s. Even more radical figures supported the idea of a European union, such as Wladimir Woytinsky (*Die vereinigten Staaten von Europa*, Berlin 1927 and also translated into French) and John Pepper (*Les États-Unis de l'Europe socialiste*, 1926).[7] A largely labour perspective was pursued at the International Labour Organization (ILO), which, under its dynamic director Albert Thomas, a socialist politician and convinced Europeanist, would strive towards European economic and social co-operation in parallel with systematic demilitarization, as instruments towards a European peace.[8] These activities of the ILO, as well as those of the Economic and Financial Organization of the League, illustrate that although a tension between internationalism and Europeanism regularly surfaced in the League of Nations, Europeanists saw no contradiction. On the contrary, they believed a European federation in the framework of the League would reinforce the latter.

The traditional peace movement, which had rather emphasized universal principles after the war, seemed to change its mind as well and accepted the need for an economic, political and social union of Europe. Although at the Universal Peace Congress of 1926 a strong current still existed to suppress any reference to exclusively European collaboration, the Congress finally accepted a motion calling for an economic *entente* between all European states and a European economic union to be established as soon as reasonably possible, with a European customs union between France, Germany and Great Britain as the first step. In the subsequent years, belief in universalism waned while that in a European federation grew.[9] In Italy, the socialist pacifist Guiseppe Modigliani increasingly argued for a European federation within the League of Nations as a step towards world peace and democracy. He also framed his arguments in 1929 in the light of the fight against fascism, which was usually still perceived as a global phenomenon, but would in the 1930s become European as well.[10]

European writers and artists also shared the European mood. The artistic avant-garde, united around, for example, the illustrious French-German *Europa Almanach* of Carl Einstein and Paul Westheim, published in 1925, opposed the nationalism and imperialism of the time and cultivated a vision of Europe in which all nations had their place.[11] Some also discussed the practical consequences of European collaboration and – an essential dimension – conciliation between the former belligerents, especially France and Germany. The Colpach Circle, where artists and writers such as Paul Claudel, Jean Guéhenno, Jacques Rivière, Karl Jaspers, André Gide, Annette Kolb and Théo van Rysselberghe convened at the domicile of the Luxemburg industrialist Emile Mayerish and his wife Aline de Saint-Hubert, became famous. Mayerish also created the French-German Documentation and Information Committee to combat misinformation about the two arch-enemies in 1926, with offices in Paris and Berlin.[12] Not all Europeanist artists shared this association with the 'captains of industry', though. The brothers Heinrich and Thomas Mann, for example, believed in a political 'United States of Europe' but they rather emphasized a spiritual Locarno (*ein geistiges Locarno*). In this context they both saw a mediating role for Germany between 'East' and West', between Russia and France.[13]

Gradually, it seems, a Europeanist ideology developed, which was presented above all as an alternative to nationalism, economic protectionism (not liberalism, incidentally) and as an alternative to communism or, increasingly, fascism. Illustrative of this ideology are the Committees for European Collaboration, established around 1927 under the dynamic leadership of the renowned French mathematician and radical-socialist politician Emile Borel. The scientist embodied the different facets of militant Europeanism in the 1920s: an intellectual of global standing and an outspoken pacifist convinced of the value of European civilization and of its 'civilizing mission'. Estimating that Europe's position in the world was endangered by nationalism and economic fragmentation, Borel tried to stimulate economic collaboration between German and French industry, trade and banking – an endeavour that was not particularly welcomed by the government in Berlin[14] – and to unite the intellectual and political elites in favour of more European collaboration. For Borel, the UK was part and parcel of Europe and should be associated with any unification project; he even believed that both Russia and Turkey, with one foot in Europe and the other in Asia, could one day join a United States of Europe.[15] He found an attentive ear in Britain, where federalism had gained popularity as a political concept.[16]

Locarno appeared as the dawn of a new era, though for very divergent reasons: some particularly valued the agreement as an expression of reconciliation between the former arch-enemies, but some observed that the peace was largely bought off with American dollars, making the continent even weaker than before – an altogether quite different motive for uniting the continent.[17] Most radical Europeanists presented their conviction as far more than a purely political objective, and phrased their thoughts in outspoken ideological, even mythical and mystical terms. The French philosopher and novelist Julien Benda would even call for a real European religion as a moral force requiring myths and heroes, as did his compatriot Gaston Riou, who considered Europe his 'fatherland'.[18] The idea of a European fatherland also animated the review *Europe*, whose first issue, in February 1923, was entitled *Patrie européenne* (European fartherland).[19] One finds such language not only among philosophers, but also in the writings of scientists and economists, such as Francis Delaisi, who spoke about the development towards an integrated Europe as an unfolding deity, compared to 'national polytheisms'.[20]

Europeanism, one can argue, became an ideology that united political, economic and cultural milieus alike. But as a political ideology it also divided and demanded compromises: Coudenhove-Kalerghi's Paneuropean ideal received a serious blow in Eastern Europe when the Austrian count endorsed German claims for a revision of Versailles in order to gain support for his ideal, explicitly demanding territorial restitutions to Germany from Poland and Lithuania in 1927, including the Polish corridor and the Free City of Gdańsk/Danzig.[21]

Towards an economic union?

Entrepreneurs, economists and labour emphasized the need for European integration mainly in economic terms.[22] The Ruhr crisis did not just lay bare the political problems of Europe, but uncovered the economic weaknesses of the continent, and demonstrated that these were as pernicious to European peace as political issues. Economists, entrepreneurs and labour leaders sharply criticized the economic and political fragmentation of the continent, which annihilated the effects of technological progress in infrastructure, as 'when one traverses Europe by railway, one find oneself blocked in a given place for an hour because there is a new frontier and customs and formalities to attend to'.[23] The crisis also revealed the interdependency of the continent, and the communication infrastructure showed that a more efficient organization of the economy was not only possible, but actually imposed itself as an essential condition for the recovery of Europe.[24] The American example demonstrated the value of a huge internal market, but there were a few who thought even that was possible in Europe, let alone a European federation. The next best thing, then, and a possible first step towards a free market, was a customs union, which would eliminate as far as possible the barriers for intra-European trade and render the customs similar in the different countries.

If France agreed with the Dawes Plan and the Locarno treaty, it was not least because the economic logic prevailed over political and military considerations. Immediately after the conclusion of the Locarno Treaty, France initiated a diplomatic initiative to establish industrial collaboration as one step towards a federal 'United States of Europe'. Such a prospect was all the more pressing as the implications of the Dawes Plan dawned: France (and now also Germany) remained indebted to the US, and France increasingly felt neglected and bypassed by Great Britain, which focused on its empire and its relations with the US. This made the restoration of an alliance between France and Germany ever more important. While the Anglo-Saxon world seemed to turn its back on the continent, the idea of a European alternative gained new strength in Western and Eastern Europe.[25]

That economic fragmentation and economic nationalism were detrimental to growth was evident when one compared the European to the American market. From this observation, several leading economists and financial experts signed a manifesto calling for a European Customs Union in March 1925, and by so doing created a very significant European pressure group, known by its French name *Union douanière européenne* (UDE), constituting national committees in different European countries.[26]

The advocates of a customs union believed politics and economics were deeply connected. 'Only economic peace can ensure peace; economic peace can only be assured through a European customs union' was their message.[27] They virulently opposed economic nationalism and fragmentation. With John Maynard Keynes, they feared that the League of Nations would become 'another Holy Alliance for the perpetuation of the ruin of their enemies and balance of power in their own interests'.[28] Norman Angell, revisiting his pre-war ideas about the obsoleteness of war, put his finger on the problem:

> European statesmanship, as revealed in the Treaty of Versailles, and in the conduct of international affairs since the Armistice, has recognized neither the fact of interdependence – the need for the economic unity of Europe – nor the futility of attempted coercion. Certain political ideas and passions give us an unworkable Europe.[29]

Referring to Keynes' *The Economic Consequences of the Peace* (p. 24), Angell – who would be one of the signatories of the Appeal which constituted the basis of the UDE – sharply exposed the lack of economic co-ordination and the short-sightedness of the politics of retaliation and reparation, which he believed were self-destructive. But his criticism ran even deeper: economic and national dynamics did not correspond.[30] Similar ideas were formulated in France by the influential publicist and economist Francis Delaisi, in numerous articles, often in trade union journals, and works of popular science such as *Les contradictions du monde moderne* in 1925 and *Les bases économiques des États-Unis d'Europe* in 1926. He gave a strong economic underpinning to the different dreams of a Europe in the image of the US, without customs hampering trade but with one single currency, where industries would not benefit from national protectionism but compete freely to the benefit of all, where neither European nor colonial wars would be deemed necessary, but where national sovereignty would be respected, with each country having its own constitution, legal system, political representation, educational system, administration and fiscal regime.[31] Delaisi would inspire virtually all Europeanist and pacifist movements during most of the interwar period, regardless of their political orientation, in France and far beyond. But industrial and financial milieus also supported such ideas. In a speech as president of the International Chamber of Commerce on 5 March 1926, the British banker Walter Leaf made it very clear that only a leap in size and scale of Europe's economy, implying the complete liberation of trade and a single currency, could give Europe 'a market of a radius equal to that of the United States'. Many, both from the left and the conservative right, compared the fragmented continent, with its small protectionist national economies, to the huge unified market of the US.[32]

The economic and political fragmentation were particularly felt in Central and Eastern Europe, where not only Germany but also Hungary and Italy felt frustrated about their territorial confinement. Their desire for a revision of the post-war treaties raised concerns among Germany's eastern neighbours, as did, in a different way, the USSR's revolutionary and imperialist ambitions. Moreover, the region remained largely rural and economically underdeveloped, which also provoked some thinkers to consider another form of political and economical organization.

The economic fragmentation incited the Hungarian financial expert (former secretary of state for finance and president of the Hungarian National Bank) Elemér Hantos to formulate an ambitious plan for the economic and technological integration of the region through the development of telecommunications – telegraphs as well as roads and canals – and lowering tariffs. He proposed creating a Central European economic union of the Danube countries or 'Grand Austria' (the Austrian variant of Mitteleuropa, including Austria, Hungary, Poland, Romania, Yugoslavia and Czechoslovakia – excluding Germany), starting from a customs union but with the aim of developing it into a close economic union. His ideas led to the establishment of the *Mitteleuropäischen Wirtschaftstagung* (MWT) in Vienna, which aimed at stimulating free trade in the area of the former Austro-Hungarian Empire. The governments of the region, however, remained sceptical.[33]

Industrial collaboration

Another, quite different but equally important way to reorganize Europe's economy implied industrial co-operation. In this respect one can refer to the process of cartelization which had developed, especially since the conclusion of the International Steel Cartel with the major steel industries of France, Belgium, Luxemburg and Germany in 1926.[34] Belgian, German and French enterprises engaged in transnational collaboration in petrol, electricity and chemicals as well as in international finance, extending their activities to Central and Eastern Europe. The idea of such an industrial organization of Europe found its most ardent political supporter in the French businessman and politician Louis Loucheur. Loucheur wanted to combine the actions of the cartels, which were capable of restructuring and rationalising industrial production on a European basis, with the customs policies of the European countries. He became the main protagonist of this particular type of European integration, motivated by a desire to counterbalance the industrial and financial power of the Anglo-Saxon world.[35]

Not all supported this line of reasoning, though, not even all industrialists: Emile Mayerisch, who nevertheless signed the steel cartel, considered it counterproductive for big industries and detrimental to the common good. However, he deemed such collaboration preferable to public control over the steel industry or even a customs union, which would entail a series of risky bi- and multilateral negotiations with a most uncertain outcome.[36] The main opponent, however, was European labour, even if unions and socialist parties took the value of transnational industrial co-operation into consideration. Labour emphasized the social and economic need for Europe to combat its economic and political fragmentation and mainly argued for lowering trade barriers. They promoted a European customs union as a first step towards the creation of a United States of Europe, although the latter idea remained vague – actually, it seems that there was little enthusiasm to go beyond an economic organization of Europe besides demilitarization, which certainly was an important issue as well. In particular, the trade unions compared the poor working conditions and lack of consuming power in Europe with those in the US, and attributed the difference to the fragmented nature of Europe's commercial system and the US continent-wide free market. A number of trade union leaders went to the US in the early 1920s, sometimes supported by the ILO.[37]

The different visions for the economic integration of Europe clashed at the World Economic Conference in Geneva in May 1927.[38] Most remembered is the opposition between a radical free-trade approach, with as its main advocate the Swedish economist Gustav Cassel on the one side, and those who favoured a Paneuropean 'protectionist' policy that was based upon transnational industrial concentration on the other. A middle ground was to some extent defended by the trade union movement, which nevertheless supported an outspoken Europeanist programme arguing for the removal of all impediments to international trade, the improvement and harmonisation of working conditions in Europe (not yet in the overseas colonies, though), the control of industrial monopolies and cartels, and an increase in agricultural production. The conference did not decide on either strategy, but called for the lowering of customs barriers and for the status of 'most favoured nation' to apply to all European countries.

Subsequent negotiations in the economic committee of the League of Nations in the subsequent years concentrated on an agreement on a possible tariff truce but in the end hardly yielded tangible results. De facto the League adopted the regionalist approach; without, however, reaching an agreement about on which format European economies should unite. The industrial strategy was not abandoned: by 1930 around 100 cartels had been constituted.[39] Clearly, economics largely prevailed over political and social issues. The latter were nevertheless present, for example in the ILO, whose director attempted to create a European social space in which similar working conditions would reign. The ILO hence supported the conclusion of labour conventions applicable throughout the whole of Europe, particularly on professional training, social insurance, the minimum wage, working time and equal wages for men and women.[40]

Briand's apogee

The Briand plan

The Locarno spirit reached its apogee in 1929 with a famous speech by French prime minister Aristide Briand to the General Assembly of the League of Nations on 5 September 1929, in which he proposed a plan for an economic union of Europe that would finally settle the remaining issues between Germany and France:

> I believe that a sort of federal bond should exist between the nations geographically gathered as European countries; these nations should, at any moment, have the possibility of establishing contact, of discussing their interests, of adopting common resolutions, of creating amongst themselves a bond of solidarity that allows them, on suitable occasions, to face up to serious circumstances, in case they arise. (...) Evidently, the association will take place mainly in the economic domain: this is the most pressing question...

Apparently Briand proposed his plan at the right time: political tensions were on the rise again, and there were signs of a weakening of the economic fundamentals, even if a few expected what was about to happen. But what was probably more important was that Germany was quickly gaining strength again, and a strong Germany, Briand understood, threatened the peace – especially as, notwithstanding Locarno, resentments in the former Central countries, as well as in Italy, remained strong. Opposition to the Young Plan, which revised the reparations that Germany had to pay according to the Dawes Plan of 1924, provoked a referendum in Germany to stop all reparations in December 1929, which heralded the breakthrough of the National Socialist Party of Adolf Hitler – while in Southeast Europe, border and minority issues reappeared.

The speech was followed by a memorandum containing a more elaborate plan for a political and economic confederation, dated 17 May 1930, which was sent to the different capitals of Europe as well as to Washington. The remarkably elegantly formulated text (actually largely written by the poet-diplomat Alexis Leger) contained a more elaborated – and notably different – proposal for a general 'pact of European solidarity', the creation of a common market and a 'European Federal Union' – respecting the full sovereignty of each state, hence a confederation rather than a federation – within the framework of the League of Nations. It foresaw a conference composed of delegates from the different European countries member of the League of Nations as 'representative and responsible organ', an executive and a small secretariat. The text was moderate and pragmatic – other proposals, such as the one Coudenhove-Kalergi formulated in response to Briand's speech, went much further. Notwithstanding some ambiguity in the formulation, Briand avoided anything that could be interpreted as a federal 'United States of Europe' and excluded any form of supranationality; his common market also stopped short of a full customs union, as the UK preferred 'most favoured nation' clauses.

Briand's plan was not just the fulfilment of a utopian dream: the French Prime Minister was far too pragmatic for that. Briand was particularly concerned about a possible unification of Austria and Germany, as openly discussed in Austria from 1927 onwards, which would fundamentally alter the power balance in Europe. That seemed to him detrimental to French interests and a possible cause for war: Briand's Europeanism was not only motivated by European idealism and pacifism, but also by France's security demands, which required Germany's power to be curtailed. Moreover, France needed the collaboration with Germany for economic and financial reasons.[41] But one should also be reminded that German post-war Europeanist politics, as continued by Stresemann, essentially aimed at safeguarding Germany's interests as well, 'the securing of a free Germany with equal rights and the inclusion of such a Germany together with all states in a stable international structure', as the chancellor explained in a speech for the University of Heidelberg in 1928.[42]

That reasoning propelled Stresemann to welcome Briand's plan as a crazy but fascinating idea. The initial reactions of most countries, and in particular the press, were also anything but negative. In Britain they were mixed, but still there existed a strong tendency among both Labour and the industry to make a fresh start with a more united Europe, even if that did not necessarily mean that the UK should join a European (con) federation. Especially, the new countries created after Versailles and allies of France (Poland, Czechoslovakia, Yugoslavia, Romania, Estonia, Latvia and Lithuania), fearful about Germany's ambitions with regard to its eastern borders, supported the plan, as did Belgium and, more surprisingly, Austria, while also in Scandinavia there was much sympathy. Remarkably, while Briand initially excluded Turkey from his European federation, several countries – particularly Greece – supported the inclusion of this country in possible negotiations.[43]

In this context one should realize that Locarno, by not providing the same guarantees to France and Belgium with regard to Germany's eastern borders, had left the door open for a revision of the political geography in Central and Eastern Europe. With its many minorities and revisionist currents, not only in Germany but also in Austria, Hungary and Italy, the flame of discontent and revision had continued to smoulder. Briand, who continued the French policy of supporting the countries of the Little Entente, repeatedly attempted to generate support for a 'second Locarno' with regard to Central and Eastern Europe and the Balkans, but had not found sufficient backing, precisely because of the lingering resentments. His plan can actually be considered another attempt to secure Central and Eastern Europe.

Too late?

Nevertheless, the 'right time' for the plan, if it was such, arrived too late. One month after Briand's speech in Geneva, his German sparring partner Gustav Stresemann died from a heart attack. Shortly afterwards the New York Stock Exchange crashed, dragging the entire world economy into the abyss. The Dawes–Young agreements that had secured the reparations issue faltered.[44] The whole endeavour collapsed. In the end, the British and German responses, in particular, left nothing to the imagination – Germany and Austria had even already initiated secret talks about unification. The proposal was effectively buried in a special commission of the League of Nations.

In reality though, things were less negative for Briand than they appeared, and certainly the European spirit was far from buried – though there were, and remained, many, quite divergent views on the subject (democratic and authoritarian, economic and essentially cultural) and governments in practice felt compelled to hark back to the protectionist economic policies, while in Germany, Austria and Italy, revanchist and even imperialist ideas surfaced. Particularly in those circles that imagined Europe as *Abendland*, Europe was more and more imagined in mythical terms. From that perspective, politicians and thinkers emphasized the need for a cultural unification of the continent. Coudenhove-Kalergi, for example, proposed creating a European Academy.[45] But the political dimension was by no means neglected. The count even attempted to create a Paneuropean party, as his movement had been dependent on governmental support that was now dwindling away as governments took refuge in protectionism and nationalism and in any case had to scrimp and economize. The initiative, as was the parallel attempt to create a Paneuropean militant movement, was still-born, as the count did not provide any permanent structure and support for a democratic popular movement. Only in Switzerland did the initiative produce the desired output with the formation of a Europa-Union. This multilingual and multicultural country, incidentally, offered a possible model for a European federation.

The Holy See in particular manifested itself as an ardent advocate of European unity. The Vatican supported Briand from the beginning, although Rome also considered his plan rather utopian. Pope Pius XI, usually a very cautious actor in international politics, nevertheless exhorted nations to collaborate internationally in the encyclical *Quadragesimo anno* (1931), and indirectly informed political leaders that the Holy See supported the development towards a United States of Europe.[46] Christian democratic politicians after much hesitation set up a common association, the International Secretariat of Democratic Parties of Christian Inspiration (SIPDIC). While actually lukewarm about Briand's project, at their (last) congress in 1931 they approved a statement emphasizing the need for market integration, support for the farmers and even a possible political union in the future, which shows how much they shared the ideas of both Liberal and more (Christian) labour-oriented European federalists:

> We must strengthen and encourage comprehensive cooperation between all European nations in order to achieve a Common Market for production and the free movement and consumption of goods...Full union, which is the final goal, cannot be achieved immediately or directly. So we must gradually remove customs barriers, and trade and financial barriers preventing the regular exchange of goods, in order to realise as quickly as possible the free movement of goods, capital, and people.[47]

Also within the peace movements, a European perspective continued to be cherished, at least until 1931–1932.[48] Moreover, a strong current of federalist support for European unity was emerging in Britain. Winston Churchill, for example, who had begun to look into federalist ideas mainly for domestic purposes, supported Briand's idea of a 'United States of Europe' in an article in 1930, but famously he considered Britain 'with

Europe, but not of it. We are linked, but not comprised. We are interested and associated, but not absorbed.'[49]

The French government continued its policy of reconciliation and found some partners in Berlin that preferred German–French collaboration over political and economic nationalism. In that respect, both Paris and Berlin supported cultural initiatives, including subsidizing journals such as the *Deutsch-Französische Rundschau* and the *Revue d'Allemagne et des Pays de Langue allemande* in the early 1930s. Especially, political contacts between the German Catholic *Zentrum* party and the (small) French Christian-Democratic *Parti Démocratique Populaire,* supported by the Vatican, helped to create a sense of connectivity and solidarity based upon a shared sense of belonging to a common Christian civilization – a sense especially dear to the new German Chancellor, the Catholic Heinrich Brüning. The rapprochement was also motivated by a common mistrust of and even outright opposition to American debt policies. The latter also brought Brüning closer to Briand. Both were on the brink of an agreement on war reparations which would actually have greatly facilitated the realization of Briand's European scheme, when 'events', such as a media storm surrounding the posthumous publication of Gustave Stresemann's memoirs in March 1932 and the appointment of Adolf Hitler as German chancellor in January 1933, torpedoed the whole affair.[50]

Associations like Paneuropa, the UDE – which changed its name to *Union économique et douanière européenne* (UEDE) in 1934 – the French-German Information Committee and the Committees for European Collaboration, among others, continued their activities, although tensions arose with the Germans, who argued for a revision of the Versailles Treaty and sometimes even viewed the Briand Plan as a French imperial project disguised as a peace plan. Overall economic concerns came more to the fore, particularly in Coudenhove-Kalergi's Paneuropa movement, partly under the influence of Minister Engelbert Dollfuss, the new Austrian Paneuropa honorary president since 1930 and, from 1932 to 1934, Austrian chancellor. Dollfuss positioned Paneuropa as an alternative to Nazism. In economic milieus it was argued that cartelization and industrial concentration offered a solution to the crisis, in particular the opportunity to stabilize prices and avoid national protectionism. Regional collaboration clashed over the very unequal economic conditions in Europe, in particular the existence of large rural areas and the difficulties these experienced in competing with more industrial and advanced regions. The latter had obstructed the negotiations for a customs union after the world economic conference of 1927 and continued to do so even more in the 1930s.

A global perspective

All these European plans had, as a double goal, the need to generate peace in Europe but also to strengthen the continent against rising new economies and world powers, in the first place the US. The representation of the US, however, was complex. In cultural terms the US was seen as related and similar to Europe, though its materialism and unbridled liberal-capitalism were scorned. The US was, however, mainly viewed in economic terms, as a formidable and threatening competitor, but also as a model – in particular because of its unified market (remarkably, its industrial model was less recognized and hardly served as a source of inspiration).[51] The USSR, in contrast, mainly constituted a civilizational and military menace against which only a politically united and culturally reborn Europe could stand up. It was sometimes associated with 'Asian barbarism', although the latter also referred to other regions of Asia. Christian authors in particular emphasized their fear of the USSR. But they also objected to the 'unbridled materialism' of the US: 'Europeanism' indeed very often represented a 'third way' between state socialism and capitalism. Japan was rarely touched upon as a direct menace, although it actually was one in economic terms. However, the possible 'awakening' of ancient Asian empires, particularly China but also Islamic ones, loomed large as a motive for European unification. Clearly, proposals for a European federation, whatever its concrete form, implied continuing the European imperial-colonial domination of the world.

In this respect, Africa occupied a central role. Notwithstanding his cosmopolitan worldview, even Coudenhove-Karlergi considered Africa in terms of economic exploitation by Europe, as he observed that 'Africa (...) could give Europe raw materials for its industry, food for its people, work opportunities for its unemployed, [and] markets for the sale of its products.' More surprising are his comments on the people: 'Eurafrica unites the most civilized peoples of the white race and the most primitive people of the black race.'[52]

The Belgian socialist Jules Destrée, an advocate of Paneuropa, likewise supported the idea of a federation of Europe with the objective of the joint exploitation of the 'black continent'. The Belgian politics that Destrée supported in the Belgian Congo shows that one should not idealize the 'civilizing' and development perspective:

> One could conceive a federation of these European countries, a federation limited to the colonization of Africa. (...) A kind of federal committee of administration could have two important features: firstly, to pursue, in general, the white civilizing mission through protecting and educating the blacks, and secondly to develop

the agricultural and mineral richness of these immense territories through major works, with broad views and considerable capital investments.[53]

This idea would remain very attractive throughout Europe in the 1930s. In Italy, fascists connected it with the ancient Roman view of the Mediterranean as a Eurafrican space. The geographer Paolo D'Agostino Orsini di Camerota, for example, presented Eurafrica as one huge autarkic region divided into three geo-political, demographic and economic zones in his popular *L'Europa per l'Africa, l'Africa per l'Europa* (Europe for Africa, Africa for Europe 1934).[54] Key elements in this perspective were, on the one hand, the need for huge empty spaces for an overpopulated Europe and, on the other hand, the idea that Africa would help Europe to resist the upcoming Asian and American forces: against the widely believed inevitable *Asia for the Asians* Europe should claim *Africa for the Europeans*. Perhaps the most ambitious of these utopian projects was the weird – but seriously considered – suggestion by the German architect Herman Sörgel: to largely drain the Mediterranean through huge dams in Gibraltar, the Bosporus, and between Sicily and Tunisia, and to irrigate the Sahara. Through altering the geography of Africa a united continent would be created, Atlantropa, which would rival the Americas and Asia.[55]

As many Germans never really accepted the loss of their colonies, the suggestion of a colonial exploitation of Africa found many followers in Germany; they associated their colonial ambitions with a vision of Europe in which Germans would actually 'preserve' 'Africa for the Europeans':

Africa, a southern extension of Europe, is to become for [Germany] a huge plantation: only Germany has sufficient excess population to carry out this transformation, without it the existence of Europe cannot be secured [...]. The current distribution of African territories has the consequence that the treasures of the black continent remain hoarded asleep: without the cooperation of Germany, Africa will remain unproductive treasure. If the great struggle of races commence, if 'Asia for Asians' should become a reality tomorrow [...] to Germany would fall the task of preserving Africa for Europe.[56]

Actually many on the French political left, such as Aristide Briand, Joseph Caillaux and Henry de Jouvenel, agreed that stripping Germany of its colonies had been an error – and saw here an opportunity to construct 'Eurafrica' in a joint effort. One of the most ardent advocates of this idea was the radical-socialist Albert Sarraut, the former governor-general of Indochina and several times minister (including Minister of Colonies), and prime minister in the 1920s and 1930s. It is as Minister of Colonies that Sarraut suggested creating Eurafrica as a 'Holy Alliance' to organize one single Eurafrican economy, directed by a 'Grand Council', in 1933. The proposal showed all the ambiguities of the project: French–German pacification and reconciliation as well as colonial exploitation, up to agreeing with the German view of the search for *Lebensraum* and the representation of Africa as a way out for the 'overpopulated' European continent, seen as a cause of war. Although most economists and colonial experts proved prudent, the idea was widely debated, and actually served as a basis for French proposals to appease Germany during the whole decennium. It found a welcoming ear at the ILO and the League of Nations as well. In 1937, the idea of an agreement on the German colonies in return for peace and stability (the 'status quo') in Europe was also suggested to Hitler by the British as part of Neville Chamberlain's appeasement policy. Hitler, incidentally, refused.[57]

Economic divergences

Les deux Europes

That the economic fundamentals in Europe diverged considerably rose to the fore of political and economic thinking after the publication of Francis Delaisi's arguably most influential publication, *Les deux Europes* (The Two Europes, 1929). In this book, the French economic publicist observed that there were actually 'two Europes', one industrial and prosperous, which experienced labour shortages, and the other largely agricultural, poorer and with a significant labour surplus, which resulted in two very different labour markets and production systems. An open market between these divergent regions could be detrimental, particularly for the underdeveloped parts of Europe situated rather in the east and the Mediterranean. These feared that industrialized countries continued to raise protectionist barriers for industrial products but demanded open markets for agricultural products.

The agricultural countries feared that the creation of an open market would completely ruin them, as they were unable to compete with the more advanced and productive countries – they were even often incapable of buying the necessary industrial machines – and would be exploited and reduced to providers of food and raw materials for the northwestern lands. Hence, they demanded special measures to protect them, such as existed between colonial metropoles and their overseas possessions and dominions. The League of Nations' Economic Committee in 1931 suggested creating a special agricultural credit organization and an international bank to stimulate investment. The Bank for International Settlements (BIS) was effectively established in 1930. With the US Federal Reserve not joining, the BIS could not really fulfil its initial purpose of aiding the reparation problem, though it functioned as pivot for the European central banks.[58] In the meantime, though, the economic crisis drove, in particular, South and Central European countries into each other's arms, though as Elemèr Hantos observed, only an association of industrial and agricultural areas had any chance of being effective. Hantos hence argued, as did Delaisi, for a European union of industrial and agricultural states in Europe which could develop a European planned economy.[59]

Delaisi's solution to the problem implied a more planned economic system, a suggestion taken on board by the World Economic Conference of 1930, though without many results, but particularly by the ILO. Europhile director Albert Thomas – who incidentally felt bypassed by Briand's famous speech – indeed offered a more thoughtful economic project for Europe in 1931, inspired largely by Delaisi's ideas on the existence of an unequal European labour market. Basically, Thomas argued for free circulation of people and goods in a regulated European free market, which would increase productivity and hence also raise living standards for the workers. With Delaisi he favoured the creation of a European employment centre, a European credit bank and a European economic five-year plan stimulating labour migration and favouring large public works in infrastructure (electricity, railways and highways), which would also make Europe more 'visible' and hence stimulate European feelings.[60]

These views shared many characteristics with the thinking of a new generation of radical-socialist politicians and intellectuals like Marcel Déat in France and the Belgian Hendrik de Man, former professor in Social Psychology at the University of Frankfurt and in the 1930s vice-president and, from 1938, president of the Belgian Workers' Party, and the leading socialist theoretician of the late 1920s and 1930s. They distanced themselves from orthodox Marxism by recognizing the nation as a source of belonging, rejecting the sole focus on the class struggle and preferring control over production rather than expropriation. Following Delaisi, they believed that only a continent-wide European planned economy, which would make use of the economic diversity of the continent to establish an integrated economic space, was able to counter the monopolistic tendencies of the international cartels, and make Europe strong enough to withstand the rising Nazis in Germany, the USSR and the US. Their federal idea implied supranational institutions and rested on a common European sentiment and common law, though it respected the nation as one of the federation's building blocs.[61]

European industry in general was not particularly enthusiastic about such plans, although the suggestion of large public works did have supporters among the interested industries. Somewhat surprisingly, organized labour – the IFTU and the CISC – initially proved reluctant, as they mainly emphasized the importance of a free market and control on cartelization. From 1932 onwards, however, when the crisis deepened and spread all over Europe, they also developed a similar programme based on German ideas of an organized *Wirtschaftsökonomie* (business economics) and the so-called Labour Plan (*Plan du Travail*) of De Man to combat unemployment and stimulate and co-ordinate the economy.[62]

Regional associations

One of the ways envisaged to increase trade was by extending the statute of most favoured nation, as the League of Nations' Economic Conference of 1930 suggested. This allowed for smaller, regional associations. Actually the Austro-German customs union of 1931, viewed as a first step towards a union, could also be interpreted from such a perspective. German and Austrian economists and intellectuals had been imagining a 'Mitteleuropean' economic collaboration for many years already, although the motive was sometimes also to curtail French ambitions. Germans and Austrians resented the French support for the Little Entente and also interpreted the Briand Plan in that light.[63] But this policy also fitted into more imperial ambitions to economically unify and direct the central European markets under German hegemony. From this perspective, German and Central European industrial concerns set up to control the German *Mitteleuropäische Wirtschaftstagung* (Central European Economic Conference, MWT).[64] This policy was furthermore underpinned by new ideas – although with antecedents in Fichte and List – about the necessity of creating large autarchic regions. The publicists Wilhelm Gürge and Wilhelm Grotkopp presented the European economy as a *Großraumwirtschaft*, a global autarkic zone independent from French and, even more importantly, British colonial imports. They portrayed such an economic organization explicitly as a pathway to a (continental) European union, an idea that would underpin Euronazi views on Europe in the 1940s.[65]

This idea clearly clashed with the interests and policies of Central and Eastern European countries, who tried to unite on economic, political and military grounds. The Balkan countries – Greece, Bulgaria, Albania, Turkey, Romania and Yugoslavia – had already attempted to associate from 1925; at the Conference of Athens in October 1930, they decided to strengthen their communication infrastructure (railways, ports, airways and postal services) as a first step towards economic and political integration.[66] It did not really imply a breakthrough, though. Also, the Little Entente, which, however, did develop into a multilateral organization that went beyond the defence against a revision of the post-war peace settlement, was not able to function as a stable base for political and economic collaboration in the Balkans.

In the late 1920s and 1930s, Elemèr Hantos, vehemently opposed to the 'Balkanization' of Southeast Europe, continued to promote the idea of a Danubian federation, emphasizing the joint economic interests and connections as well as the common culture of the countries around the 'blue river', beyond the Austro-Hungarian realm. His concept of a Danubian federation excluded Germany, though, as Hantos opposed Prussian imperialism. In May 1931, he gained the support of France for his plan, which suggested a system of preferential custom tariffs in Central and Eastern Europe (the 'Tardieu Plan'). However, both Berlin and Vienna perceived it as aimed at their political and commercial interests. Mussolini shared that view and looked for allies against what he perceived as French imperialism. Others, such as the writer Dezső Szabó, imagined a union of all Central and Eastern European people who shared a similar culture between Germany and Russia. As one of the most vehement Hungarian anti-Semites, though, Szabó's Central-European Union excluded 'impure' races such as Jews. Some, in contrast, supported the Paneuropean ideal, among them the aforementioned Oscar Jászi, who would be one of its fiercest defenders during WW II, as an emigrant in the US.[67]

Although some in the Hungarian government sympathized with the idea of a Danubian federation, it finally clashed with the ambition to revise the Trianon treaty. Since 1932, the latter perspective in particular had come to dominate economic concerns. Hungary mainly attempted to associate countries that would help to revise the Trianon treaty, but without handing over to German imperial ambitions. However, this policy failed, and notwithstanding an agreement with Austria and Italy, Hungary could not impose its agenda and would fall into the German orbit.[68]

The idea of a Danubian federation was nevertheless adopted by the Romanian government and in particular Prime Minister Iuliu Maniu, though he included Germany. His quite concrete plan contained a four-step model: (1) an economic alliance of the countries from the Baltic to the Black Sea; (2) a customs union; (3) a military defence alliance (against the USSR); and (4) the establishment of a federation with common institutions but maintaining each state's sovereignty. This federation should associate with Italy in the first place, and then extend further into the rest of the continent. Hence, Europe would be built upon the base of the Central European federation, an idea that would be followed up later, from 1938 onwards, by the better known Grigore Gafencu whose ideas would contribute to a post-war European Movement.

Further north, Polish intellectuals and political activists dug up an old idea of a Jagiellonian federation referring to the former Polish–Lithuanian Commonwealth, which would, for example in the proposal of Stefan Gużkowski, encompass not only Poland and Lithuania but Estonia, Latvia, Bulgaria, Austria, Czechoslovakia, Romania, Yugoslavia and Hungary as well. These should federate, following the Jagiellonian motto of *cooperare sine violentie* (collaborate without violence), though the dominance of Poland would be such that one is entitled to view the *Imperium Jagellionum* as the Polish version of a Mitteleuropa or even *Großraum* developed in Berlin. It would constitute both a political buffer state able to contain its powerful neighbours, and an economic union that would compete effectively with the rising powers in the East and the West, being at the same time independent from them.[69]

In Northwestern Europe, the emphasis was mainly on the need for a liberalization of trade. However, as the First International Conference on Concerted Economic Action or Customs Truce Conference, organized by the League of Nations (February–March 1930), fizzled out, the UK withdrew its attention from the continent, focusing on its Empire instead. As a reaction, Norway, Sweden, Denmark, the Netherlands, Belgium and Luxembourg signed a convention in December 1930 on economic co-operation and information exchange with regard to monetary policies. The 'Oslo-states', as they became known, also declared their intention to promote international, particularly European, collaboration. In fact, they hoped to establish a Western European free market zone which would include the UK as well as France and Germany. However, the UK reoriented its policies towards its dominions (Conference of Ottawa, 1931), while Germany developed more imperialist plans for Mitteleuropa and France prioritized its economic interests above international engagements. Quite limited in content – the signatories agreed to avoid customs increases or if they felt compelled to impose an increase, to announce it two weeks in advance, allowing the other members of the convention to respond – the Oslo convention nevertheless initiated some spill-over effects with respect to trade policies (such as the extension of the status of most favoured nation) and even the suggestion of creating a common currency. In June 1932, Belgium, the Netherlands and Luxemburg established a customs union. The alliance remained vulnerable, though, to the economic policies and protectionism of the other major European powers. Extending the union to the other Oslo states and the UK, as was the intention, proved impossible, but gradually the attitude of France changed.[70]

The economic and financial crisis went into another phase when monetary means were shed in the struggle, especially when the UK abandoned the gold standard and devalued the British pound in September 1931, followed by several other nations – including the Scandinavian members of the Oslo convention – and particularly the US in April 1933. The resulting financial chaos and economic and financial struggle was addressed by the League of Nations, which convened an international economic and monetary conference in London in July 1933 but yielded no tangible results. The European countries that still clung to the old monetary order and aimed at restoring the gold standard tried to establish a 'Gold Bloc' between France, Belgium, the Netherlands, Switzerland, Italy and Poland. Their attempt failed, as France continued to prefer bilateral agreements with the other major powers rather than the 'smaller' nations and maintaining the gold standard proved economically detrimental: Belgium felt compelled to give up the gold standard and to devalue the Belgian franc in 1935. The others followed suit.[71]

Fascist and nationalistic Europe

Eurofascism

Gradually the idea of European unity was resurrected by the extreme right, albeit as an 'anti-Europa' – by which fascists and radical nationalists mainly meant that they rejected the existing liberal and democratic Europe. As the chief publicist of 'fascist Europeanism', Asvero Gravelli, stated in the first issue of the influential journal *Antieuropa* in 1929, 'The anti-Europeanism of fascism is not an end in itself, but a provisional historical position, which will last till fascism has enabled Europe to regain its ideal and spiritual equilibrium, the starting point of a new European role in the world.' He went on to define what fascism, for him, actually meant. His statement is worth quoting extensively, as his words obviously appealed to wider circles at the time, even if fascist 'ethics' were far from humanitarian and fascist Italy in reality looked very grim:

> Fascism transcends democracy and liberalism; its regenerative action is based on granite foundations: the idea of hierarchy, of the participation of the whole population in the life of the State, social justice in the equitable distribution of rights and duties, the infusion of public life with moral principles, the affirmation of religious values, the prestige of the family, the ethical interpretation of the ideas of order, authority and liberty.[72]

Fascists in this respect imagined an alternative hierarchical and organic European order based upon nation states. At first glance it seems as if the fascists emphasized the nation state. However, certainly in Mussolini's view, a fascist European order implied a hierarchical structure in which larger states would dominate the smaller ones, as was the main purpose of the Four-Power Pact that the 'Duce' proposed in March 1933 to Germany, France and the UK.[73] It came to little, especially after Germany left the League of Nations after the referendum of November 1933, but significantly (and perhaps prophetically) the UK would long cling to the idea as a way towards a stable peace in Europe – the idea would ironically make a comeback in 1944.

The Eurofascist conception of Europe, referring to a hierarchical model of an association of fascist or corporatist states maintaining their territorial integrity, national traditions and (relative) independence, and often phrased in 'universal' terms (as the Italian fascist principles were believed to be applicable elsewhere as well, not restricted to Italy or even Europe), was forcefully advanced by Mussolini and his fascist supporters in the late 1920s and early 1930s.[74] They could build upon a transnational network of fascist organizations in Europe that were already familiarized with the idea of fascism as a European regeneration movement, but one that was now more explicitly phrased in European terms through publications, magazines and journals such as *Antieuropa* and *Ottobre: Quotidiano del Fascismo Universale* (1932, referring to the 10th anniversary of the March on Rome), and organizations such as the International Centre for Fascist Studies, established in Lausanne (Switzerland) in 1927 and headed by the British Major James Strachey Barnes, the *Istituto Europa Giovane* and the *Comitato per l'Universalità di*

Roma (CAUR, 1933), which was to co-ordinate the different activities but quickly failed as a result of divergences between 'Roman' fascists and proponents of a *völkisch* Europe based upon ethnicity and race.[75] Fascist ideas about Europe were widely publicised and discussed at the time, and often received appreciative comments from conservative politicians and intellectuals such as Winston Churchill, Julius Evola and Mircea Eliade.[76] Illustrative is the Volta Conference of 1932, organized by the fascistic Royal Academy of Science in Rome to debate the future of Europe, though undoubtedly it was also conceived as a platform to propagate Mussolini's vision of a fascist Europe.[77] Although the conference particularly appealed to conservative Catholics, fascists and Nazis (including Hermann Goering and Alfred Rosenberg), certainly not all attendees and speakers were fascists. Indeed, among them one would encounter the likes of French diplomat Joseph Avenol, who would become director-general of the League of Nations in 1933; the Dutch socialist politician Hendrik Brugmans (later one of the leading European federalists and founder of the College of Bruges), the British Catholic historian Christopher Dawson, and the pre-eminent German sociologists Werner Sombart and Alfred Weber. The Austrian-Jewish pacifist writer Stefan Zweig had accepted the invitation but cancelled his participation *in extremis*. Nevertheless, the conference emphasized the need for a strong Europe, be it a Europe 'liberated' from British influence, or Europe as a union of independent nation states emphasizing its superior position in the world.

> Essentially, the war and peace made Europe fully aware of its relativity in the world, compared not only to the American world, but also to the Japanese, Chinese, and Indian ones. Such considerations already lead to pessimism as there is a danger of Europe being dethroned from its position of ruler of the world. The current economic crisis – for some, even a crisis of civilization – has confronted Europe with an examination of conscience: few and far between are the ideal fixed points in modern Europe; almost all beliefs are disputed or discredited.[78]

The solution was in a new 'Roman' empire based on a common cultural base, but hierarchical and diverse, referring to its rich history of arts and ideas, which legitimated its dominance of the world. The interpretation of Europe's diversity incidentally provoked an interesting debate, when the Nazi representative Alfred Rosenberg sharply criticized the discourse of a universal fascistic revolution, emphasizing the inequality of European cultures and associating national with racial purity. Remarkably, the fascist philosopher and president of the conference, Francesco Orestano, defended the ethnic mix and plurality of the European fabric.[79]

Certainly not all attendants endorsed either Nazi or fascist views, but there are nevertheless clear parallels with, especially, Catholic conceptions. Many Catholics, who were very predominant in Rome in 1932, emphasized the need for a new 'Roman-Catholic' European order as a stable foundation to establish peace as well as a European Christian rebirth. Their ideal was a Europe based on human rationality and Christian conscience, which needed to be grounded in a new order, as the Swiss Catholic historian Gonzague de Reynold argued.[80] But not all Catholics followed that logic – Christopher Dawson, for example, emphasized the Roman heritage of Europe as 'a bridge between East and West, and its achievement consisted not so much in its own independent contribution to culture as in its organization of the alien elements that it incorporated in a new unity' – not exactly the fascist interpretation of Roman heritage.[81] Later he would particularly emphasize the Christian values that should underpin European unity.

A Germanic 'Mitteleuropean' empire

Somewhat similar ideas were developed in Central Europe in the late 1920s and 1930s. Conservative German rightist intellectuals, many present at the Volta conference in Rome, spoke about Mitteleuropa as a restored Holy Roman or – mainly in Vienna – Habsburg Empire. Prince Karl Anton Rohan, for example, sought support for such ideas not only among those who dreamt of the restoration of the Habsburg Empire, but also in Bavaria and southwestern states that equally felt dominated and marginalized by Prussians. Rohan even drafted a 'minorities statute' in June 1930, according to which national minorities should be protected and free to establish transnational associations. Such policies, including the right to education in one's own (minority) language, can be viewed both as a continuation of long-standing imperial policies of granting different rights to different peoples, but also as a strategy to undermine the new post-war national order, especially as Rohan presented Germans as the 'leading cultural people in Central Europe' and capable of 'bringing order' in a region that he considered 'chaotic'. In view of his authoritarian, anti-democratic convictions, this certainly meant turning away from the democratic regimes that were in place. Such views brought the movement into fascist and national socialist waters. Themes such as the supremacy of the white race as core of Europe's identity and the Jewish problem came to dominate the *Europäische Revue* in the 1930s. Nevertheless, Rohan, though he considered himself a fascist and affiliated to the Austrian NSDAP in 1935, stopped short of advocating a 'violent' repression of minorities.[82]

Similar views can be found among other conservative thinkers, such as Carl Schmitt, Giselher Wirsing, or the *Abendland* movement. The latter in particular increasingly spoke of a Mitteleuropa as 'Holy Roman Empire of the German Nation', focusing on the centrality of the Rhine in the European imagination, and supported the idea of a German 'Third Reich' – paving the way for an alliance with the national socialists. From this perspective, the Catholic concept of a sacred order was gradually eclipsed by imperial ambitions.[83] Giselher Wirsing (*Zwischeneuropa und die deutsche Zukunft*, 1932) particularly emphasized the leading role of Germany in a Central European *Großraum* which rejected the centralized, democratic state model associated with France as well as American democracy (in particular in his *Der maßlose Kontinent* published in 1932), which he considered manipulated by Jews.[84] Carl Schmitt, who had already abandoned the Catholic Church in the mid-1920s, reformulated his view of Europe as a new Holy Roman Empire and based it on a similar Germanic concept of Mitteleuropa as the heart of a European *Großraum* standing against Russia.[85] Rohan, in contrast, favoured a fascist alliance of Austria, Italy and Germany centred around the Italian-Austrian 'Roman' interpretation of Europe as proposed by Mussolini. The Nazis, however, sidelined him and took over the direction of the *Europäische Kulturbund*, though allowing the *Revue européenne* to continue.[86] It contributed to Nazis being associated with the idea of a European unity. Their view, however, was not only fundamentally different from those of liberal and socialist European federalists, but from those of the Italian fascists and Catholic conservatives as well. Their more radical conceptions did show some parallels with radical-socialists, though, when these argued for 'transcending' the nation in a new European order.

Transcending the nation: The Nazi nation-empire

The 1920s and 1930s are often represented as the culmination of nationalism. In many ways, however, that was not the case. Certainly, the idea that every nation or people should govern its own state – especially in Wilson's interpretation of self-determination – seemed omnipresent and in that sense nationalism appeared as a major political force, while the different European states established bureaucracies to promote exclusive forms of citizenship (passports) and erected tariff walls to protect domestic industrial and agricultural production from outside competition. Also, fascism exalted the virtues of the nation and pleaded for a national rebirth, or 'palingenesis' in Roger Griffin's apt phrase. However, it also dawned on many that the nation was not necessarily the most appropriate form to cope with the demands of the modern age. Economic forces did not stop at borders, while the breakthrough of the masses appeared to be making the existing institutional framework of national party politics obsolete. Hence, the very idea of state sovereignty came to be discussed by politicians, businessmen and scholars from all sides of the political spectre. Such a reflection often started from a reflection on the nature of the state, though.

Euronazism

In Germany, mainstream thinking emphasized the nation as the source of political and legal order. Especially, Hans Kelsen, Carl Schmitt – that brilliant but 'dangerous mind' (Jan-Werner Mueller) – and the lesser known Hermann Heller offered poignant reassessments of the relationship between sovereignty and the state, with Schmitt arguing for a new absolutism ('sovereign is who decides upon the exception') and Heller, observing that the breakthrough of the masses and totalitarianism undermined the rule of law, offered the foundations of a *sozialer Rechtstaat* through the construction of a political community which would integrate the masses into the system.[87] Still, this new emphasis on the nation generated a view that would 'transcend' traditional nationalist interpretations of the nation and develop into a Euro-imperialist ideology, which I will call Euronazism, and which should be distinguished from Eurofascism.[88]

The Nazi view on Europe was indeed quite different from the Italian fascist one, though they shared many features, such as the idea of an international order based on hierarchy instead of equality between nations and the rejection of socialism and communism as well as liberal democracy. Alfred Rosenberg, the main ideologue of the NSDAP, already in 1925 had presented a vision of Nazism as a force that would 'unify' Europe under the Swastika.[89] Euronazism, however, was based on pure racism: the Nazi objective of a European utopia implied the racial 'purification' of the continent.[90] This implied not only the systematic exploitation of Jews and other 'inferior races' or persons, but also their physical elimination. While Eurofascists might or might not be racists (particularly anti-Semites), racism and anti-Semitism constituted an essential component of Euronazism. In that respect Nazism had a universalism of its own and certainly opposed the 'liberating' and 'ecumenic' aspirations of Italian fascism and its theoretical emphasis on the nation state. Nazis, and in particular Hitler, only had the interests of one nation in mind, the Aryan Germans, and actually considered 'real' European unity as the extension of *Germanentum* in a 'Teutonic Empire of the German Nation'. By the mid-1930s, the Nazi views of a German-led 'Third Reich' overpowered all others; Mussolini also politically aligned himself with Hitler and embraced the Nazi concept of race as the constituting element of a new Europe. However, during the war not all collaborative forces shared that vision, least of all the nationalistic extreme right of Vichy France and the supporting *Action française*.

The Großraum theory

Already since the mid-1920s, German conservatives, right-wing Catholics and racist nationalists had developed the idea that Germany, as the principal nation in Europe, should expand and establish a 'third' German Reich as the framework for the unification of all 'greater Germans' in Central and Southeastern Europe. The idea, popularized by Arthur Moeller van den Bruck's *Das Dritte Reich* (The Third Reich, 1923) but also adopted by the NSDAP in 1921, was further developed into a concept of European unity. Hitler, incidentally, objected to the use of the term 'Third Reich' because of its historical reminiscence and chiliastic connotations, and preferred the phrases 'German' or 'Greater Germanic Reich' based on racial superiority.[91]

This actually indicates that national socialism cannot be reduced to an extreme variant of nationalism, as it did not take the ethnic understanding or palingenesis of the nation as its point of departure but rather race, which is transnational and universal by nature even if the Nazis in practice confounded race and nation. Moreover, the state in the *völkisch* perspective was a useless concept, as the *Volk*, or race, held predominance over any political form, certainly over such a highly structured, constraining and thus inapt one as the state. The *Volk* needed protection, reinforcement and *Lebensraum*, threatened as it was by the dangers of liberalism, communism and, especially, as a result of interbreeding with Jews or non-whites (referring to the role of colonial troops in fighting Germany during WW I).[92] It was not to be curtailed by something as obsolete as state borders. While conservatives, traditionalists and liberal nationalists valued the diversity of the European fabric, national socialists, in contrast, only had eyes for the interests of the 'core-state', and of the 'people' as opposed to a privileged elite (the traditionalist position) or class (as Marxists argued). While perhaps for Italian (and most Austrian) fascists a hierarchical European order respecting national sovereignty in Europe corresponded to their fascist ideal, for Nazis, and particularly for Hitler, such an order could only be accepted as temporary and insofar as it did not conflict with the interests of the German nation or *Volk* (nation, *Volk* and race overlapping). And the instrument to express these interests was not the nation but the *Reich* – hence, one could argue, national socialists are not nationalists.

The idea of a Nazi European empire did not only appeal to Germans, but enjoyed widespread support all over Europe. Gradually in the latter half of the 1930s, fascism adopted the rhetoric and policies of Aryanism and anti-Semitism.[93] *Abendlanders* and other Catholic conservatives, for example, drifted towards similar ideas but with a neo-Habsburg Reich as their focal point. But for them too, the interests of the Austro-German *Volk* determined the shape of the empire as well as relations with other nations.[94] The appeal of an integrated Nazi Europe, however, dwindled quickly as the politics became effective.

Within the national socialist realm, some thinkers developed a particular 'Euronazi' programme which was not entirely shared by all Nazis and particularly not by Hitler, whose aim seems rather to be simply the overall dominance of the Germans. Among the theoreticians of Euronazism a prominent role must be attributed to the legal scholar Carl Schmitt, who developed a comprehensive political scheme, associating several likeminded nations or states into a *Großraum*, of which the political course would be determined by the leading nation or Reich. Hence, Europe would be constituted of several largely autarchic and homogenous *Großräume*, which would avoid inner conflict – an idea reminiscent of Fichte that we have already found in Polish and Hungarian European plans during and after WW I, and which would make a remarkable reappearance in British and American plans for the post-war period.[95]

The German-led *Großraum* would cover most of continental Europe, as the interests of France, Great Britain and even Italy lay overseas. Schmitt's European vision actually corresponded very closely to that of Mussolini's Four-Nation Pact. In contrast to his critics such as the SS jurist Werner Best and certainly also Hitler, Schmitt did leave space for national states. European unity was seen mainly in its relationship with 'external' powers, to strengthen it (or rather the Reich) vis-à-vis the US, the USSR and the British Empire. This model was, according to Schmitt, meant to reconstruct a European legal order, which in his view had been eroding since the mid-nineteenth century by the growing instrumentalization of the law by the states on the one hand, and by the American-inspired 'moralization' of war and international politics expressed in the demand for unconditional surrender and the 'total' humiliation of Germany at Versailles. In the perspective of hardline Nazis though, the central concept was rather that of the Greater Germanic Reich of the German Nation, which would assimilate all 'Germanic' nations into a Pan-German state stretching from the Netherlands and Alsace-Lorraine to Scandinavia in the north and Northern Italy in the south, on to Bohemia and Slovenia, finally ending in Silesia or, after 1941, up until the Urals.

Alongside the political *Großraum*, there corresponded a *Großraum* economy, or *Großraumwirtschaft*. The publicist Wilhelm Grotkopp and the economist Werner Daitz presented themselves as the main propagandists of an economic organization of Europe as a self-supporting and autarchic economy, based on race and territory, controlled by Germany and the Germans. This *Großraumwirtschaft* included a pure Germanic 'welfare' and labour policy and a European planned economy, with a common monetary union based on a 'labour' standard (referring to productivity) instead of the gold standard. It also implied a monopolization of trade or a Europe-wide distribution of labour between industrial and agrarian states, but always under German leadership, with the agrarian states as suppliers of food and raw materials for the German industry, and extending its application to include Africa as supplier of food and raw materials.[96]

The latter idea referred to pre-war conceptions of Eurafrica, which certainly could appeal to French proponents of this concept. Hitler and Mussolini actually agreed to work towards a Eurafrican system in October 1940, albeit as a long-term perspective after the war was over. It would include the French, Belgian, Italian and newly established German colonies and protectorates under German leadership.[97]

The ideas about a European *Großraum* and *Großraumwirtschaft* were particularly influential in the Nazi Ministry of Foreign Affairs. In March 1943 – Germany already occupying most of the European continent – the Minister of Foreign Affairs, Joachim von Ribbentrop, who had always been particularly interested in questions of European unity (he had attended the Volta Conference of 1932), presented a comprehensive plan for a European 'confederation' uniting Germany, Italy, France, Denmark, Norway, Finland, Slovakia, Hungary, Romania, Bulgaria, Croatia, Serbia and Greece, as well as Spain; other occupied states could also join. It would establish a fierce block against the USSR and the allies, who would have to accept that they were 'not liberating European states, but attacking a Europe which stood firmly against them'.[98] As Hitler had no intention of compromising on the absolute leadership of Germany and on the *Führerprinzip*, he obviously rejected the plan, as it implied respecting the political sovereignty of its members (and therefore was welcomed enthusiastically by the collaborationist movements and regimes in Europe).[99] However, it nevertheless contributed to the contamination of the concept of European integration, all the more so as Nazi propaganda systematically spoke of a 'War of Continents' and represented national socialist Europe as a fortress and a bulwark against 'Asian Bolshevism', American capitalism and Jewry.[100] But also in the late 1930s the Nazis had presented the (imminent) war as a war of liberation and European unity, phrases that went beyond rhetoric, as in the words of one of von Ribbentrop's closest collaborators:

> The present war is also a war for the unity and freedom of Europe. Its aims are: To bring about and guarantee lasting peace for the European countries. Security against economic strangulation and interference by foreign powers; Britain and the US. Europe for the Europeans![101]

This essentially Eurofascist view included a colonial perspective as well, representing Africa in particular as a space for colonization, peopling and exploitation.[102]

In the collaboration

Eurofascist views on Europe found followers among fascists and collaborators outside the German lands as well, although these supporters rather emphasized an association, on a more equal basis, of fascist states, also after 1940. Some, such as Marshal Pétain in Vichy France, collaborated out of pragmatism and the refusal to wage a lost war, adopting a nationalist-fascist position, including anti-Semitism, but not the broader Euronazi perspective, including a rejection of its profound racist underpinning. Others, though – such as Scandinavian fascists and the Walloon Rex or the Flemish DeVlag in Belgium (albeit for different reasons) – accepted a complete integration into the German Reich as Germanic or Nordic Aryans. Many Christians, Catholics as well as Protestants, were attracted by fascist anti-communism and ideas about a corporate order, which seemed similar to Christian views, all along the 1920s and 1930s.[103] Euronazi views on a new European economy, however, found support especially among neo-socialists in Belgium and France, such as Hendrik De Man and Marcel Déat. They were thrown into the orbit of national socialism in the later 1930s and early 1940s, although most of them initially rejected anti-Semitism in principle, as well as nationalism and dictatorship.

The motivations behind the neo-socialists' move are complex and diverse.[104] Just like Nazis, they believed that the traditional concept of state sovereignty and the representation of the people through parties should be left behind. Not only neo-socialists but also a former Marxist such as Jacques Doriot recognized the nation as a platform for socialist action, but opposing nationalism, they argued for 'transcending' national sovereignty in an integrated, planned European economy. Francis Delaisi, for example, had tirelessly promoted the cause of an organized European economy as opposed to a purely liberal-capitalist one, and seemed to find such an economy in the Euronazi schemes.[105] In addition, they shared a belief in a European common culture – though its content varied considerably – and a desire to eliminate the communist menace. Racism and anti-Semitism did not rank high in their priorities – Déat and De Man certainly were no racists – but they gradually embarked on that road too. Other factors played a role as well, such as the perceived need to strengthen Europe against the USSR and the US, and sometimes also the British Empire or the awakening of Asian peoples. No doubt the impression of the overwhelming power of the Nazis, making resistance appear futile, must be taken into consideration as well. In addition, pacifists and all who opposed war between France and Germany – we may call them 'neutralists' – and who believed that the origin of the disastrous economic and political situation lay in Versailles often demonstrated a remarkable willingness to appease and collaborate with Germany (though initially only in the general meaning of the term). Examples include Jean Luchaire, a close ally of Aristide Briand, a brilliant militant of Paneuropa and advocate of French–German reconciliation in the 1920s. To some extent they hoped that reason and a common integrated European economy would take away the root cause of the conflict. Some continued to do so even during the war, such as Pierre Laval, a socialist politician, a close collaborator of Briand in the 1920s and a radical pacifist who in the early 1940s came to share the 'Euronazi' ideal and became Prime Minister of Vichy France. It is in this capacity that he gave a famous speech in June 1942 in which he outlined his conviction and motives:

> I aim at restoring with Germany and Italy a normal and trusting relationship. From this war inevitably a new Europe will arise. [...] To build this Europe, Germany is waging huge battles [...] I desire the victory of Germany, because without it, Bolshevism tomorrow will

take power everywhere. [...] This war, as I have already said, is a war like no other. It is a revolution from which must arise a new world. You have nothing to fear from the regime that will be installed here, but everything to expect. A younger, stronger, more human Republic has to be born; Socialism will be established throughout Europe, and the form it will get in France will be shaped by our national character.[106]

One should note in this quotation, and in virtually all texts of these 'to fascism converted neo-socialists', that they continued to claim that they strove towards a socialist society. This was, in my opinion, not mere propaganda, though it may have been self-deceiving rhetoric.

An important role in this remarkable evolution can be attributed to the Sohlberg Circle, the initiative in 1930 of a German teacher and art lover, Otto Abetz, to bring French and German youth movement leaders together. Abetz, however, agitated not only for Franco-German rapprochement, but also for a revision of the Versailles treaty. As a member of the NSDAP from 1933 (?) onwards, he used the meetings to influence his French and Belgian guests, who included many of those previously mentioned, such as De Man and Luchaire, his brother-in-law. Besides the Sohlberg Circle, Abetz created the German-French Committee, which published the bilingual *Cahiers franco-allemands*. The latter emphasized a racist European spiritual and cultural unity, announcing 'a millennium of peace' that would generate from the reconciliation of 'Teutonic Germans' and 'Celtic Frenchmen'. This movement strongly appealed to such conservative French Catholics as Alphonse de Châteaubriant. During the war Abetz became German ambassador to Vichy, which allowed him to stay in contact and influence his friends.[107]

By 1942, Euronazi views came to dominate in occupied and collaborationist Europe, even if some – in particular the Vichy regime of Marshal Pétain, who collaborated for nationalist and opportunist reasons – continued to reject the idea of a Europe in which national states were subordinated to general principles, fascist or otherwise. Illustrative of the Euronazi view was the 'Exposition on European France' held in Paris in the summer of 1941, which portrayed a new vision of a prosperous and rural French economy as a result of a united European market in which cities were connected through efficient railways, canals and highways. Euronazis and Eurofascists recalled European history, with Charlemagne as a symbol of a European empire and culture. However, as the tides of war turned, some resorted to more confederal Eurofascist models. A number of prominent European Nazis and fascists headed by the Italian diplomat Giuseppe Bastianini, for example, proposed establishing a European Magna Carta in March 1943, in the aftermath of the Stalingrad debacle, proclaiming a new European corporate order under joint German-Italian tutelage that respected the autonomy of nation states within the Germanic Reich. The project, however, was not discussed with Hitler, who would certainly have rejected it.[108] Although the European dreams of Eurofascists and Euronazis, and 'neosocialists converted to national socialism', remained pure chimera, the idea of an integrated European order did exist as a motivation and an image from which others had to distance themselves.

Beyond the nation-empire: The federal alternative in the 1930s

As Eurofascists lauded the values of a united Europe of nations and Euronazis extolled the virtues of an organized European economy, albeit for the benefit of the leading German nation, the European idea seemed effectively appropriated by the extreme right. However, in the late 1930s a federalist alternative, often presented as a 'third force' or 'third way', found new life amid different ideological milieus.

The idea of a third force had many fathers – fascists also presented themselves as such. In this context, perhaps one should mainly remember some Catholic perceptions of the nation. While many Protestants developed an 'intimate' relationship with nation states through state churches – which hence does not apply to dissident churches – and Catholics, including followers of Charles Maurras' 'integral nationalism', could also embrace the nation as the paramount principle of social organization, many Catholics considered the state as just one of many communities and of relatively recent origin, of which they were wary as they associated it with French ('Gallican') centralism and secularism.[109]

Since the nineteenth century the Catholic Church had gradually developed a social and political doctrine of complementing communities, of which the nation state was one (besides family, corporation and the – transnational – Church itself). Christian personalists recognized the 'person' as a spiritual being, which implied rejecting both capitalist and Marxist materialism, and emphasized man's imbedding in different communities who shared and divided 'sovereignty'. Similar ideas were developed among non-Christian intellectual circles considering ways to overcome the spiritual crisis of Europe, among which the *Ordre Nouveau* (New Order) movement of Alexandre Marc (born Aleksander Markovitch Lipiansky) in France and other 'Non-Conformists of the 1930s', which found inspiration in Nietzsche and Proudhon rather than Thomas of Aquino, opposing liberalism, fascism, communism and democracy in favour of a 'spiritual' renewal and 'person-oriented' economic and political system.[110] However, they all shared the assessment of the crisis as an existential one, which demanded a complete reformulation of the social and political system and considered the nation as part of the system. They actually all advocated a solidaristic, 'corporatist' organization of society in contrast to the French 'Jacobin' association of state and nation and state absolutism. The concept of 'subsidiarity' – which delegated decision-making authority to the 'most appropriate level' (from the family to the corporation or the region to the state or even a supranational authority) – became the magic instrument to reconcile the human person to the society. Illustrated by the conversion of Marc to Catholicism, a connection between Catholicism, the *Ordre nouveau* and the Non-Conformists was established.

Many of these somehow recognized personalist principles in fascist and national socialist ideas in the 1930s, particularly in Germany, Austria – where a Catholic 'Austro-fascist' state was installed with the support of the local hierarchy and the not entirely tacit approval of the Holy See –, Hungary and further in Central and Eastern Europe. Western European Catholics also followed such a road, including Léon Degrelle and his Rex movement in Belgium and the French writers Pierre Drieu La Rochelle and Alphonse de Châteaubriant, who had previously been active in Karl Anton Rohan's European Cultural League and in the late 1930s embraced national socialism. Blending Aryan racism and traditional Christian anti-Semitism, Châteaubriant even engaged in a missionary crusade for a 'purified' Aryan Europe which would get rid of Jews and communists. The Catholic philosopher Jacques Maritain, in contrast, argued for an inclusive humanistic Christian ideal that respected the plurality of secular society in *Humanisme integral* (*Integral Humanism*, 1936), one of the most influential Catholic books of the twentieth century. It helped other personalists, such as Marc, opposing absolutist ideas and orienting them towards the Resistance.

Building upon these various ideas, some personalists such as Emmanuel Mounier, Don Luigi Sturzo, Denis de Rougemont and Alexandre Marc gradually became influenced by federalist and even (especially in the case of Marc) Proudhonian ideas by the end of the 1930s and during the war. Others, Catholics and Protestants, rather followed German traditions of Europeanism and French–German reconciliation, as was the case with the later German Chancellor Konrad Adenauer, who had pushed through his Europeanist views at the SIPDIC congress of 1931. The Swiss Protestant Denis de Rougemont, however, was one of the first to explicitly associate personalism with federalism, presenting the Swiss federal system as a possible model for Europe at least from 1937 onwards. Still, only a few Christian democratic voices considered a European federation as an alternative to fascist or national socialist utopias for Europe. Notwithstanding the ephemeral SIPDIC they were, moreover, hardly connected internationally and – in contrast to the mythology grafted onto Christian Democracy later – not particularly 'internationalist'. Most Christian personalists and Christian democrats began to conceive of a European union only after 1940; examples include the influential exiled leader of the Italian Christian democrats Don Sturzo, as well as Maritain. It is not by accident that they developed their personalistic views about a European union in the US. Some German Christians developed an alternative to the Nazi economy during meetings in the Kreisauer Circle. There, a 'subsidiarity' model for Europe was imagined, including a European constitution and parliament.[111]

Emphasizing that planism and neo-socialism had a lot in common that facilitated their rapprochement does not imply that all neo-socialists went along this road. Questioning the nation state could very well lead to anti-fascism and anti-Nazism. European federalism was largely conceived from that perspective, as the case of the Italian anti-fascist movement around the journal *Giustizia e Libertà*, founded by the political activist and Paris exile Carlo Rosselli in 1929, illustrates. Rosselli had, by the late 1920s, developed liberal-federalist views in the wake of ideas that had existed in Italy since 1918 (Enaudi, Ciabiati) but he was further inspired by De Man's *Au delà du Marxisme* (Beyond Marxism, 1927) and the anarchism of Proudhon and Jaurès. He actually tried to imagine a 'liberal-socialist' federalist order as a reaction to the centralization that fascists imposed in Italy. Rosselli's European federation imagined a social space in which people, money and trade would circulate freely, aimed at limiting the totalitarian ambitions of state power, which he saw as the root cause of fascist degeneration. Rosselli connected with Italian anti-fascists such as Ernesto Rossi – who would later co-author the federalist Manifesto of Ventotene – and socialists who opposed the Marxist orientation of the socialist party (Filippo Turati, Claudio Treves, Giuseppi Saragat, Eugenio Colorni, Guido Calogero) and embraced his federalist ideas.[112]

German socialist exiles in particular imagined new federalist forms of international collaboration, though similar ideas flourished in Austria and Czechoslovakia as well. As exiles, they felt estranged from the socialist parties in their host country, and in particular members of the German *Internationaler Socialistischer Kampfbund* (International Socialist Vanguard) and the socialist splinter group *Neu Beginnen* (Starting Anew) developed ideas of a 'Third Force' between the Soviet model and the Western powers and imagined new federalist forms of international collaboration in Central Europe, conceived largely as a sort of 'competition' with Nazi plans. They certainly opposed coercion but particularly favoured a federalism based on voluntary associations, creating socialist *Lebensräume* centred around a Germany independent from the USSR or great Western powers.[113] The latter concept was absent in British labour circles, where several groups imagined a federal Europe as a possible future for the continent – it always remained unclear whether that included Britain or not.[114]

A very different perspective was defended by the Austrian economist and professor at the London School of Economics, Friedrich von Hayek, who in 1939 argued that political integration and economic liberalization were inextricably linked: one could not happen without the other. In this sense he radically opposed fascist, socialist as well as Christian democratic proposals, a position that he would continue to defend after the war.[115]

In the late 1930s Hayek's star had already waned considerably in London, and his impact was rather marginal. Nevertheless, European federalism got the wind in its sails in the late 1930s. In 1938, a number of prominent British federalists set up the Federal Union (FU) in London to promote European unity; in 1940, they established the Federal Union Research Institute (FURI), chaired by William Beveridge. The movement mainly attracted politicians and intellectuals from the political left, such as the British labour leader Ernest Bevin, but reached out to more right-wing figures as well, such as Robert Boothby, R.A. Butler and Duff Cooper who considered a European 'third force' if the US would return to protectionist and isolationist positions, as they anticipated would happen. Some of them also feared for British colonial possessions. These milieus supported a French–British alliance in 1940, though there were others who also considered an Atlantic federation.[116]

One of the most famous representatives of this current was the *New York Times* journalist Clarence Streit. In 1938, he published the mega-bestseller *Union Now*, in which he appealed to all democracies to unite with the federal model of the US, after which he founded the Federal Union as an international pressure group and think tank. The suggestion was shared by Ernest Bevin, who saw a European 'Peace Bloc' emerge which would encompass the UK, Western Europe and

Africa.[117] In a review of Streit's book, George Orwell, however, exposed the colonial logic of such proposals:[118]

> [...] all phrases like 'Peace Bloc', 'Peace Front', etc. contain some such implication; all imply a tightening-up of the existing structure. The unspoken clause is always 'not counting niggers'. For how can we make a 'firm stand' against Hitler if we are simultaneously weakening ourselves at home? In other words, how can we 'fight Fascism' except by bolstering up a far vaster injustice? (...) What real settlement, of the slightest value, can there be along these lines? What meaning would there be, even if it were successful, in bringing down Hitler's system in order to stabilize something that is far bigger and in its different way just as bad?[119]

In a still profoundly racist and imperialist Europe, however, Orwell's sharp criticism found little response – very few of those promoting European federalism opposed imperialism and colonial racism. In contrast to a widespread assumption, WW II would not change that.

8
Pacification by Division

For all these things have been done by Europeans to other Europeans in Europe. That in itself should be enough to remind us that the story of recent European history that we have been telling ourselves and our children is little better than a fairy tale. And yet our politicians go on telling it.

Timothy Garton Ash, 1999[1]

Between Spinelli and Morgenthau

The road to unity of the Resistance?

Even more so than WW I, there is a tendency to consider the experience of WW II as conducive to peace and harmony.[2] The world conflict appears somehow to have increased the appeal of an integrated Europe and stimulated both new initiatives and the formulation of more radical concepts of renunciation of sovereignty in return for stability, economic growth and peace.

An earlier generation of historians of European integration strongly emphasized how among major resistance movements and exiles during the war, the idea that national oppositions had to be overcome gained currency, in parallel with a critique of the weakness of the League of Nations, paving the way for the idea of European integration to materialize after 1945. However, recent scholarship seriously questions the impact of either exiles or Resistance movements and argues that their strong stance in the historical representation of European integration is largely a myth developed later.[3] The political impact of exiles on the post-war European construction was marginal, while most resistance fighters battled for the independence of their country from occupation. That is not quite the same as fighting for a united Europe. Moreover, if

157

there was one issue on which resistance movements may have agreed upon, it was the need for harsh treatment and punishment of the perpetrators of the war. The emphasis of Nazis on a common European core, their representation of a united Europe as a Nazi ideal, the collaboration of many conservatives and aristocratic reactionaries with the Nazis and the 'nazification' of several conservative and rightist movements, moreover, all discredited Pan-European views of a renaissance of the continent on the basis of a common culture. 'Only a few spoke out in favour of European unity [in 1945] – faint voices indeed amid the din of nationalism aroused by the war and the Occupation', the French jurist and political scientist Maurice Duverger recalled at the beginning of the first session of the Council of Europe in Strasbourg in August 1949.[4] Nevertheless the idealistic representation of the Europeanist orientation of the Resistance is not entirely devoid of reality: there were quite a few resistance leaders and intellectuals who effectively imagined the formation of a federal Europe with supranational institutions and even a common European army, even if the concrete modalities clearly varied considerably and their impact was more indirect than immediate. The evidence assembled by the now often overly disparaged Walter Lipgens c.s. cannot be that easily dismissed.[5]

The most famous expression of a radically federalist vision of Europe is the so-called 'Manifesto of Ventotene', *Per un' Europa libera e unita* ('Toward a Free and United Europe'), which was drafted by the Italian communist Altiero Spinelli and the anti-fascist Ernesto Rossi, one of the co-founders of *Giustizia e Libertà* in 1929, before and during their detention at the Island of Ventotene and which became the Magna Carta of the European Federalist Movement, created clandestinely in Milan in late August 1943.[6] The manifesto states the key principles of European federalism very clearly. It argues that the many problems of Europe would be easily solved by a European Federation, presented as a strong super-state possessing a European army 'that will have sufficient means to see that its deliberations for the maintenance of common order are executed in the single federal States'. The Ventotene Manifesto, however, was not only a federalist statement, it was also a socialist one, calling for a radically new Europe, even if this was to be realized in pragmatic ways. The originality and uniqueness of the text lies in the fact that it calls for the unification of Europe as a precondition of a socialist transformation of the continent, and not the other way round.

Such views also implied the integration of an undivided Germany into the greater European scheme – it was also considered the only way to pacify this European giant. The former French socialist prime minister

Léon Blum, also imprisoned, reached a similar conclusion from reading history, as he realized that neither the harsh treatment of Prussia after the Battle of Jena–Auerstedt in 1806 (when Prussia was defeated by Napoleon) nor of Germany at Versailles had prevented Prussia or Germany from resurrecting itself and coming back with a vengeance. Hence, 'to obtain the innocuousness of Germany in a peaceful and safe status of Europe, there is just one way', he concluded, 'which is the incorporation of the German nation into an international community that is powerful enough to re-educate her, to discipline her, and, if necessary, to control her'.[7]

Especially in Western continental Europe, there were a number of socialist groups that followed Spinelli's radical ideas. Some went even further, advocating a European socialist revolution, opposing any alignment with the US.[8] Others, in contrast, emphasized a democratic Europe opposed to both fascist and communist models. The German socialist Willy Brandt, for example, taking refuge in Stockholm, imagined an integrated Europe which included a European planned economy but with a particular emphasis on the establishment of a strong international legal order, which would also protect the rights of minorities. As he starkly put it, 'The Europeans face the choice between a new imperialistic power solution or a democratic, federal new order.'[9] Others emphasized the right of self-determination of nations; the Hungarian-Swedish political scientist and journalist Stefan Szende even recalled the idea of Renner's dissociation of state and nation. The (small but significant) Socialist Vanguard Group (SVG), operating within the ranks of the British Labour Party, argued for a European federation – Europe mainly conceived as a federation of northwestern 'democratic' nations – as 'It would be a catastrophe to allow Europe to return to the old multitude of sovereign States, or to be once more divided. ... A United Europe, on a free basis, promises greater guarantees for peace ... because it would mean a progressive solution to the European problem.'[10]

In 1943, the SVG organized a European resistance symposium in London, 'The Future Order of Europe', to which socialists from all over Europe were convened, and which concluded in favour of a European federation.[11] German socialists still proved somewhat inspired by plans referring to a German-led Mitteleuropa, but the conference envisaged the division of Germany as a preliminary phase before Pan-European unification. In the spring of 1944, another European resistance conference was convened in Geneva, at the home of the Dutch Reformed theologian Willem Visser 't Hooft. The latter's mediating role incidentally illustrates that exiles and resistance members tried to bridge political and ideological divisions between socialists, communists and Christians. Though Spinelli hoped to write a common declaration on the future of a European union, it proved impossible to reach an agreement on essential aspects, such as the degree of supranationality (or renunciation of sovereignty) and on who would be included and who would not – in particular, the UK and the USSR caused problems (Turkey, as usual, was not included). As the Dutch host of the meeting recognized in his memoirs, not everyone was reconciled, while those who would be the main decision-makers after the war were not present in Geneva.[12]

Perhaps the most 'Europeanist' were some industrial and entrepreneurial milieus. Overall, leading industrialists and economists favoured the re-establishment of Germany as a condition for the overall recovery of the European continent, though that did not necessarily translate into support for European associations. A notable exception to the latter is the leading French steel magnate Alexis Aron, a former close collaborator of Louis Loucheur, who in 1942 and 1943 designed a plan for a global industrial co-operation on a European foundation based upon his experience with the International Steel Cartel before the war. Notwithstanding his personal experience during the war – as a well-known Jew, he risked his life by remaining in France – his plan implied a reconciliation of Germany and France, which respected the territorial situation of 1943 (with the Saar and Alsace-Lorraine annexed to Germany). His views were ignored by the French Resistance, but would be picked up during the negotiations for the European Coal and Steel Community (ECSC).[13] Most of these plans however, especially as developed after 1946, limited European co-operation to inter-state, 'confederal' forms.

Redrawing the European map to contain Germany

Some European governments appeared willing to give up sovereignty in order to unite in a stronger federation in the first months and years of the war, though that perspective dwindled further the longer the war lasted. Illustrative is the initiative for a far-reaching Anglo-French Union that the British war cabinet approved in order to avoid a French capitulation on 16 June 1940, which had been suggested earlier by the head of the Anglo-French Coordinating Committee Jean Monnet and was supported by both Prime Minister Winston Churchill and General Charles de Gaulle, then French Under-Secretary of State for National Defence and War. However, it failed as a result of French hesitations, which meant that no time was left for thorough negotiations. It would remain in the margins in subsequent years, without really being considered any further.[14]

Similarly, the Polish government in exile, headed by General Sikorski, suggested creating a Polish-Czechoslovakian federation as early as September 1940. The idea of a Central European Union appeared attractive to others as well, in Yugoslavia, Greece and even the Baltic States. The final Polish-Czechoslovakian agreement of January 1942, however, fell short of the federation that was initially contemplated and the momentum was lost. The main reason for the failure was in fact Stalin. Although after the German invasion of the USSR in June 1941 Sikorski supported a Soviet-Polish rapprochement, Stalin either distrusted Sikorski's aims or was not interested in having powerful neighbours. As soon as he felt strong enough, he demanded the pro-Soviet leader of the Czechoslovakian Resistance Edvard Beneš tear up the agreement with Sikorski in January 1943, and he broke off diplomatic relations with the Polish government in exile three months later.[15] Central European exiles in New York, among them the renowned Polish historian Oskar Halecki, established a Central East European Planning Board in New York in 1942, dreaming about a strong post-war Central-European federation, but collaboration, even in exile, proved more difficult than imagined and the endeavour soon collapsed.[16]

One of the strongest forces against European unity was indeed the USSR, which, whenever possible, forcefully opposed projects for either Pan-European or regional Central European federations; Stalin instructed communists all over the continent to follow its directions.[17] The USSR, during and after the war, insisted on guarantees for its own security against Germany, such as troops to be stationed in Eastern European countries (including Finland). The Soviet policy, however, also reflected the opportunities and limitations of the changing power relations and developments.[18] Illustrative is that Stalin accepted the idea of a 'Balkan federation' under the leadership of the Yugoslavian communist leader Josip Tito. Tito attempted to forge both multi- and bilateral alliances, but largely failed due to the many local antagonisms, among which was Kosovo.[19] However, the Soviet Union also increasingly aimed at territorial expansion, at least restoring the boundaries of the former tsarist Russian empire, maintaining as strong as possible a position in the countries east of Germany and avoiding any alliance that may have been considered a threat to Soviet interests and integrity. In the long run the USSR hoped that Europe would turn communist, so eradicating any prospect of a European attack against it, but this was not necessarily a goal for the near future: in its eyes, history was on its side anyway. Keeping the continent, and especially Germany, divided and weak, however, obviously was in its immediate interest, as well as policing and economically exploiting the countries under its control.[20] Post-war (West) European leaders, incidentally, did not demonstrate not much insight into Soviet policy. Particularly the French, but also Italian politicians looked to the USSR to reinforce their position towards the other Allies in the immediate post-war months.[21]

Also, other European countries, most of all France, mainly envisaged a European order that would contain Germany in the future. The French Committee of National Liberation imagined a Western European union of France, Belgium and the Netherlands – with eventually Italy and Spain and perhaps also the UK joining – that would contain Germany. In contrast to the people engaged in Spinelli's federalist movement, the leading French Resistance leaders – from the radical-socialist adminis- trator and businessman René Mayer in Alger to General de Gaulle in London – suggested the detachment of the Western German indus- trial heartland of the Rhine-Ruhr-Saar area from the German Reich and its integration into this Western European union,[22] which would, 'inevitably', operate under French leadership. Jean Monnet, the Direc- tor of the French Plan Commission (competent for establishing five-year plans), however, insisted on including Germany – or the different German lands, if the country was to be divided up. The French Com- missioner for Foreign Affairs in the UK, René Massigli, believed the UK would have to take part in such a union, but de Gaulle and others firmly opposed that suggestion. A wartime report commissioned by de Gaulle under the direction of the civil servant Laurent Blum-Picard concluded in October 1943 that 'a united Europe is the example of a false good solution which attracts by its apparent simplicity'.[23]

Still, the idea of a Western European Union without Germany was taken on board. It was tied in with the French view of disarmament, de-Nazification and an occupation of Germany, and increasingly also presented as a parallel organization to the one the USSR was envisag- ing in Eastern Europe. But de Gaulle also understood that France by itself could not recover its former position, and that it could only play a major international role again in a broader, French-dominated Western European economic union. A customs union with the open economies of Belgium and the Netherlands would help to modernize French indus- try. But it was also, as René Massigli recalls, a means to create a union of colonial empires to remain a strong international power.[24]

De Gaulle seemingly realized his main objective of neutralizing the German threat through the Franco-Soviet agreement of December 1944, which committed both signatories to supporting each other against any German menace. The French policy towards the USSR was, incidentally, based on a misperception of Soviet interests: the USSR forcefully objected to the reconstitution of a strong French colonial power and would allow France only a limited role in Europe. In that they joined the British perspective, as the UK was not keen on seeing French power restored overseas either. However, neither they, the Americans, nor the French left for that matter, were inclined to offend the Russians in this respect in 1943 and 1944.

In contrast to the USSR, the British supported the formation of large federations in Europe. Churchill in particular suggested constituting Scandinavian, Danubian and Balkan federations in March 1943 – though he remained eloquently silent on Sikorski's Central European Union, knowing Stalin's reaction and apparently already accepting a division of Europe into zones of influence. The British actually envisaged eliminating the smaller states in Europe altogether and seriously thought of redrawing the European political geography on the basis of larger states and conglomerates, an attitude shared by the US government. In part inspired by Coudenhove-Kalergi, who, while residing in the US, continued his crusade for a united Europe along the Paris-London axis, and the British diplomat-historian E.H. Carr, British and Americans blamed nationalism for the failure of Versailles and the world war – a view which has become part of the standard mythology of twentieth century history.[25]

Such views of a Europe dominated by just a few large states were actively fought against by the Belgians and the Dutch in London and Washington, who emphasized the value of smaller nations in organizing and facilitating international collaboration.[26] Though some accepted the principle of transmitting sovereignty to a higher authority, most opposed the very idea, and only conceived a loose coalition with the British and the Americans, a position that was defended by, for example, the Belgian socialist Paul-Henri Spaak, who nevertheless would later become one of the most outspoken advocates of a transatlantic brotherhood.[27] Their perspective, which came to dominate after 1943, was that of an alliance that would contain Germany but perhaps not destroy it – the Netherlands, especially, counted on German industries to reconstruct its economy. The small western states were not yet completely opposed to the USSR, and even less concerned with the idea of unifying Europe. The prospect of a United States of Europe appeared rather as a Nazi ideal, and Coudenhove-Kalergi was effectively portrayed as a Nazi agent.[28]

The American policy towards the reconstruction of Europe during and immediately after the war shows some similarities with the Soviet one. According to Klaus Schwabe, President Roosevelt in public held a universalist discourse of disarmament, self-determination, equal treatment of all nations great and small, and equal access to the trade and raw materials of the world, as formulated in the Atlantic Charter of August 1941, but actually followed a quite different, hidden agenda. As he was convinced that the cause of the war lay in nationalism, the 'smaller' European nations, including France, were to be disarmed, stripped of their colonies and controlled by the superpowers, which would effectively rule the world as a 'world police'.[29]

As regards Germany, draconian measures were considered in the summer of 1944, including the dismemberment and deindustrialization of the country – the so-called Morgenthau Plan – to prevent Germany from becoming a menace ever again. The American Secretary of the Treasury, Henri Morgenthau, was not only convinced that an agrarian economy would maintain a reasonable standard of living, but also believed that working the land would educate the Germans in the values of civility and democracy – a curious conviction rooted in his Christian beliefs, which nevertheless shows some similarities with certain ideas of communist leaders such as Mao Zedong and Pol Pot about the value of rural re-education. However, the plan was not implemented: it was hard to imagine how an agrarian state would be able to pay compensation and reparations, let alone contribute to the reconstruction of Europe. Even more, it risked the US having to assist the German population, not a popular prospect for the American taxpayers. Hence, it was quickly abandoned, although restricting Germany's industrial production capacities constituted an important component of the post-war peace.

When Allied troops advanced, they ended up de facto occupying large parts of Europe and, in particular, Germany. Gradually, an effective partition of Germany into zones of influence imposed itself. For Roosevelt an inter-allied common government would guarantee security to the USSR in exchange for free elections for the Germans. After the Yalta Conference and the signing of the 'Declaration on Liberated Europe' in February 1945, which pledged free elections in the whole of Europe, emphasis shifted to military security, while maintaining the territorial integrity of Germany. President Truman initially followed this reasoning, until he realized that the USSR went much further in controlling politics in her occupational zone. By 1946, the tide had already turned towards a clash of influences.

Uniting by dividing

The end of the war

In hindsight, WW II appears as a break, as the continent seems to have undergone a transformation from centuries of warfare to an 'unprecedented' 60 years of peace, with the Europeans becoming 'doves' instead of 'hawks'. In European self-representation, and certainly in the main narrative promoted by the EU, the war had revealed to some visionary minds that a federal organization of the continent would offer an alternative to the nationalistic bidding that lay at the root of the last two world wars, while WW II, in addition, demonstrated the moral superiority of democracy and human rights. In fact almost everything in this representation needs to be qualified, including the idea that postwar Europe became the land of the doves, that the continent overcame its demons – which are ill-defined anyway – as well as that the war made people peaceful and forgiving. But most of all it ignores the global context.

Postcolonial scholars have emphasized that this narrative disregards the continuing colonization by major European powers and the violent and cruel colonial wars fought afterwards.[30] This colonial dimension, which I explore in the next chapter, in addition raises questions as to the impact that both colonialism and decolonization had on the process of European integration in the 1950s, especially as maintaining European power and prestige had been an important motivation in arguing for European unification in the past. The traditional narrative quite obviously also downplays the importance of the emerging Cold War and of both the US and the USSR, although American historians have emphasized this dimension as well. The proverbial elephant in the room in this respect, however, are the atomic bombings on Hiroshima and Nagasaki in August 1945. These are certainly often discussed with respect to the end of the war with Japan, the relationship with the USSR – the well-known discussion of to whom the bombings were actually addressed – and even the rearmament of Germany. But the American possession of the bomb also altered the security issue in Europe in another way. To put it simply: with the bomb in Allied hands, Germany no longer posed a threat to European peace. Hence, all plans with regard to the 'containment' of Germany actually lost their meaning. If such plans about the division and containment of Germany continued to be pursued, it was arguably for other motives. Nevertheless, the security issue was rarely, if ever, posed in these terms.

Without the A-bomb, Europe could not be anything other than a minor player in the world and dependent on decisions made elsewhere – one reason why the USSR, the UK and France prioritized obtaining it, though that proved to be far more difficult than initially imagined.[31] The USSR mastered the technology surprisingly quickly in 1949, Britain in 1953 and France only in 1960, after which it was years before it possessed effective nuclear arms. By then, these were exclusively viewed in the context of the Cold War. Nevertheless, as the Korean War and the colonial wars in Indochina demonstrated, conventional warfare remained possible in a nuclear age; perhaps, then, it was also possible in Europe. But in the immediate post-war years the US still imposed itself as the playmaker, reducing its European allies to the role of bystanders, largely because of the A-bomb.[32]

The agreements that determined the end of the war not only redrew the map of Europe and the world, they also clearly exposed the redundancy of European politics. At the conferences of Tehran (November–December 1943), Yalta (February 1945) and Potsdam (Summer 1945), which de facto settled the post-war order, only one European state was present, the UK, and nobody will argue that it had a decisive impact – if only because Churchill did not attend the final meeting at Potsdam. France was not even invited, although the fate of Indochina was decided at Tehran. Smaller nations had even less chance of being heard. Although Germany's continuation as a state was guaranteed, it lost the territories that it had conquered from 1938, as well as historically disputed lands east of the (newly established) 'Oder–Neisse line' to Poland, including the German Free City of Danzig. A reduced Germany was sliced up into three (after Potsdam four) occupation zones controlled by the Allied Control Council. Its industrial capacity was reduced to 75 per cent of that of 1936, and agreements on reparations guaranteeing the subsistence of the German population were agreed upon in principle; practice remained another matter.

'A clear sweep'

The territorial adjustments demonstrate the cynicism of geo-strategic thinking to an extreme degree; they also show that the drive to homogeneity still pervaded the thoughts of the negotiators. The Allies at Tehran and Potsdam continued the logic of ethnic cleansing after the war. It was quite obvious, indeed, that the division of Europe as designed at the politicians' table implied mass 'transfers' of people, especially Germans who were to move to Germany, and Poles ending up 'the wrong side of the border'. As Winston Churchill admitted in a speech in December 1944: 'There will be no mixture of populations to cause endless trouble . . . a clear sweep will be made.' A clear sweep indeed: an alleged 12 million Germans were expelled from their *Heimats* in Eastern and Central Europe to the newly constituted and reduced (occupied) Germany. Exceptions were not allowed, and the criterion was ethnic: the whole German third of the Czechoslovakian population was transferred, including resistance fighters and children of mixed descent. Although excessive violence was gradually prevented, Germans faced starvation in many places. Several million other people, including some 2 million Poles from Ukraine, Lithuania, Russia and Belarus, were deported or reallocated. Their fate depended on many factors, among them the state of their country of destination – for many of them their trail of tears ended in a grave.[33]

In the Soviet occupation zones, a political and economic 'Sovietization' policy was pursued that left little room for nationalist agitation: it 'pacified' Eastern Europe by oppression but also by imposing an ideology that prioritized class interests over national and ethnic ones, which were considered 'bourgeois' and reactionary. Nevertheless, communists initiated genocidal politics of political purification and ethnic cleansing, particularly of Germans and their allies, as well as Jews, who almost faced a second Holocaust.[34] Myths of national homogeneity made life hard again for minorities, particularly in Poland and Czechoslovakia. For political reasons, Romania and Yugoslavia remained relatively spared as more ethnically mixed states, although, particularly in the first case, the longing for homogeneity emerged. Nowhere were the foundations of a lasting peace laid, as memories of injustice linger on to this day.

In the western zones, no similar policies were implemented, as the Western Allies soon realized the disastrous effects of their policies in the east. In the most problematic area, the Saarland, France pursued a policy of conciliation, hoping that the population would finally embrace an annexation. It would not happen, but the relationship between France and Germany had evolved in such a way that the Saarland was able to 'return' to Germany without even causing ripples. In that sense, the institutional integration in Western Europe effectively worked: increasingly, the national antagonism was controlled. That, however, was not simply the outcome of a process of increasing consciousness, but of a complex political process, tightly connected to – though not limited to – the emerging Cold War. The significance of the recognition of guilt by, in particular, German political authorities, the process of punishment and repression, as well as local initiatives of post-war reconciliation of the population, supported or not by international and European organizations, should not be underestimated in this context.[35]

In the meantime, the global international situation had also changed. The League of Nations had given way to the United Nations (UN). The UN was to be all that the League of Nations was not: universally representative, powerful and effective – at least, so it seemed in the popular contemporary European understanding. Of course it was not, even if it was more than just 'a means of keeping the wartime coalition intact necessary at whatever cost (was) to avoid the fate of its predecessor'.[36] The UN provoked the emergence of a new wave of internationalism, and particularly in the UK and Scandinavia leading voices would, as in the past, consider Europeanism opposed to internationalism and argue that a (Western) European federation or union, by its very formation, would only increase the polarization.[37]

Europeanists, however, did not put much faith in the UN: in contrast to the 1920s when the League of Nations offered a framework for developing European ideas, European plans were conceived entirely outside the UN framework after 1945 – which, however, does not mean that there was no interaction, as with regard to human rights.

Uniting Europe, east and west

No later than June 1946, the Soviets started setting up a new European organization to replace the Comintern. It would mainly co-ordinate and synchronize the political actions of the communist parties under the leadership of the USSR.[38] In the west, the situation of economic deprivation and distress also jeopardized the future of the liberated countries, even if democracy was restored or reinvented. It did not look as if the French goal of dismantling the Reich and establishing a Western European alliance with the Rhineland as its 'axis' – in de Gaulle's famous words – had any chance of being realized, though de Gaulle stuck to this hardline policy until 1948. The British continued to focus on their alliance with the US.

Economists and politicians both sides of the Atlantic in the immediate post-war period realized that the reconstruction of European economies – of the individual nations in the first place – imperatively required transnational, European arrangements. Especially, the supply of coal raised concern and gave way to some speculation about the circulation of coal between Europe and the US. In May 1945, the US and Great Britain set up the European Coal Organization to assist in the distribution of coal supplies between the victorious countries (Belgium, Denmark, France, Greece, Luxembourg, the Netherlands,

Norway, the UK, the US and Turkey). Although the USSR was involved in the negotiations, Eastern European governments hesitated. Poland and Czechoslovakia, however, joined after a few months. However, it soon proved impossible to deny coal to other countries, including the vanquished ones. Hence other countries de facto also joined, such as Italy, Portugal, Sweden, Switzerland and Austria, demonstrating the interdependency of European economies. From that perspective, the UN set up the Emergency Economic Committee for Europe (EECE) and the European Central Inland Transport Organization (ECITO).[39] Nevertheless, in February 1946, France, with the Director of the Plan Commission, Jean Monnet, as the main architect of the concrete proposals, went a step further by suggesting the creation of a supranational industrial authority with regard to the exploitation of the industrial production in the Rhine, Elbe, Danube and Oder regions. However, as the Monnet Plan de facto excluded German participation, the proposal was bound to fail.[40]

As the impact of the USSR on Eastern Europe increased, so did tensions between the USSR and the 'Western' nations. In the process positions shifted. As the Soviets were not inclined to give France satisfaction on the question of the Rhineland area – the USSR even objected to the integration of the Saarland into France, opposing a French occupation zone in Germany while claiming co-determination in the Ruhr – the French policy moved away from the USSR towards the US and the UK in the course of 1945. Increasingly, France resisted a unified Germany not only because of the danger of its becoming a menace again, but because a unified Germany risked falling under Soviet control, thus transferring the menace to the USSR.[41] The British shared the same apprehension, worried that the economic degradation of Western Europe would also drive the western lands of the continent into communist arms; it also made them realize that some sort of European unification would enforce democracy and liberalism in Europe.[42] But many issues divided the Western Allies, not the least of which were the German reparations, as the USSR, which suffered by far the most from the war, insisted on exploiting German and Eastern European resources to the maximum, while the Americans in particular feared economic collapse and mass starvation in Germany. The Western Allies also refused the drastic social and economic reforms that the USSR demanded.[43]

Tensions increased globally after 1945, coming to a head in early 1946 in Iran, where the USSR, which had agreed to withdraw from the country, in fact supported two Soviet puppet republics and the US backed the counter-attacks of the Shah; in the Greek Civil War, where the UK had to withdraw in early 1947 and the US stepped in to combat communist rebels; and in the success of Mao's communist forces in China as well as in the Korean War, which started in June 1950 and suddenly appeared to make the prospect of a new world war far more real, among other events.[44]

By 1946, the overall perspective in Europe was already moving away from securing the post-war order by settling the German problem and accommodating Soviet security concerns, towards a clash of influences between the western Allies and the USSR.[45] This made room for envisaging new ways of thinking about Europe's future. Still, there was more than one possible scenario. Surprisingly, the UK – or forces in Britain – strove towards European unity, although the British finally focused on their empire and the Commonwealth rather than Europe. It was hence the US that gave an important, though finally less than decisive push towards both economic recovery and European integration, burying Soviet–Western understanding in the process.

Britain for Europe?

Although the British mistrusted the French, especially de Gaulle's 'flirtations' with the USSR, and suspicions were further fuelled by the political strength of the communists in immediate post-war France, obtaining 26.1 per cent of the votes in the first post-war elections in October 1945 (though their impact would dwindle quickly afterwards), Britain moved towards support for a European federation after the war. In particular, the Federalist Union commanded formidable intellectual support for a federal Europe, from, among others, the economist William Beveridge, the historian Arnold Toynbee and the philosopher Bertrand Russell.[46] Their ideas found an attentive ear in the British Foreign Office and in particular with the former trade union leader Ernest Bevin, who became Foreign Secretary in the first post-war cabinet. The latter regarded a British–French axis as a springboard for a broader Western European alliance, from Scandinavia to the Mediterranean. Also within the Labour Party, several 'ginger' groups existed that supported a European federation.[47]

The Foreign Office had been contemplating the idea of a British-led political-military union since the last months of the war, partly with the ambition to remain an important international player afterwards, and aware of Britain's being the 'weakest link' of the Allies (France not considered anyway, as it was not part of the victors – it was *liberated* – and no longer a world power). Bevin, who had little confidence in the durability of British-American relations, followed up on these ideas, and actually went further. He envisaged economic co-operation, supported the idea of an 'internationalized' Rhineland (hence detached from Germany, as demanded by France) and even considered a joint exploitation of the Ruhr with France. He gradually imagined a 'third world force' of European colonial empires – from Scandinavia to Africa – that would effectively counterbalance the two main superpowers, the US and the USSR.[48]

Bevin's rather vague plans, however, initially found little response in the Attlee government and collided with the reality of Britain's rapidly deteriorating industrial capacities, to which an alliance with an equally declining French economy or poor African territories appeared to offer no solution: severing ties with the US and the Commonwealth looked far more promising. Finally, the British government largely preferred the continuation of the allied alliance of the US and the USSR. Its main interest remained with its empire. This implied a particular focus on the Mediterranean, Greece, Turkey and the Dardanelles in particular, but apart from preventing Germany from becoming a danger to the international order yet again, it had little interest in what happened elsewhere on the continent. As the British understood the Soviet need for security at their western borders, they (like the US) could live with a division of spheres of influence there, although they believed that even as part of a Soviet sphere of influence these countries in Central and Eastern Europe could be free and democratic, as the USSR had agreed at Yalta.[49]

Nevertheless, the British feared Soviet expansionist ambitions, particularly towards Turkey and the Dardanelles, and from 1946 increasingly felt ignored by the US. Hence, the idea of a more unified Europe resurfaced. However, if Winston Churchill in September 1946 famously advocated a 'United States of Europe', he was referring to an intergovernmental association but not a federal transfer of sovereignty, and not one that would include the UK, which would perhaps associate with it together with the Commonwealth, and was mainly envisaged as a buffer against the USSR.[50] Bevin, however, went further and in 1948 suggested establishing a Western European Union which would include the colonial possessions and dominions of each (see below). Especially in colonial milieus, it was believed that 'Britain's only salvation lay in realizing that the country formed part of Western Europe; to commit Britain's destiny to the USA would be the worst disaster'.[51]

The rapprochement between France and the UK mainly resulted in military co-operation. The Dunkirk Treaty of Alliance and Mutual Assistance between France and the UK (4 March 1947) against a possible German attack not only addressed France's continuing concern about

Germany, but also signalled a willingness to engage into a broader engagement. The collaboration between the Western Allies in this period increased again, including in occupied Germany, while the communists in France and Italy lost ground. On 17 March 1948, a far wider military agreement than the Dunkirk treaty was signed in Brussels between Belgium, France, Luxembourg, the Netherlands and the UK, setting up the Western Union Defence Organization (WUDO) a few months later. The European interest of the UK waned though, giving way to an Atlantist perspective on the one hand, and an increased orientation towards its empire and the Commonwealth on the other. On 4 April 1949, NATO was established, which included the US, and which would incorporate the WUDO. This development opened space for the US to take the lead.

The European Recovery Plan

The European Recovery Plan (ERP), officially launched by Secretary of State George Marshall during a famous speech on 5 June 1947 but already in the making for several months, included massive US aid to European countries to rebuild their economies. This, the US realized, was the only way not only to ensure European economic recovery, but also to bridge the dollar gap, allowing Europeans to pay back their loans and buy American products. Ideological factors weighed heavily as well, with no doubt more than economic calculation, securing European commitment to liberal capitalist and democratic values, which seemed threatened by the domestic communist advances not only in the regions liberated (or occupied) by the USSR, but also in the western zones, especially in Greece, Italy, Germany and France. Liberal values required both prosperity and stability, which further stimulated the growth of these principles.[52]

From that perspective, the US imposed two conditions: participating states had to formulate a joint recovery programme, which implied mutual consultation, and to give the US the right of supervision, implying that technicians of the ERP would have full access to economic data. Moreover, the US, as well as the UK, opposed the idea that economic gains would be used for reparations to the USSR. Although Moscow was initially interested in a programme that would help the European economy, including the USSR itself, each of these conditions was unacceptable, including the first one: a united Europe under American supervision would obviously jeopardize the USSR's European politics. Hence, the Soviets stated that none of the countries in their zone of influence would accept the American offer, although Poland

and Czechoslovakia in particular appeared more than willing at first.[53] France and Great Britain, incidentally, invested quite a lot of energy in trying to bring the USSR and Central and Eastern European countries of the Soviet zone into a European collaboration scheme, but to no avail.[54]

This was perhaps less a foregone conclusion than it may appear in hindsight. In Yugoslavia, Tito's plans for a Balkan federation, imagined as a way for smaller nations to 'safeguard their independence', entered a decisive phase. In November 1946, Yugoslavia established a customs union with Albania, which was extended to Bulgaria in August 1947. The latter agreement included a clause on the recognition of the rights of the Macedonians – the first step towards integrating the Macedonian lands into the federation. At that point the USSR still supported the project, but the Soviets soon changed tack as Tito followed his own policy, ignoring Stalin's directives. The issue lay at the root of the estrangement and split between the two leaders in June 1948, after which Stalin forced Bulgaria and Albania to tear up the project.[55] Yugoslavia, however, withstood the pressure and accepted Marshall help in 1950.

Where possible, communist parties under Soviet direction seized power and swept aside liberal democracy, as in Czechoslovakia in February 1948. In Austria though, even if a communist putsch appeared imminent in 1947, the communists were not strong enough to stage a coup, and the social democrats opted for a pro-American course. Hence, the Austrian government did accept the American offer.[56]

The ERP required the economic consultation of the European beneficiaries and the US and Canada. In this respect it could build upon the pioneering role of the Benelux, which was established in 1944 as a customs union between Belgium, the Netherlands and Luxemburg. Though initially not intended to lay the foundations of a Pan-European federation and notwithstanding its very limited initial competences, it did show the way for later regional agreements. It was not by accident that it started with a monetary union – an echo of the Oslo Convention and the Gold Bloc, but also a lesson learned from Keynes (whose insistence upon stable monetary relations seems to have been later forgotten). Although it was two years more before it actually went into operation, it proved not only an economic but also a political success story, as the three countries often acted as one in international politics, and by so doing magnified their political clout. But finding an agreement on a common European economic project, or a customs union among the 16 'West' European countries that accepted the ERP, proved another matter. The 16 did, however, constitute a Committee on European Economic Co-operation (CEEC) in June 1947 to discuss different possibilities. At a European economic conference in July 1947, the US suggested creating a European customs union among them, but reactions remained lukewarm.[57] An Italian proposal to start with a customs union between France and Italy initiated an at times hilarious set of negotiations in which the Benelux also became involved, partly to try to convince the Americans about the 'seriousness' of European commitment to economic collaboration. The UK, incidentally, favoured the Italian initiative but refused to consider entering a European customs union itself without its dominions, which was unacceptable for the French.[58] Also, the degree of sovereignty transfer, if any, remained disputed.

Apart from the question of how far economic collaboration would go, the position of Germany constituted a formidable obstacle, especially for the French. When in March 1948 the western zones of Germany were 'invited' to participate in the ERP, this signalled the end of the post-war order in which the four Allies administered Europe. It could do so only because the Western European countries, France in particular, changed their tactics towards Germany. Germany became less and less perceived as a potential menace, neither in military nor, in the short term at least, in economic terms – if only because in reality the country was divided up into a western and an eastern part, industrial Silesia largely incorporated into Poland, the Saarland a French 'protectorate' and the Ruhr under Allied command. No-one actually anticipated that West Germany would recover as swiftly as it did. In fact, the ERP stipulated that it would not be allowed to grow faster than its neighbours. Still, the idea of Germany as a partner in international relations remained hard to swallow.

The Organization for European Economic Co-operation (OEEC) was constituted in April 1948, uniting the European 'Sixteen' plus representatives of the western German occupation zones and Trieste. I will not venture into its policies, but limit myself to pointing out a few important elements. Above all, the OEEC supported a certain economic and political model, one that emphasized productivity growth in particular, and in that respect proclaimed the values of an open market, to the model that the US constituted itself. It aimed at stabilizing the international and, in particular, European financial system and payment balance with the US, as well as facilitating international payments by regulating receivables and payables and reducing roaming costs; with this purpose it established the European Payments Union in 1950.[59] The OEEC required a strong control by the US, which installed a central Economic Cooperation Administration (ECA) with commissions in each country, which were also used for propagating its liberal and capitalist values in Europe.[60] The OEEC constituted the first effective European organization and stimulated systematic interactions between officials from Europe and the US at different levels. Such contacts and interactions created a fruitful base for later talks on other subjects as well, as, for example, with regard to the Schuman Plan.[61] Although France had always opposed the integration of Germany in a European order, the ERP actually helped it to achieve at least some of its long-term goals: an economic recovery, recognition as a major international power, as well as establishing a framework that secured peace with Germany – after all, the result was a breaking up of the latter country, albeit not in the way the French initially envisaged it. Still, the ERP turned out to be ambiguous: it certainly proclaimed further European economic and political collaboration, but also strengthened the British–American relationship. The Brussels Treaty of 17 March 1948, incidentally a British initiative to demonstrate European willingness and capability to co-operate, made clear that military collaboration largely prevailed in British and American eyes – the British firmly refused to extend the collaboration to other political and economic issues.

The ERP fitted into the Truman Doctrine of 'containing' the communist menace in Europe and the world, which would lead to further military integration of European and American states in NATO in April 1949. From this wider perspective the ERP contributed to, but perhaps mainly expressed the division of Europe between a Western Europe that largely followed American political, economic and cultural modes, and an 'Eastern' bloc that was more directly and forcefully integrated into the Soviet Empire and introduced a 'communist' culture that proclaimed a break with older 'bourgeois' traditions.

The Soviets responded to the ERP with the creation of the Cominform, though the decision to create such a platform predates General Marshall's speech and must probably be seen within the overall perspective of the increased Soviet control over the European communist parties, particularly in Eastern Europe.[62] The Cominform contributed to the circulation of Soviet directives and propaganda through what could be considered the Soviet Empire in Eastern Europe, and helped the USSR to streamline economic policies in its 'empire'. In the first place, the Eastern European countries, particularly East Germany, were, for years, mainly considered as resources for the recovery of the USSR itself. Hence, while thanks to economic planning living standards in Eastern Europe may have been fairly decent, certainly compared to those in the American, British and French occupation zones in Germany – one reason why the communist model remained attractive – they did not match the pace of economic recovery after the implementation of the Marshall Plan in the West and the economic and political 'liberation' of Germany, which very soon recovered economically.

In 1955 the USSR established the Warsaw Pact, similar to but more 'European' than NATO, in response to the FRG joining the western military alliance, equally with the purpose of securing peace in Europe. It should be noted that Yugoslavia, which searched for a 'Third Way' in its domestic socialist politics as well as in its international policy, was excluded from the Cominform in 1948 and able to remain outside the Warsaw Pact. The latter became notorious for crushing democratic protest against Soviet policies in Central and Eastern Europe.

Wind in federalist sails?

The Federalists' moment

The context of peace and the Cold War actually blew wind into the sails of the European movements in western Europe. These were, however, not really focused on participating in subordinating Europe to grand political schemes which made the continent dependent on others, though most European federalists ultimately envisaged a strong European organization as part of either a trans-Atlantic one or of a world organization. Federalists from the left and the right realized a synthesis between socialism, Christian personalism and British federalism in the Union of European Federalists (UEF), already established in December 1946 by Altieri Spinelli, Hendrik Brugmans and Alexandre Marc, which was part of a global federalist movement.[63] These federalists claimed to represent a 'Third Way' in international politics, though it was never very clear what that actually meant as they also supported a close alliance with the US.

In the first post-war years, there existed in Western Europe an important intellectual current that rejected the division of the world into a communist and a liberal capitalist bloc and strove towards 'neutrality'. As Hubert Beuve-Méry, the director of the leading French journal *Le Monde*, wrote in October 1945,

> The organization of a western association (entente) of comparable importance as the USA and the USSR, situated geographically, economically, politically halfway of these two powerful partners, normally seems logical, desirable, beneficial to all. On one condition, however: that the new organization is as independent from Washington as from Moscow.[64]

The chairman of the Swiss Europa-Union Hans Bauer described similar sentiments when, in November 1945, he stated that Europe had become 'some kind of protectorate' of the world powers of America and Asia. Only 'European self-determination' could save the continent, he concluded.[65] Likewise the Holy See opposed a clear choice of one side, looking for a way to protect the Catholics living in communist countries while at the same time advocating an international order that was based upon natural law and Catholic morality.[66]

In the subsequent years, Christian democrats in particular played a major role in the development of European federalism, if only because they were so prominently present in post-war European governments in the six countries that would unite first in the framework of the ECSC. In this respect Geneva remained an important centre of contact and interaction for progressive Protestant and Catholic intellectuals and political leaders, particularly from France, Germany and Switzerland, after the end of the war. Such contacts, as well as those leading to the establishment of a more formal Christian democratic association, the *Nouvelles Équipes Internationales* in 1947 (no real European Christian democratic party, though), allowed for the discussion of different concepts and ideas on the organization of society at regional, national and European level, which would gradually establish the foundation for a highly successful and flexible Christian democratic ideology as a 'Third Way', which adopted the subsidiarity principle for domestic as well as international politics – allowing competences to be shared by the state at supranational as well as subnational level (allowing a decentralization of the German state, which became a federal republic in the West).[67] The European orientation of these Christian democrats, however, is far less evident than is often imagined and to some extent contrasts with pre-war hesitations.[68]

The impact of Christian democracy gave way to a popular and persistent myth of a 'Vatican conspiracy', a fallacy in all respects.[69] The myth nevertheless points to the role of the Vatican in the process of European integration. While its role is obviously overstated, the Holy See supported the idea of European unity as it had done in the 1930s. But in contrast to the Christian democrats, who distanced themselves from an overly clerical influence and fully embraced a democratic Europe including the UK and Northern and Eastern Europe (with the exception of the USSR), the Vatican clung to a vision of a 'medieval' Catholic Europe, supporting dictatorships in Spain and Portugal. Its influence was rather indirect, as Christian democrats made use of the Catholic Church's structures for transnational contacts.[70]

Gradually, first within the socialist movement as a result of the strong impact of British Labour, but soon also among Christian democrats, anti-communism got the upper hand and both movements adopted a transatlantic perspective. Apart from some isolated leftist Catholics or radical-socialists, Christian democratic and social democratic politicians had fully subscribed to the Atlantic world order by 1947–1948; this, however, did not prevent the Christian democrats, in particular, from advocating a Third Way in politics, economy and international relations that in principle rejected both communist and liberal capitalism, pleading for a middle way based upon Christian personalism.[71]

There is also a tendency to underestimate the role of socialists, as socialists focused on the development of the welfare state at national level and did not support major initiatives such as the Treaty of Paris in 1952, establishing the European Coal and Steel Community (ECSC) (Italian and German Social democrats even voted against) nor the Treaty of Rome (1956), as they considered them too much favouring economic liberalism. They preferred actually more European collaboration and planning. Although one should not overestimate its importance within European socialism, the Socialist Movement for the United States of Europe (SMUSE), created in February 1946, for example argued for the creation of a social-democratic United States of Europe. As social democrats strongly opposed any sort of Catholic Europe – imagining some Catholic conspiracy in favour of a 'Vatican Europe' – this socialist federation should include Germany as well as the UK and Scandinavia. The question of the eastward borders remained an issue, but clearly the movement rejected the communist model and emphasized liberty in contrast. In line with pre-war ideas on a planned European economy, in 1949 the movement suggested European planning of basic industries. This planned organization required supranational institutions per industry – in the first place coal, steel, electricity and transport – to avoid cartelization, co-ordinated in function for the common good of the workers. This suggestion would be of paramount importance to Jean Monnet when he imagined the basis of the Schuman Plan.[72]

Some still consider European federalism as an essentially liberal project, referring to the input of liberals and of big business and the entrepreneurial milieus, organized in different associations. Among these the European League for Economic Cooperation manifested itself most prominently as part of the European movement. Essentially liberal, it was nevertheless more open towards other political movements, including Labour, than most other business associations.[73] Among the liberal thinkers addressing the question of European reconstruction and the reintegration of Germany, one should particularly note the contributions of Friedrich von Hayek. To be sure, his influence had already waned in Europe since the late 1920s and 1930s, but his ideas were taken seriously in the US. Already in 1939 he had argued that European integration and liberalization of the economy were inextricably linked, and he would continue to develop his basic insights with other like-minded thinkers in the so-called Mont Pélerin Society, named after the Swiss village near Vevey where the group first met in 1947. Free trade, Hayek believed, was the only way to unite different European nations – planned economies, in contrast, would pull them further apart. His ideas, with those of the German economist Wilhelm Röpke, would inspire Ludwig Erhard, the German Minister of Economics from 1949 to 1963 and widely considered to be the architect of the German economic reconstruction or *Wirtschaftswunder*. Erhard manifested himself as a staunch advocate of economic liberalism and of creating a European customs union as a first step towards a free market, but opposed more interventionist policies as advocated by, for example, Jean Monnet.[74]

The federal movement and the creation of the council of Europe

The different federalist groups – from all over Europe, east and west, north and south, socialist, liberal and Christian-democratic – to some extent converged in their European ideal, even if, as would soon become clear, they did not all mean the same thing by it and more conservative forces would predominate over progressive movements. The ideological convergence is nevertheless remarkable. Some of the groups met regularly in the Anglo-French United European Movement, which prepared a European federalist congress in The Hague in May 1948, where a resolution was passed in favour of a political, economic and monetary union of Europe. The final resolution stated explicitly that such a union or federation was needed in order to assure security and social progress. In the wake of the congress, the European Movement (EM) was founded as an umbrella association for all European federalist movements. Though some advocated a 'Third Way' for Europe in international politics, the EM quickly moved towards a more Atlantist position which supported a strong Europe as a buffer against communism. One of its first achievements was the creation of the Council of Europe, responding to Winston Churchill's call for 'some sort of United States of Europe' in a lecture in Zürich in September 1946, reiterated at The Hague and recalling his words of 1930.[75]

The Congress in The Hague and the subsequent negotiations, however, laid bare the deep divergences between the federalists, who

advocated a quick evolution towards a political and economic federation of Europe, with a supranational authority, and those, mainly but
certainly not exclusively the British and Scandinavians, who advocated
a confederal or intergovernmental structure which would respect the
national sovereignty of the affiliated states. By and large the latter prevailed, as the final institution, the Council of Europe – a far cry from
the United States of Europe or European Union – established in May
1949, had very limited authority and competence and was in no way a
supranational body. It did not prevent the Council from being presented
as a major success in an age-old quest for peace. However, attempts to
increase the political authority of the Council in subsequent years failed.

The Council of Europe would mainly become known for its cultural
activities. The Council effectively set out to promote some common
values of Europe and with that aim adopted the European Convention on Human Rights (ECHR) and established the European Court of
Human Rights – not quite the Court of Justice that the Congress of
The Hague had demanded, but significant nevertheless. It illustrated
the commitment – or rather the connection – of Europe to human
rights. Europeans had played a major role in drafting the Universal Declaration of Human Rights by the UN as well – even if the impact of
non-Europeans was significant, the idea of a set of human rights that
needed to be listed and protected is fundamentally a European one.[76]
However, the European Convention on Human Rights was based on a
limited set of values – the right to free elections was only included in
1952 – and accepted reservations that seriously undermined its significance: the Convention did not need to apply in overseas colonies and
its application could be suspended during periods of war, as it was by
the UK during the Mau-Mau uprising in Kenya in the early 1950s.

Belgium, Denmark, France, Ireland, Italy, Luxembourg, the
Netherlands, Norway, Sweden and the UK were the first members of
the Council. Greece, Turkey and Iceland were allowed to join, clearly
indicating an ambition to represent the whole of Europe, even if some
feared that the USSR would consider it an anti-Soviet alliance (which it
could have been if it had possessed political clout). Only free and democratic states could affiliate, which excluded the communist Central and
Eastern European countries as well as the authoritarian states of Spain
and Portugal, but the prospect of joining the 'club of free countries' was
real nevertheless. That Spain and Portugal were excluded contributed to
giving the organization credibility in the field of democracy, liberty and
human rights. Germany, as well as Austria, could also join, albeit after
difficult negotiations (France actually wanted the Saarland to become

a member on equal terms with Germany, indicating how difficult the German question remained for France), as could Greece and Turkey.

The Monnet method and the (non)formation of European communities

To the naïve observer, with or without the advantage of hindsight, it may have appeared that by 1949 Europe had made decisive steps towards unification, though admittedly fewer than some had dreamt of. After all, a number of important new institutions had been created for political, economic and military collaboration. However, as the European economic collaboration within the OEEC demonstrated, in reality the European nations still thought that they could do well without collaboration, and if they spoke about Europe it was, to paraphrase Bismarck, from the perspective of realizing their own particular objectives – such as defending the pound sterling for the British or the economic modernization of the French economy.[77] Accepting the Marshall Plan, moreover, had been perceived as a humiliating experience and at times an impediment to national sovereignty, which was particularly hard to swallow for the French. The negotiations for the Council of Europe furthermore taught the latter that containing Germany within a supranational federal Europe, a main motive for eventually supporting a European organization, was impossible because of British opposition. The Germans showed a particular interest in creating a European organization, political as well as economical, in which their country would be recognized as a full partner – not quite the prospect France looked forward to. The US insisted on the rearmament of Germany without much consideration of European fears both with regard to Germany and the USSR – for many in Europe, German rearmament appeared a dangerous provocation of the Soviets. Hence, the idea that Europe was well on its way to integration largely rests on *Hineininterpretierung* – at the time, the reverse was the case: it seemed more likely that the movement towards European federation had already reached a dead end and that national considerations would take over again.

However, the tide had again turned in favour of more integration. The coal and steel industries entered a deep crisis as a result of uncoordinated (over) production. Also, increased American pressure against the cartelization of the coal and steel industry raised much concern in France.[78] It is in this context that the Schuman Plan to create a supranational organization to regulate the coal and steel production in Western Europe must be viewed. The Schuman Plan, the outlines of which French foreign minister Robert Schuman proposed in a speech to the French parliament on 9 May 1950, actually retained the essence of Monnet's earlier plan of 1946 to gain control over the coal reserves of the Ruhr for the reconstruction of France and the French needs for economic development and military security, as it secured continuing American support for its modernization (in reality including its colonial policies), but added to that a realistic perspective of integrating Germany into a broader European institutional framework which would control it, making war between France and Germany 'not merely unthinkable, but materially impossible'.[79] In fact this was the idea Aristide Briand had already defended in 1929, but Schuman and Monnet, in association with the US administration and other contacts in the US and Germany, reformulated it in a more concrete way, starting with economics (as Briand and Coudenhove-Kalergi actually initially suggested as well) and industrial co-operation, reminding one of pre-war proposals for an industrial organization of Europe. However, through the High Authority, the Schuman aimed at avoiding the creation of just a huge cartel – to which the Americans as well as labour organizations strongly objected. That this supranationality implied that the UK would not join was not such a big price to pay in French eyes, as France was very wary of a possible British domination of Europe, a prospect which it considered a 'nightmare'.[80]

After thorough negotiations, the Benelux countries, as well as Italy and the two major protagonists, France and the FRG, established the European Coal and Steel Community (ECSC) through the Treaty of Paris in 1951. Unlike any other previous European association, it possessed a real supranational executive, the High Authority (HA). It was composed of 'independent' representatives and was competent to decide economic and social policy (thus far more than regulating production). It actually created a common market for coal and steel, with the HA acting on behalf of the whole community in its external relations. Besides the HA, the ECSC contained a Special Council of Ministers of the affiliated states, a legislative Common Assembly composed of national parliamentarians and – not least – a European tribunal. According to the signatories of the treaty installing the ECSC, this signalled 'the true foundation of an organized Europe'. With its supranational High Authority it is indeed the forerunner of the European Communities and the European Union that was created in 1993, though it was still a far cry from what economists and politicians had been arguing for since the mid-1920s. But in 1950 this was as far as one could go. As pleas for a rearmament of West Germany increased in the wake of the Korean war, the French proposed organizing a European Defence Community (EDC). It was signed by the same six countries of the ECSC but never executed. Also, the ensuing project for a European Political Community that would encompass both the EDC and the ECSC collapsed, as the French national assembly opposed it, along with many other countries. In fact, the French were not prepared to continue on the path towards a further transfer of sovereignty and European federalism – as Richard Griffiths commented, the proposal for a EDC probably aimed at appeasing French public opinion in view of German rearmament rather than really containing Germany, let alone creating a real political union. France had achieved its main objective, and would in the following decennia put the brakes on further integration, emphasizing the importance of national sovereignty instead. Hence, West Germany was granted full sovereignty and allowed to join the Western Union Defence Organization (WUDO) and NATO.[81]

Nevertheless, in view of new, important challenges with regard to atomic energy, which required concerted action from several countries, and agriculture – a potentially lethal issue for European political systems – the 'Six' further extended their collaboration more or less following the model of the ECSC, by accepting supranational interventions where needed but maintaining sovereignty in a complex institutional setting. The European Economic Community (EEC) and Euratom were established in 1957, constituting (with the ECSC) three European Communities (ECs). With these, the Six established the common market that many had dreamt about. The ECs were far more than a common market, though, as they developed highly protectionist external economic boundaries and intervened actively through extensive subsidizing in several economic sectors, in particular transport and communication, energy and, above all, agriculture – pre-war economists such as Delaisi had already strongly emphasized the need for a Europe-wide policy to tackle the deep economic disparities, while the subversive potential of the peasant class was widely recognized.[82] Euratom gave European nations (including Germany) a prospect of nuclear might. Although these institutions maintained the sovereignty of the member states, the Court of Justice, newly established in the framework of the EEC, gradually gained authority over national courts as European legislation came to override national law (with major exceptions). In 1965, the three communities merged to constitute the European Community (EC, singular).

Some countries that were not willing – or allowed by the Six – to engage in strong European economic communities but still saw the benefit of lowering trade barriers constituted the European Free Trade Association (EFTA) in 1960 (the 'outer Seven': Austria, Denmark, Norway, Portugal, Sweden, Switzerland and the UK). But while the EEC acted as a common market, adopting a common external customs tariff and organizing the market by directly intervening, by regulations and subsidies (particularly with regard to agriculture), the EFTA only lowered customs within the free trade zone and for industrial products. In its own way it proved very effective, but it lost the ideological battle to the European Communities, which slowly also gained political power. Even the UK preferred to join the EC, but saw its entry blocked by France.

9
Epilogue: The EC's Colonial Empire

> In the nineteenth century the white has made the black into a man; in the twentieth century Europe will make a world out of Africa. To remake a new Africa, to render the old Africa amenable to civilisation, this is the problem. Europe will solve it.
>
> Victor Hugo, 1879[1]

Not yet the end of the affair

WW II signalled the end the European colonial era, although it took a decade or more before Europeans realized how much the world had changed. Italy lost its colonial possessions: Libya and Ethiopia became independent, while Eritrea, at first occupied by the British, was finally invaded by Ethiopia. Italian Somaliland, also conquered by the British, became a Trusteeship of the UN but under Italian administration, before gaining independence together with British Somaliland in 1960. The fate of the Italian colonies shows that the continuation of colonial rule had ceased to be self-evident. The Dutch, driven out of the Indies by the Japanese, proved unable to regain control over their former colonies. They faced not only a violent uprising in 1945 but also worldwide protest and a condemnation by the UN Security Council. France was confronted with a similar situation in Indochina, which it reoccupied after the retreat of the Japanese, only to confront a massive anti-colonial resistance by the Viet Minh. It found itself trapped in a colonial war it could no longer win. The British Empire gave up its 'jewel in the crown' in the face of successful moral campaigns for independence. Only Central West Africa, in particular the vast Belgian Congo, remained rather untouched, although in French and British colonies and protectorates anti-colonial voices arose.

185

Still, Europeans, even the British with regard to the Middle East and sub-Saharan Africa, continued to cultivate ambitions of global power and colonial empire, although the state of their domestic economies after the war hardly allowed them to do so. The ambition to regain strength was certainly one of the main motives for France to stimulate European integration. Decolonization was not on the French agenda, as the country counted on the supplies of raw materials from its overseas territories for its recovery, although at the same time the productive capacities of these territories were seriously damaged and needed to be reinforced as well, while everywhere in the empire anti-colonial calls for *égalité* were heard. France constituted the *Union Française* between the metropolis and the overseas territories in response, declaring all inhabitants 'equal in rights and duties without distinction of race or religion'. In reality, metropolitan France was definitely more equal than other places: the *Union Française* distinguished between the metropolis, overseas departments (such as Algeria), overseas territories (colonies no longer called such), and associated territories and states (Indochina, Morocco and Tunisia), and only the metropolitan French enjoyed full citizenship rights, including the right to vote (unless otherwise specified, I use the term 'overseas territories' as an encompassing term for all except the metropolis). This *Union Française* did not, however, constitute an impediment to European integration per se – the latter, though, was viewed as instrumental to the former.

The motives of the Netherlands for supporting European integration likewise cannot be dissociated from their colonial experience, albeit in a different way, as they were unable to hold onto their colonial empire in Southeast Asia. Initially they certainly prioritized regaining their colonial position above engaging in common European initiatives, including military collaboration. They turned to Europe when their 'rightful claim' on Indonesia was not supported by the main powers and they felt baffled and betrayed by the world. They reasoned that Europe had to unite in order not to be overpowered by others and to face such 'violations of international justice', as a leading politician noted after the condemnation of the Netherlands by the United Nations Security Council in 1948, expressing a widespread feeling in the Netherlands. But the loss of the Indies opened up political space for a reorientation of Dutch foreign policy towards a European common market and an Atlantic defence system, as the Dutch Foreign Minister Dirk Stikker pleaded for from 1948 onwards. Surprisingly, the loss of their colony actually proved beneficial for the Dutch economy and more prospects for growth and prosperity appeared through European collaboration.

Hence, the Netherlands, after the failure of the European Political Community and the European Defence Community in 1952, even took the lead in proposing a common market.[2] Only for Belgium and Italy did the colonial perspective seem not to have played a major role in their decision to support European unification, although Belgium certainly shared the French view on colonization – actually it did not consider that decolonization of its African colonies and protectorates could happen in any foreseeable future. Italy focused on its own disastrous economic situation.

The British actually shared similar ambitions to the French, and initially believed that their empire might survive and give them a position of power in the new world. Nevertheless, they realized that even the British Empire was no longer a match for the US. A joint European colonial federation might offer an alternative. In particular, the British Foreign Secretary, Ernest Bevin, imagined a 'Third Force' of European colonial powers (at least, as Anne Deighton observed, as 'a fallback position if international collaboration through the United Nations Organization and other multilateral institutions that favoured British interests could not in fact be achieved'). Bevin believed that only united European countries, with their colonies, dependencies and dominions, had a chance of 'being able, in the long run, to compel our two big partners to treat us as an equal', while in the short term enabling Europe to bridge the dollar gap. It would require American help in the beginning, but eventually, 'as soon as we can afford to develop Africa, we can cut loose from [the] US', the reasoning went. Whether it could really make 'the whole world richer and safer', as was the official motivation, is another matter.[3]

However, Bevin's strategy was not followed up. Though the UK still engaged in expanding its imperial influence in the Middle East and sub-Saharan Africa, it decided to focus on the British Commonwealth, which after the affiliation of India in 1949 turned into a multiracial and multicultural conglomerate of former dependencies and colonies, and to fully engage in a trans-Atlantic association with the US. As its dominions remained economically and culturally tied to the former metropolis, the latter was inevitably able to further dominate the network even after decolonization. The financial crisis of 1948–1949 and the global advance of international communism also pushed the UK towards a closer relationship with the US. Especially joined to the US, this British Commonwealth of Nations would allow London to continue to play a major role in global politics. This certainly offered more interesting prospects than an uncertain alignment with weakened

European partners. Hence, London remained on the sidelines, support-ing European integration as a strong and prosperous Europe was also to its advantage, but, as Churchill indicated, 'not part of it'.[4]

The French, incidentally, viewed the Commonwealth mainly as a competitor, the main reason why De Gaulle opposed British member-ship of the EEC in the 1960s. Britain would indeed look for ways to associate with the burgeoning European economy in the 1950s and 1960s, in addition to entering negotiations for joining the EC, and set-ting up the EFTA when that prospect failed in 1960. France opposed the entry of the UK into the ECs, although it suggested joining the Com-monwealth itself. That proved quite unattractive to the British, though their 'Plan G' to create a free trade zone with all 16 members of the OEEC – imagined in the mid-1950s – aimed at a gradual rapprochement of the EC and the Commonwealth in the long term.[5]

The US opposed European colonialism in principle, albeit rather inconsistently in practice, as it was much more interested in the raw materials of the European colonies in Africa and in preventing the spread of communism. In general, in the late 1940s and 1950s, the US would therefore emphasize the need for the development of European colonies and dominions. European colonial powers, especially France and Belgium, subscribed to this demand in terms of their alleged civilizing mission, but opposed any questioning of their colonial poli-cies. The French in particular supported that perspective and imagined grandiose, though not always very realistic plans for Africa, which could be (and effectively were, to a large extent) executed using ERP funds – which was not quite what the US intended. Nevertheless, assessing the amount of funds France received in the framework of the ERP and what it spent on its colonial projects, including the war in Indochina, the American historian Irwin M. Wall concludes that the US actually subsi-dized the continuation of the French colonial empire.[6] But the French and the Belgians remained very wary of the US, as the latter also inter-vened directly in Africa, in part to buy strategic raw materials, but also to pursue their own development policies. The Europeans considered these interventions as intrusions on their sovereignty and potentially undermining their colonial legitimacy.[7]

Eurafrica

To some extent, colonial ambition was projected upon the ECs. European federalists harked back to pre-war ideas about Eurafrica in which Europe and Africa would constitute a closely knit economy and

Africa functioned as a way of accommodating Germany in Europe.[8] The UEF in its Draft of a Federal Pact, presented at the Conference of The Hague in 1948, saw in a European federation a unique opportunity to continue the colonial project, defined in terms of mutual benefit and development:

> Europe as an entity will be viable only if the links which unite it with countries and dependent territories [...] are taken into account. The era of national ownership of colonial territories is past. [...] From now onwards a common European policy of development for certain regions of Africa should be taken in hand.[9]

The Dutch president of the UEF, Hendrik Brugmans, referred to the need for 'living space' (!) *on a bigger scale* than the nation state as the prime motivation for Europe to unite with Africa.[10]

In the Council of Europe, Europeans diverged on almost everything but not on the need to exploit African resources, as they provided the necessary means to fill the dollar gap. The French Prime Minister Paul Reynaud pulled no punches when he stated that 'We must also, if free Europe is to be made viable, *jointly* exploit the riches of the African continent, and try to find there those raw materials which we are getting from the dollar area, and for which we are unable to pay.'[11] As a Danish representative observed, echoing similar statements made before the war, as Europe had lost Asia, it could not risk also losing Africa. This view illustrates the increased geo-strategic importance of Africa in the European imagination, which would particularly surface in the framework of the plans for a European Political Community. Africa would offer not only raw materials (minerals especially), energy, foodstuffs and space, but also a strategic base of retreat in case of a new world war. From that perspective, Africa was no longer a project of colonial metropoles, but also of Europe as a whole, including the nations without colonies. In this respect, proponents of a European investment in Africa claimed support from, in particular, German and Scandinavian resources in capital and manpower. For Germany, the association with the (French) Overseas Territories constituted an asset in itself. Belgium, though, adopted a cautious, rather rejecting tone, as it feared intrusions of European institutions (particularly if an EPC was established) into its sovereignty and had no intention of having other European countries 'benefit' from its colonial riches.[12]

A number of developments in the late 1950s further increased the Eurafrican perspective. In April 1955, a major international conference was held in Bandung, Indonesia, where representatives from Asia and Africa discussed international co-operation and economic development, opposing colonialism and neo-colonialism. Quite clearly the death knell for European colonialism had sounded once more, but the Suez intervention of late 1956–1957, when joint French-British troops landed in Egypt to safeguard their authority over the Suez canal after Egyptian president Abdel Nasser had nationalized it, demonstrated that European leaders in London and Paris still stuck to their old habits. However, the US veto once again laid bare the redundancy of European powers and the opposed interests and policies between them and the US, and from that perspective was of crucial importance as well. While the costs of maintaining a colonial empire were rising beyond French and British capacities, the debacle increased their demand for nuclear arms and for European solidarity. Especially, France concluded that it could not count on the US. Belgium too started to feel the need for European solidarity with regard to the Congo, as Paul-Henry Spaak – who was also the chairman of the negotiations leading to the Rome Treaties installing the EEC and Euratom – realized after his trip to Congo in August 1956: an association and partnership between the ECs and Africa could offer a viable alternative to a violent decolonization and create a foundation for a different, more equal and mutually beneficial relationship in the image of the British Commonwealth.[13] Far more than the French and Belgians, the British realized that more and more Asian and African countries would move towards independence. Instead of fighting a hopeless rearguard action, an alternative strategy could reside in investing in the development of Africa and the Commonwealth, a strategy that was already well in place in the mid-1950s but was accelerated after the Suez crisis.[14]

The French but now also the Belgians (some at least) rather saw a solution in a Eurafrican association. This would have as an additional advantage that other European nations would be involved in the maintaining of a strong connection between the two continents, as they could also benefit from the raw materials and the new markets that would open up. However, creating a market for European products demanded important funds – that, of course, was the main motive. Understandably, the other Europeans, for different reasons – not necessarily out of principle – proved very hesitant in accepting the Franco-Belgian perspective.[15] Italy for example rather feared the competition for its economic policy in the *Mezzogiorno*. But for France the association was vital, and it pushed its vision through. Surprising as it may seem, the US supported the idea and considered Africa to be Europe's hinterland and of strategic importance in the Cold War. Moreover, Eurafrica might offer a way out of the Algerian crisis. But the Americans realised quickly that the colonial objective of the plan counteracted the inevitable push towards independence.[16]

The Treaty of Rome (25 March 1957) installing Euratom and the EEC effectively associated – not integrated – the overseas territories and colonies to the EC, from Algeria – which was an integral part of France, though a special arrangement was foreseen – to the Belgian Congo, and opened the door for independent states to affiliate. Needless to say, a major impediment for the accession of the UK to the EC existed here, although the EEC model actually appeared very attractive to the UK, as it pooled important resources for the development of Africa.

The invention of 'Europe the fair'

Soon, though, – actually already during the negotiations – a new wave of anti-colonial protests and revolts stripped the European colonial powers of their overseas members or associates, including Algeria in 1963, which seceded from France after a pernicious war that cost up to 1,000,000 lives.[17] Hence, the EC had to give up its colonial ambitions. Remarkably swiftly, the continent adopted a discourse of peace and progress unspoiled by its colonial past – in fact the colonial dimension of the ECs vanished from European memory: virtually all representations, textbooks and overviews on European integration and the Foreign Relations of the EU remain silent on it, though the tide is turning. How could the EC make that transition so easily?[18]

The answer to that question lay not only in Europe but also outside it, in the interiorization of Europe's discourse on values of progress, democracy and equality that took root, notwithstanding the racism of European colonialism: in that respect the civilizing mission had been successful. Even anti-colonialist ideologies largely found inspiration in western ideologies.[19] Illustrative is the enthusiasm of African intellectuals and leaders for being part of Eurafrica *'à la française*, based on real respect and equality' in the words of the Senegalese member of the French Parliament (later president of Senegal) Leopold Senghor in 1952, though his words can also be read as a warning.[20]

The amazing transition from a colonial empire to 'Europe the fair' is not only a question of forgetting and some sort of collective 'Stockholm syndrome' on the side of the colonized, though. Europe in general has a long history of claiming to defend liberty and equality as well as development and civilization. Though arguably the inventors of the cruellest slaveholding practices in history, Europeans also abolished slavery in the nineteenth century (A parallel springs to mind: Europeans developed extensive and explicit theories of religious toleration because of their extremely intolerant past.). Europeans also developed ideas about *global* human rights, even if these served their imperial objectives.[21] The British, for example, presented themselves as the consciousness of the world by the suggestion of bringing Turkish authorities to trial because of 'crimes against Humanity' against the Armenians in 1919.[22] Development and the 'civilizing mission' were at first considered a way of legitimizing and strengthening the colonial endeavour. That was also the perspective as the European institutions continued, for example when the Hague Conference of 1948 demanded that a European union should 'assist in assuring the economic, political and cultural advancement of the populations of the overseas territories associated with it', although significantly 'without prejudice to the special ties which now link these territories to European countries'.[23] Under American pressure, development became a prime objective of the OEEC, pleading for extensive works to be initiated in Africa to maximize Africa's production. Development also became part of the discourse of the Council of Europe as well as the ECSC and later the EC: 'With increased resources Europe will be able to pursue the achievement of one of its essential tasks, namely, the development of the African continent', Robert Schuman stated when calling for the creation of the ECSC.[24] The Dutch Foreign Minister Jozef Luns foresaw for the ECs an even greater role on the occasion of the signing of the Treaty of Rome in 1957, 'to assure the conditions of an increasing prosperity to our old continent and permit *the continuation of her grand and global civilizing mission*' (emphasis PP).[25] From this perspective, the EEC created an Overseas Development Fund (ODF) financed by all members of the Community – Germany in particular contributed large sums. The perspective of decolonization, however, remained conspicuously absent from such development calls. For the French, and certainly also the Belgians, the very idea was still inconceivable in any foreseeable future, even at the time of the signature of the Rome Treaties in 1957.

It was different for the British, who already in the famous British proposal for a West European Union in 1948 contemplated the possibility of self-government, as the aim was 'to secure that when African territories attain self-government they do as part of the Western World', even if that was not necessarily envisaged in the immediate future.[26] From 1957, however, it was. Hence, the UK invested in development policies in order to safeguard its influence on (former) colonies, members of the Commonwealth. Its resources remained limited, however. And if the Commonwealth turned into a liability, the EEC looked like an appealing prospect: leadership of the organization would bring the UK back to the position of world power, while the EEC Overseas Development Fund could mobilize more funds.[27] However, the French in particular were not thrilled by the prospect of British leadership – their worst nightmare – and blocked its entry.

Around 1960, and certainly after the French finally gave up their fight in Algeria in 1962, the EC renounced its colonial objectives. Jean Monnet, a lukewarm supporter of the French colonial development policies after 1945 anyway, indicated the change:

> One impression predominates in my mind over all others. It is this: unity in Europe does not create a new kind of great power; it is a method for introducing change in Europe and consequently in the world. People, more often outside the European Community than within, are tempted to see the European Community as a potential nineteenth century state with all the overtones this implies. But we are not in the nineteenth century, and the Europeans have built up the European Community precisely in order to find a way out of the conflicts to which the nineteenth-century philosophy gave rise.[28]

He was no doubt sincere, but whether the transition was so clear-cut can be doubted. Recent assessments of EU foreign policy documents suggest its discourse shows many parallels with the old 'civilizing mission' of the colonial powers since the nineteenth century, while there is much continuity in EU development policies as well.[29]

Epilogue

As this book has already surveyed 1,000 years of conceptualizing European unity, I do not assess the developments since roughly 1950–1960, as from that period onwards European countries effectively constituted some sort of European union – albeit different in east and west. However, there exist plenty of excellent books that analyse and discuss these developments, certainly with regard to Western Europe, although the previous pages suggest that I would prefer a less linear story to be told: less exclusively focused on Western Europe and the less than self-evident road towards the present EU, taking into account the different forms of European unity and collaboration with other institutions and not only looking at the supranational 'inner sphere' of the EC/EU but also at the relationships between affiliated states and manifestations to the outer world, as well as different institutional manifestations such as the European jurisprudence,[30] and more critical towards the EU's complacent self-representation as a moral beacon for the world. The following paragraph contains just a few major steps to make the transition to some concluding remarks.

After 1968, France no longer opposed the affiliation of the UK, initiating increasing political co-operation and opening the gates of the European communities to others: in 1973, the UK, Ireland and Denmark joined the ECs. Turkey, however, which in 1959 had already requested membership, was kept waiting. Enlargement proved a powerful argument to intensify the institutional co-operation: the decades after 1973 were far more dynamic in this respect than the stagnating years of the 1960s, when proposals for a political union as well as the issue of the affiliation of the UK resulted in a decennium of crisis. The enlargement of the EC also provoked a need for a reflection on Europe's 'identity', which would only intensify after the Soviet empire in Europe crumbled in 1989, and one year later when the former DDR merged with the FRG and hence became part of the EC. The EU motto 'united in diversity' suggest that the EU considers this unity as remarkable, though this book has shown that the countries involved – to some extent apart from Turkey, which is a special case – had considered themselves and been considered by others to be European and included in plans about European unity for centuries. Such a sense of a common history is something the states that constitute the US never had (certainly not those that belonged to New Spain in 1800), nor those states and regions that constitute India today: although external observers did distinguish a distinct South-Asian culture for centuries, Indians themselves only started to view themselves as belonging to one 'nation' or culture after the uprising of 1857.

Whatever the EC's increased competence and authority since the 1970s, it proved ill-equipped to deal with the disaster that happened in the former Yugoslavia, where since the death of President Tito in 1980, ethnic tensions had been mounting. The disintegration of the Soviet empire and the claim of democratic self-determination contributed to raising the stakes as different ethnic and religious groups, starting with Slovenia, aimed at breaking away from Yugoslavia and becoming independent. While in the west such ambitions had also provoked violent reactions from the states concerned – witness the conflicts in Northern Ireland and the Basque country – in Yugoslavia things got completely out of control. Nevertheless, the EC did intervene actively in trying to pacify the situation though diplomatic pressure and consultation, but though it extended its competences and political instruments considerably, they failed due to lack of military backing and the obstruction of the US and NATO, who refused to intervene in any way. Uncoordinated diplomatic interventions of European countries, in particular Germany, in favour of certain parties as well as discussions on the authority to intervene, furthermore considerably complicated the situation. Finally the US did step in and forced the issue. Its failure in the Balkans seriously discredited the emerging EC's foreign policy.[31]

The EU reinvented itself with the Treaty of Maastricht in 1993, establishing the European Union, which possessed considerably increased supranational competences and foresaw the introduction of a single currency, the Euro, which became effective in 2002. Notwithstanding the scepticism of monetary experts, particularly in the Anglo-Saxon world, the Euro proved highly successful. However, as the EU still did not obtain real authority to impose a common social and economic policy upon the member states, it ran into problems with the all too divergent economic performance of member states after the global financial crisis of 2007–2008. The Eurocrisis reintroduced existential tensions between member states that may jeopardize the whole European edifice, although the EU has proved to be far more resilient than critical observers thought.[32] Foreign policy remained underdeveloped though, even if the EU tried to present itself as a 'soft' power, emphasizing its values of democracy, human rights and sustainability. Some scepticism towards such benevolent European foreign policy is in order, however, as it is structurally grafted upon the imperial discourse of a European civilizing mission and is characterized by a sometimes astounding lack of empathy for non-European sensibilities and considerations.[33] Still, one should not underestimate the power of words in this respect either: emphasizing the values of democracy, the rule of law – however it has been abused to legitimize European imperialism in the past –, international co-operation, human rights and fundamental freedoms has become part and parcel of European identity. And promoting these, even sometimes ambiguously – imposing typical European sensitivities and values upon others, at the same time defending national as well as common European interests – is still largely preferable to politics of war, terrorism or other power politics that seem to be increasingly dominating international politics again. In this respect the current EU's representation as a beacon of peace is not completely unfounded.[34]

Conclusion: In Search of European Unity

> The unification of Europe is an age-old dream. It has been attempted by conquerors, pondered by philosophers, sought by scholars – and sabotaged by as many politicians as have extolled it, with not infrequently the same doing both.
>
> Dirk U. Stikker, 1966[1]

In his speech accepting the Nobel Peace Prize in 2012, the then president of the European Commission, José Emmanuel Barroso, referred to the values that inspire the European Union and that find their roots deep in European history, especially in the history of humanism and the Enlightenment:

> 'Peace is not mere absence of war, it is a virtue', wrote Spinoza (...). The European Union is not only about peace among nations. It incarnates, as a political project, that particular state of mind that Spinoza was referring to. It embodies, as a community of values, this vision of freedom and justice.[2]

In this book I have portrayed a slightly different picture of the history of European integration. But perhaps Europe has changed since the horror of WW II, during which Europe met its nemesis? At the moment the answer must indeed be yes, even if the story of the change is less straightforward than some sort of sudden enlightenment, and the agency lies not solely in the hands of some illuminating 'founding father'.

Though undoubtedly operating within the margins of political decision-making for centuries, people in Europe have sought to unite the lands which they conceived of as 'European', not just as conquest of their surroundings – the way the Chinese Empire(s) expanded from some tiny kingdoms in the Yellow River Valley to the giant subcontinent that it now is – but as a federation of states. Their reasons for doing so varied. I have in this book emphasized the quest for peace and stability as well as the longing for global power. Peace, to be sure, was not always the prime motive. Some of the earliest plans called upon Christians to unite in order to fight the infidels and conquer the Holy Lands. Nevertheless, while fear of the Islamic menace from the east may have contributed to forging a European consciousness, as many scholars believe, it was not a trigger to unite in common defence. Organizing a common market to withstand economic competition from new upcoming powers – the US in the first place, the BRICS more recently – in contrast, certainly was, as was Europe's fear of losing its dominant position in the world to an awakening Asia. That fear haunted the European imagination already long before the heyday of colonization – one may wonder whether that illustrates how strong the will to dominate actually was, or rather expresses a deep-rooted 'minority complex', as has been argued.[3]

Though scholars of European integration by and large ignore the remarkable parallelism between European integration and decolonization,[4] there is undoubtedly a close connection. Nevertheless, the relationship between European integration, colonialism and decolonialization is complex: colonial ambitions were above all national ones, and calling for a united Europe to defend these interests appears rather contradictory. Only in very specific circumstances could the European way be an option. But that option was very real, in particular for France in the 1950s. In addition, as Michael Collins recently observed, decolonization in general provoked new thinking about federalism among the colonizing powers.[5] Federalism appeared as a way to counter nationalist demands of anti-colonial agitators. The ECs, however, made the first effective steps towards some sort of new European colonial empire, implying a deep association with Africa, a continent rich in resources but 'underdeveloped'. The association of the 'overseas territories' with the ECs was not just a technical issue as it is presented in the literature – if it is mentioned at all – but part of a (neo-) colonial project in which the ECs would benefit from the exploitation of Africa's resources in return for the latter's 'development' – mainly to create a market for European products. This the current Europe (not just the EU) has conveniently forgotten; it does not fit well into the contemporary discourse of Europe as moral beacon and origin of universal values of humanity and enlightenment, and the EU as global harbinger of peace, human rights and sustainability.

The role of the US merits special attention, as the US figured as an economic competitor and cultural foe throughout the nineteenth and twentieth centuries, a main motivation to unify Europe. But its open internal market and democratic federal system functioned as a powerful model and ideal for where Europe should be heading – although its interpretation diverged, also because the American system naturally evolved too: the US of George Washington and that of Barack Obama have little in common.[6] However, the US repeatedly and decisively intervened in the continent, militarily during the two world wars, economically and politically afterwards, entailing a cultural 'Americanization' of the continent (mainly embodied within the west during the Cold War era). Incidentally, periods of non-intervention – referred to as periods of 'isolationist' politics – were often seen as problematic as well. The relationship was all the more complicated as European states became heavily indebted towards the US after WW I and WW II, which considerably contributed to the economic woes of the continent. The US helped to solve these political and economic problems in the 1920s, with the Dawes Plan making the Locarno Peace possible, and after WW II with the ERP. Though European historians tend to downplay the impact of the US on the European integration process between 1950 and 1960 (in contrast to scholars working on American archives perhaps tending to inflate it), it remains hard to imagine how the plans for a new post-war order that were developed by Europe's leaders, especially in France, might have led to a unified Europe or even a lasting peace, as the most likely result would have been a 'Versailles with a vengeance'. That a growing Soviet menace in itself would have sufficed to unite Europeans seems highly unlikely, given the accommodating policies favoured by the continental European governments. Also, the opposition between the former belligerents, notwithstanding genuine and important efforts at reconciliation, remained strong. In any case, apart from the USSR and the UK, no European state possessed enough remaining political and economic leverage to decide upon its own future, let alone that of the rest of the continent, though the US was also unable to realize its goal of a strong Europe as a 'third force'.[7]

Russia must be mentioned here as well – *with* and *in* Europe from its own perspective, at least until WW II (in contrast to the British Isles, *with* but not *in* Europe according to Winston Churchill), but looked at with mixed feelings from the western parts of the continent that at times considered themselves more enlightened and advanced.

With the coming to power of communism, the (former) Russian/Soviet empire in Western Europe was perceived increasingly as part of barbaric 'Asia', though its ideology without doubt was quintessentially European. The USSR fought an existential war with that other quintessentially European phenomenon, Nazi Germany, and afterwards, as part of the Allies, found itself firmly tied into Europe once more. Its ambitions had changed, however: it started constructing a reliable buffer zone around Germany and transformed into a Eurasian empire, de facto splitting the continent. The split only lasted some 40 years, though, before collapsing, as the USSR lost the ideological competition with 'the West' – Western Europe integrated with the more 'informal' American empire – which performed so much better in terms of economic and military performance, as well as with regard to political legitimacy, offering prosperity, progress and even equality to its population to a far larger degree. However, the Soviet menace and the resulting Cold War proved a decisive factor in Western European integration, offering the conditions for a new relationship between the former belligerents under an American nuclear umbrella. It is this new condition that opened the way for European federalists to steer European politics in the direction of more unity. Hence, it was not the European institutions that generated peace in Europe but the 'armed peace' of the Cold War that made the constitution of European institutions possible.

The main motive for striving towards European unity was, however, 'internal'. Christendom, as it developed from the late Roman Empire, and continued and reinforced in medieval times, already contained an ideology of homogeneity (there was no truth beyond the Church), considering difference as detrimental to the godly order, which was much reinforced through the association between worldly and religious power. However, the world of Christendom was torn apart by the struggle for the highest authority between the papacy and the emperor – or rather between the Church and the secular powers – as well as between different religious factions in Christianity. The solution that gradually emerged from the fifteenth century, and which offered the framework of thinking about European unity, first of all implied the gradual secularization of international politics: in plans for European unity, power was allotted to secular princes, not to the ecclesiastical authorities. This also implied the introduction of toleration in international politics – the reason why Christian monarchs could do business and conclude alliances of friendship with each other irrespective of confession, but also with the Ottoman Turks. Rules of toleration were also introduced at domestic level if the population was too diverse or the minorities too powerful or important to do otherwise. But the main strategy for over-coming the problems of diversity within the European lands was striving towards religious homogeneity and confessionalization, meaning a close relationship between monarch and Church dominated by the former.

In this respect, the concept of the nation state, ideal-typically homogenous, was developed as a means to ensure peace, internally as well as externally. It allowed for the politics of power balancing, which would become part of the diplomats' main tools for peacekeeping in Europe, and elsewhere, from the eighteenth century. But as the pow-ers which convened in Vienna realized in 1815, neither justice nor power balancing sufficed: there should be institutions of consultation, arbitration and international law. Moreover, as the early nationalists understood, nation states could perfectly associate in (con) federations, perhaps the best way to ensure peaceful relationships in theory. How-ever, two problems haunt the nationalist imagination: the definition of the nation – in the end always somewhat subjective and ever-changing – and the relationship with other nations, as nations have the unfortu-nate habit of sharing territory with others. Hence, nationalism became a factor of instability and conflict as well, especially if one nation claimed territories 'occupied' by others. With the development of social Darwinism and racism, full equality between nations was increasingly seen as obsolete. Homogeneity remained the ideal; it was pushed to the extreme by Hitler, but in a way the Allies reasoned similarly in 1944–1945 when they wanted to divide Europe into 'large states' and avoid too much 'mixing'. The essentially nationalistic idea that ethnic mixing leads to conflict, and that separation produces peace, became a strong trope in politics and international relations: it motivated the post-war politics of ethnic cleansing in Central and Eastern Europe as well as today's concentration of migrants in ghettos in contemporary cities.

Some liberals saw the dangers of nationalism very early on, consider-ing nationalism already obsolete before it was actually invented. They argued that commercial ties and trade relations would soon make war irrational. It is a powerful idea that underpins much contemporary pacifist and federalist thinking, but the evidence is rather against it: the British used it as a pacifying instrument in the 1860s, a period of intense technological and commercial interaction, but it did not pre-vent any war – perhaps, as Fichte and List in particular predicted, the opposite. At the very least the relationship between commercial and also technological interaction and war and peace is far more complex.

The most attractive political concepts in Europe in the nineteenth and twentieth century were not those of the nation state and a European federation, but that of the modern European 'nation-empire' (actually what Jan Zielonka unhappily calls a 'Westphalian empire').[8] In contrast to premodern and most non-western empires based upon a loose confederation of lands with separate rules and institutions,[9] the modern European nation-empire to a large extent introduces common laws and institutions for all inhabitants of the empire, addressing the individual instead of collectivities – the final result looks more like a huge centralized nation state than a 'traditional' empire. Certainly within Europe, all major states were in fact such modern nation-empires, or at least strived towards it, from Napoleon to Bismarck to the Nazi *Third Reich*. Certainly some European federalists may have dreamt of organizing Europe as such a modern nation-empire as well. However, that was not the way followed. Zielonka compares the EU after the enlargement wave of the early 1990s to a 'neo-medieval' empire corresponding to the imagined traditional empire I have spoken about above, referring to the polycentric way of government and divided sovereignty within the EU, the cultural and economic heterogeneity between the affiliated member states, and the changing borders. Luuk van Middelaar has argued that within the ECs and the EU a complex decision-making scheme developed in which different levels interact, sometimes even conflict, which, however, does not correspond to traditional conceptions either of nation states or empires.[10] Chris Bickerton also showed that the relationship with the member states of the EU changed profoundly over time, becoming more intense and complex, changing the very nature of the affiliated states themselves as well as the European frame.[11] This all points to the EU becoming a particular political form *sui generis*, for which adequate terms and analysing tools still seem missing.

At this point two more observations must be made. Firstly, it needs to be emphasized that the nation state remained or rather *became* the standard political form within Western Europe, and notwithstanding the lesser national sovereignty also on the east side of the former Iron Curtain. After 1945, the ideal of the nation state was the ultimate dream of political activists, for the native anti-colonial elites in Asia and Africa who detached from the European metropoles as much as for the people of the former communist Eastern European states in the 1990s and the peoples that strove, violently or otherwise, towards their own autonomous or independent state, such as the Basques, the Irish (in Northern Ireland), the Flemish and the Scottish (at least some of them). But it was also the case for the Western European states that timidly searched for ways to unite at European level after WW II. As A.S. Milward forcefully argued, the early ECs offered the (only) way for war-devastated Western European countries, up to their ears in debt, to recover and modernize their economies, with the help of the US. The economic growth and productivity increase served to develop the European welfare state, carefully designed at national, not European level. That is most obvious in the case of France, but actually applies to all European states. In the previous chapter I showed that even the concept of a Euro-African community cannot be dissociated from national colonial objectives. As Mazzini already knew in 1840, nationalism and Europeanism should not be considered exclusive: even fascist or Nazi ultranationalism proved perfectly compatible with either confederal models of collaboration or with supranational institutions (albeit in an imperial framework). This allows me to observe that a vested interest in advancing national causes in no way impedes larger ambitions. Indeed, one cannot understand the advancement of European integration without taking into account the 'synecdochal' desire for 'grandeur' also,[12] as well as elevated ideals of establishing if not a perpetual, then at least a lasting peace and justice in Europe – and, if so, then why not in the world?

Still, the ECs and the EU have inherited some features from the model of the nation state (or perhaps rather of the modern nation-empire). Especially since the economic crisis of the 1970s and the first wave of enlargement (with the UK, Ireland and Denmark in 1973), the EU has sought a common identity and political legitimacy; the latter became ever more pressing as more countries from the Mediterranean and former Eastern Europe joined, the institutions democratized, and the EU was transformed into a monetary union.[13] As the latter happened without much consideration for accompanying economic policy instruments, the Euro crisis of the 2010s provoked important tensions between the member states and generated a spectacular increase in Euroscepticism. The search for a common identity and history shows a few results up to the present time – and it has certainly not hampered the rise of Euroscepticism.

As I have tried to illustrate throughout this book, European history shows a few notable constants, such as its difficulty in coping with diversity. Still, it is too easy to see in the medieval 'persecuting society' (R.I. Moore) a prelude to the Holocaust. What I argue is not that this is so, but that there are some deep-rooted features – 'habits of thought' and practice – that are dealt with and even solved but nevertheless keep on popping up in completely different guises.[14] Europe overcame what it saw as existential problems such as religious diversity and the tension between religious and secular political authority, but in a paradoxical way these determined the way solutions were sought – in confessionalization as well as theories of tolerance – and returned in nationalism. Likewise, the crusades are something completely different from the nineteenth century colonial wars, let alone the EU's 'normative' power, but they do share some basic features.

Nevertheless, Europe has departed from the old longing for homogeneity. The Council of Europe not only developed a discourse on human rights as quintessentially European but also imagined Europe as a mosaic already from the 1950s, giving a positive twist on what for centuries had mostly been seen as a source of conflict and weakness. The ECs (the EU after 1992) borrowed the idea in the 1970s as part of their quest for a common identity.[15] As the Irish nationalist politician John Hume powerfully testified in his speech accepting the 2008 Nobel Peace Prize, the EU's example of dealing with diversity set an inspiring model for those trying to solve bitter national and religious conflicts, as in Northern Ireland:

> But it has happened and it is now clear that European Union is the best example in the history of the world of conflict resolution and it is the duty of everyone, particularly those who live in areas of conflict to study how it was done and to apply its principles to their own conflict resolution.[16]

Gradually the idea that diversity is detrimental to peace appears to have vanished in post-war Europe; 'diversity' even came to be evaluated positively. Many post-war European countries from somewhere in the 1950s onwards stopped emphasizing racial divisions, allowing, albeit not all to the same extent and following different modalities, (post-) colonial migrants to acquire national citizenship. Anti-Semitism all but disappeared from the political vocabulary. Also, the so-called 'guest-workers' were relatively well accommodated (at least they did not face persecution), notwithstanding sometimes substantial discrimination.[17]

Today, however, it seems that old demons are resurfacing. As the continent has become far more diverse as a result of postcolonial and global migrations, many (if not all) European countries have witnessed reactions against expressions of culture and, in particular, religious belief that are deemed different, such as the headscarf. Even anti-Semitism appears to have re-emerged, in extreme right parties such as the Front National in France as well as in reactions against the anti-Palestinian politics of Israel, which affect 'progressives' and young militant Muslims. The EU has reacted to the popular pressure by desperately seeking to keep out the migrants and asylum seekers since the 1990s. Moreover, the 'Unity in Diversity' discourse sometimes sits uneasily with the EU's search for a common identity – the idea that identity is homogenous has proved more resilient than postmodern scholars imagined. Given the difficulties the continent had with relatively minor differences in the past, one is entitled to find some contemporary developments worrisome – it is significant that the old fear of diversity has to some extent returned in the negative appreciation of the concept of 'difference'.[18]

Finally, has European unity as expressed so far in the ECs/EU bought Europe everlasting peace, or has war in Europe become inevitable? The historian, remembering his mentor Leopold von Ranke and his misreading of the period after the Congress of Europe,[19] will always be cautious. After all, although European unity has been advocated as a means towards peace, the actual establishment of the ECs was the result of far more ambiguous motives and complex processes, even if the ambition to make peace was systematically invoked. Moreover, the representation of a post-war peace is partly flawed, as it downplays many conflicts at Europe's margins and especially the colonial violence and wars of liberation, among them the Algerian liberation war. The optimistic view of post-war European peace somewhat recalls the perceptions of the period after the Congress of Vienna in 1815. The Yugoslavian wars of the 1990s have awakened old fears, and while I have been writing this book Ukraine has broken up as a result of civil war and Russian intervention, while incidents on Baltic borders bode little good. That the Cold War did not degenerate into an open war was certainly in part due to the clear recognition of the boundaries of the main spheres of influence (or of the two 'empires') backed up by a strong military deterrence – the possibility that the boundaries are being questioned and tested today is more dangerous than many seem to realize. However, with regard to Western Europe, at least the French–German antagonism appears to have been overcome, and this can be fully ascribed to the collaboration within the framework of the ECs: no minor feat. What made it possible were a series of factors. Certainly the Cold War drove the former arch-enemies into each other's arms, and firmly kept them there. Undervalued are the many very concrete actions of conciliation – certainly an important avenue for further research. But it seems that the intense negotiations and increasing intertwining of decision-making procedures and practices generated the necessary basis for easing the antagonisms and creating the conditions in which the prospect of war between the partners gradually, but quite soon after the war, dwindled away. Institutional entanglement, more than economic interdependence, appears to be the key factor. Transnational networks and interactions between individuals and organizations played a decisive role in the shaping of European institutions as well. Last but not least, the discourse of peace and reconciliation in itself, dissociating the responsibility for the war of enemy politicians and leaders from the people, allowed the former belligerents to overcome their hatred. That it perhaps also required a mythical interpretation of our own history is a price even historians are glad to pay, at least for a while more.[20] The suggestion that Europe has finally overcome its demons and that it can sustain 'permanent peace' without common institutions and permanent interaction, however, strikes me as criminally naive. This admittedly 'political' conclusion of course does not in any way preclude a profound discussion about the nature of the European Union. I hope that this book can contribute to make such a debate informed.

Notes

1 'Peace for Our Time': The European Quest for Peace

1. https://www.gov.uk/government/history/10-downing-street#number-10-at-war. Benjamin Disraeli upon returning from the Congress of Berlin in 1878 used the same phrase, which echoes the verse in *The Book of Common Prayer* 'Give peace in our time, O Lord'.
2. Cf. Sheehan 2008.
3. Cf. http://www.nobelprize.org/nobel_prizes/peace/laureates/2012/
4. Ash 2005, 199.
5. Hansen and Jonsson 2011; 2012.
6. Bhambra 2009.
7. Kaelble 2001; Kaelble and Kirsch 2007.
8. Gollwitzer 1951 distinguishes between inclusive and exclusive views. The distinction is not always helpful, though, as much depends on the threshold and perspective one adopts: exclusiveness and inclusiveness are often ambivalent.
9. On the latter see Shore 2000; Sassatelli 2009.
10. The literature on European identity is endless. For a brief overview, see Wintle 2013.
11. 'Indeed, drawing distinctions among and between themselves have been one of the defining obsessions of the inhabitants of the continent.' Judt 2011, 46.
12. For discussions of such representations of European history see Huistra, Molema and Wirt 2014; Leggewie 2011.
13. Delanty 2013 is actually one of the most interesting histories that take the diversity of the continent as a constituent element of its identity seriously.
14. Alesina et al. 2003 publish indices for ethnic, linguistic and religious fractionalization for about 190 countries. These indices can only be used with caution, though. In particular, the index on religion is highly questionable, as the text shows a little reflection on the definition of religion and on how religious diversity was measured – different denominations were apparently treated as different religions. See also Kymlicka and He 2005.
15. The Indian constitution recognizes 22 official languages. The actual number of literary languages in India, however, is much higher. Lewis 2009 counts 438 living languages. The Indian census recognized 1,652 different languages in India (including languages not native to the subcontinent) in 1961; the 1991 census limits the amount at a total of 122 languages and 234 'mother tongues' of at least 10,000 speakers. http://www.censusindia .gov.in/Census_Data_2001/Census_Data_Online/Language/Statement1.htm. The EU currently recognizes 35 official languages; there are not many languages that do not benefit from official recognition.
16. For an overview see Prügl and Thiel 2009.
17. Mamdani 2001.

18. Kymlicka and He 2005. An interesting comparative study of premodern societies around the Indian Ocean based on Cantor's set theory in Chaudhuri 1990. See also Burbank and Cooper 2010.
19. Stepan 2011.
20. The Malaysian government launched a very successful campaign to promote itself as multicultural and diverse under the slogan 'Malaysia, truly Asia' in 1999.
21. The issue is not that straightforward, though, and is disputed by, among others, Bruce 1996.
22. For a recent, albeit controversial, assessment see Gregory 2012.
23. Maleševića 2012; Reynolds 2011; Wolff 1994.
24. Gat 2013.
25. Perhaps with the significant, but partial, exception of Jews, though Judaism was increasingly – but not exclusively – defined in racial terms. Compare Boyarin 2009.
26. In this respect, see especially the work of Mann 2005; Ther 2011; Wimmer 2002; 2012 and 2013.
27. Labrie 2011; Mergel 2009. See also Kraus and Sciortino 2014.
28. Compare Burbank and Cooper 2010, which emphasizes the homogenizing politics of Europe in comparison with non-European empires. See also Boyarin 2009.
29. Weitz 2005: 20; Nirenberg 1996: 1–17 and 241–245.
30. Habermas and Derrida 2003, 293, quoted in Bhambra 2009, 3. Delanty 2013 makes this representation of cosmopolitan Europe the core of his long-term narrative.
31. Cf. Bhambra 2009. On the cooperation and peace-building features of EU Foreign Policy see Keukeleire and Delreux 2014, especially chapter 6.
32. E.g. Milward 1992. See also Moravcsik 1998 and Collins 2013.
33. A state of the art in Nexon 2009, chapter 8.
34. Burbank and Cooper 2010, 182.
35. Dickinson 2008. See also Ther 2004.
36. Cf. Semmel 1993; Fitzpatrick 2012.

2 Peace in Christendom?

1. Dante, *Monarchy*, edited by Prue Shaw, Cambridge University Press, 1996, 26.
2. Swedberg 1994.
3. Dussel 2000, 465.
4. Sen 2005.
5. Brague 1992.
6. Wickham 2009, 563. On the legal changes more below.
7. Brown 2013, 408–433.
8. Wulfstan of York, *The Institutes of Polity*, ca. 1010, quoted in Smith 2005, 250. For a broader discussion, see ibidem 217–252.
9. Vian 2004.
10. Barbero 2004; Lieberman 2013, 43–87.
11. Barbero 2004.
12. Reuter 1992.

13. Fischer 1957, 46.
14. Hay 1968, 25, erroneously identifies the author as Isidorus Pacensis (Bishop Isidore of Beja). The document has been edited and translated by J. Eduardo Lopez Pereira, *Continuatio Isidoriana Hispana Cronica Mozarabe de 754*, León, 2009. English translation by Wolf 1990 (passage 145).
15. Heather 2010.
16. Gollwitzer 1951, 31.
17. Siedentop 2014, 151–162 and ff. See more detailed in Bellomo 1995; Lesaffer 2012; Povolo 2013; Schröder 2013; Stein 1999.
18. Rietbergen 1989, 138.
19. William of Malmesbury, *Chronicle of the Kings of England*, translated by Rev. John Sharpe, edited by J. A. Giles, London: George Bell and Sons, 1904, 360 (orig. *Gesta regum Anglorum*, 1126, quoted in Den Boer 1993, 28). Hay 1968 gives a more ample discussion of the meaning of Europe for the Middle Ages.
20. Rietbergen 1998, 138. For a reassessment of the significance of the European–Islamic opposition, see Rich 1999.
21. Yapp 1992, 134–155.
22. Balzaretti 1992.
23. Bartlett 1994.
24. Especially Delanty 2013 and in a different (more sophisticated) way Brague 1992.
25. Similarly Crom 2009, 86. I use the term 'Cathars' as a generic term. According to Moore 2012, no such sect existed and the Cathars were an invention of contemporary elites.
26. Hrabanus Maurus, *Expositio in Epistolam I ad Corinthios*, 2 quoted in Smith 2005, 231. An overview in Lieberman 2013, 43–87 ('Word and sword in the making of Christian Europe').
27. For a brief but brilliant presentation see Berend 2013, 1–13. Compare Nirenberg 1996.
28. Kater 2006, 20–25. For an extensive analysis of Augustinus' conception of peace, see Budzik 1988.
29. Boyarin 2009, 6.
30. Smith 2005, 217–230.
31. Moore 2007; 2012; Landes, Gow and Van Meter 2003.
32. Crouzet 1990.
33. Nirenberg 1996, 18–40.
34. Delanty 2013, 35.
35. Virk 2014 gives an extensive list of authors and figures.
36. An example would be the great Muslim mapmaker Muhammad al-Idrisi at the court of King Roger II of Sicily in Palermo. See Rich 1999, 441; Wintle 2008, 29–30.
37. Abu-Lughod 1989. For the idea of a 'cosmopolitan Christian Europe of the twelfth and thirteenth centuries', see for example Smith 2005.
38. Cf. Helfers 2005, who emphasizes the heterogeneity of medieval and early modern culture (in reality limited to the borderlands though) in his introduction, but admits that Europe did not share today's multiculturalism as 'as an ideological stance [valuing] just this diversity and the tentativeness that comes from valuing it' (7).
39. Brown 2013, 383–404.

40. Rietbergen 1998, 136–142.
41. Höfert 2007.
42. Hay 1968, 58–61.
43. Rietbergen 1998, 139–140. On Marsiglio, see Nederman 1995. For a broader situation, see Nederman 2000.
44. Geyer 2003, 129–139.
45. Quoted in Höfert 2007, 216.
46. Höfert 2007.
47. Al-Azmeh 2007, 351–352.
48. Beaune 1994, 35–56 (includes a French translation of Podiebrad's *Tractatus*).
49. For example, Philpott 2001. Compare Beaulac 2004 (the whole book is a devastating critique on the sovereignty 'myth of Westphalia'); Osiander 2001 and Nexon 2009, chapter 8.
50. For example Loriaux 2008, 138–147.
51. Middell and Naumann 2010. On the issue of corporate sovereignty, see Stern 2011. In contrast to the Hanseatic League or monastic military orders, corporations did associate with states.
52. Loriaux 2008, 138–147 (especially 146); Balibar 2001, 22.
53. Justus Lipsius, *Six Books of Politickes or Civil Doctrine*, done into English by William Iones, London, 1594, Book IV, 3 quoted in Tuck 1988, 21–22.
54. John Locke, *Epistola de tolerantia: A letter concerning toleration* (1689), 64 f, quoted and translated by Oberman 2010, 16. See also Marshall 2006. More in general Louthan, Cohenand & Szabo 2001; Ragnow and Phillips Jr. 2011; Grell and Scribner 2002.
55. Beneke 2008; Pellegrino 2013.
56. Kaplan 2007, chapter 8.
57. Bély 2007, 248–255; von Greyerz 2008; Nexon 2009; Schilling 2007.
58. Wangerman 2011, 209–218.
59. Kaplan 2007; Onnekink 2009.
60. Van Rooden 1996.
61. Jacobs 2009 (in contrast to the more conventional, romanticized view in Shorto 2004). Elsewhere the picture is mixed: in Southeast-Asian Dutch colonies, Catholics were not tolerated – they were suspected of being allies of the Portuguese or Spanish – but Jews and dissenters usually were. In the Dutch Republic itself Jews enjoyed a relatively privileged position.
62. Kooi 2012.
63. See Muchembled 2006–2007.
64. Bély 2007, 481.
65. *Mémoires sur le grand projet de Henri le Grand pour établir en Europe une police générale, un arbitrage permanent, une protection réciproque entre les souverains chrétiens*, 1638, in *Mémoires*, Vil. III, 168–169 (quoted in Spector 2011, 45). The context of Sully's plan is analyzed in Bély 2007, 103–130; Roberts 2013 (who, however, seems unaware of Sully's peace plan).
66. Gollwitzer 1952, 44–45.
67. Emeric Crucé, *The New Cyneas*, ed. and trans. by Thomas Willing Balch, Philadelphia: Allen, Lane and Scott, 1909, xv (orig. *Nouveau Cynée ou Discours d'Estat représentant les occasions et moyens d'establir une paix générale et la liberté de commerce pour tout le monde*, 1623, 57). See Fenet 2004; van Heerikhuizen 2008; Mansfield 2014.

68. William Penn, *An Essay towards the Present and Future Peace of Europe by the Establishment of an European Dyet, Parliament, or Estates*, London, 1693 in William Penn, *The Political Writings of William Penn*, introduction and annotations by Andrew R. Murphy (Indianapolis: Liberty Fund, 2002), Section 2. Accessed from http://oll.libertyfund.org/title/893 on 2013-11-11. On the association of justice and peace see Kater 2006.

69. Ibid.

70. Charles-Iréné Castel de Saint-Pierre, *A Project for Settling an Everlasting Peace in Europe* (London, [1714]), ii, viii–ix (orig. *Projet pour rendre la paix perpetuelle en Europe*, Utrecht, 1713–1717, 3 vol.), xix–xxi.

71. Schröder 2012, 35–50.

72. Pernot 2003.

3 Enlightenment, Revolution and the Evaporating Dream of a Perpetual Peace

1. Novalis, *Christianity or Europe: A Fragment* (orig. *Die Christenheit oder Europa. Ein Fragment*, 1799) in Beiser 1992, 77.

2. For a compelling assessment see especially Bukovansky 2009.

3. Johann Gottfried Herder, *Briefe zu Beförderung der Humanität* (1793–1797), trans. Michael N. Foster, Herder: Philosophical Writings, Cambridge, University Press, 2002, 365, quoted in Nakhimovsky 2011, 17.

4. Kater 2006, especially 18–19.

5. See Knutsen 2007; Van De Haar 2008.

6. Gat 2013, 132–243. Modern socio-political theories define the nation differently, mainly as a product of modern communications and theorizing (for an overview see Smith 1998, 70–96). Gat's assessment has more eye for historical contextualization and is far more in accordance with historical evidence. In the seventeenth and eighteenth century, the terms 'state' and 'nation' were used interchangeably.

7. Burbank and Cooper 2010, 219.

8. In contrast to the East India Company (EIC), the major companies had already collapsed before 1800 (the Dutch *Vereenigde Oost-Indische Compagnie* in 1799 and the French *Compagnie des Indes orientales et chinoises* in 1793); the British government took over the EIC's possessions in Asia only in 1858.

9. Cf. Burbank and Cooper 2010.

10. Middell and Naumann 2010. Even as late as the 1880s, private companies were given sovereign rights to rule European colonies in Africa and Asia. Koskenniemi 2001, 117.

11. Gollwitzer 1951, 71ff.

12. Compare Moyn 2010.

13. On the concept of 'Ossianic' see Loriaux 2008, 20 (and passim).

14. Spector 2013, 371–393.

15. Jean-Jacques Rousseau, *A Lasting Peace through the Federation of Europe*; and *The State of War* (1756), trans. Charles Edwyn Vaughan, London: Constable and Co., 1917.

16. The project is presented as a general European project in Tschubardjan 1992 (unfortunately without proper referencing), quotation 48. Other authors

rather present it as a Polish–Lithuanian–Russian federation (e.g. Borodziej, Brzostek and Górny 2005, 45).

17. See supra the plan of V.F. Malinowski, who was one of his main collaborators. On Czartoryski's ideas, see Borodziej, Brzostek and Górny 2005, 44 ff; Horel 2009, 295–296; 332–335, on his significance and influence on Tsar Alexander I, Rey 2003 and Jarrett 2014, (here) 37–42 and passim.
18. Quoted in Jarrett 2014, 41.
19. Quoted in Wolff 1994, 358 (orig. *Memoires*, 1859, vol. I, 300).
20. Custine, *Lettres de Russie*, 1839, cit. Wolff 1994, 365.
21. Gollwizter 1951, 81–84.
22. Cavallar 2006, 12–34; Kater 2006; Mazower 2012, 15–18. English quotations from Immanuel Kant, *Toward Perpetual Peace and Other Writings on Politics, Peace, and History*, edited and with an introduction by Pauline Kleingeld, translated by David L. Colclasure, with essays by Jeremy Waldron, Michael W. Doyle and Allen W. Wood, Haven (Conn.): Yale University Press, 2005.
23. Burgdorf 1994, 401–408.
24. Jeremy Bentham, *The Principles of International Law*, essay 4: *Plan for an Universal and Perpetual Peace* (orig. 1789) in *The works of Jeremy Bentham, Now First Collected under the Superintendence of John Bohring*, William Tait: Edinburgh, 1839, Part VIII, 546–560, 548.
25. Eze 1997, 103–140; Kleingeld 2007; Muthu 2003; McCarthy 2008, 42–68.
26. Marie-Jean-Antoine-Nicolas Caritat, Marquis de Condorcet, *Outlines of an Historical View of the Progress of the Human Mind, Being a Posthumous Work of the Late M. de Condorcet* (Translated from the French) (Philadelphia, 1796) (orig. *Esquisse d'un tableau historique des progrès de l'esprit humain*, 1794) (Accessed from http://oll.libertyfund.org/title/1669 on 2013-08-22).
27. Dicke 2006, 41–42.
28. Quoted in Voyelle 2003.
29. Kant, *Perpetual Peace*, in *Kant's Political Writings*, Hans Reiss, ed. H. B. Nisbet, trans. Cambridge: Cambridge University Press, 1970, 104, also quoted in Nakhimovsky 2011, 66.
30. Herder, *Briefe zu Beförderung der Humanität* (1793–1797), trans. Foster, *Herder: Philosophical Writings*, quoted in Nakhimovsky 2011, 17. On Herder's view, see Muthu 2003, 210–258.
31. Nakhimovsky 2011, 15–62 (quotation 17).
32. *Mémorial de Saint-Hélène*, by Emmanuel de Las Cases, E. Boudin: Paris 1942, vol. II, 417 (1816).
33. Edmund Burke, *Two Letters Addressed to A Member of the Present Parliament, on the Proposals for Peace with the Regicide Directory of France by the right honourable Edmund Burke*, vol. III: *Letters on a Regicide Peace*, London: F and C Rivington, 1796, 104 (Letter II: 'On the Genius and Character of the French Revolution as it regards other Nations'). It is easily overlooked that France was not yet a modern nation, and regional allegiances largely eclipsed national ones.
34. Burgdorf 1994, 403–405; Gollwitzer 1951, 114 ff. Compare Loriaux 2008 and supra, 23–24.
35. Burbank and Cooper 2010, 225 ff.
36. Broers 1996; Broers, Hicks and Guimera 2012; Englund 2008.
37. Compare Steven Englund's harsh criticisms (2008, especially 227–250) of Michael Broers' view on Napoleon's politics as a colonial civilizing mission.

38. See for example Jean Jaurès, *Histoire socialiste de la Révolution française*, rééd. présentée par A. Soboul, Editions Sociales, Paris 1968 (orig. 1901). Non-French observers and historians see in the French conquest a little more than an ordinary imperial war: for example, Blanning 1983; Forrest 1988.

39. Karl Christian Friedrich Krause, *Entwurf eines europäischen Staatenbundes*, 1814, cit. in Cavallar 2006, 46.

40. Tschubardjan 1992, 62–66.

41. A. Thierry, *L'industrie* (1817), quoted by Piguet 1993.

42. A. de Saint-Simon and A. Thierry, *De la réorganisation de la société européenne ou de la nécessité et des moyens de rassembler les peuples de l'Europe en un seul corps politique en conservant à chacun son indépendance nationale*, Adrian Egrion: Paris, 1814, 60. For an original assessment see Lützeler 1982, 25–29; 283–310 and Thompson 1994, 55.

43. Burgdorf 1994; Loriaux 2008. On Gentz see Zimmermann 2012; Dorn 1993; Bond 1973. These depict a quite different portrait of Gentz from Golo Mann's *Friedrich von Gentz* (1947).

44. Quoted by De Rougemont 1962, 192; Thompson 1994, 56.

45. Benjamin Constant, *De l'esprit de conquête et de l'usurpation dans leur rapports avec la civilisation européenne*, Le Normant: Paris, 1813.

46. Fontana 2002.

47. Novalis, *Christianity or Europe: A Fragment* (orig. *Die Christenheit oder Europa. Ein Fragment*, 1799) in Beiser 1992, 59–80. On Novalis and other Romantic visions of Europe see extensively Lützeler 1982 and Svenungsson 2014. Our assessment, however, is mainly inspired by Thompson 1994 and Kleingeld 2008.

48. Edmund Burke, *Two Letters* (...), 113, 135 (letter I: 'On the Overtures of Peace'). On Burke's view see Welsh 1996.

49. *Kritische Friedrich-Schlegel-Ausgabe*, edited by Ernst Behler, München, 1958, vol. VII, 208, quoted by Timms 1991, 904.

50. For an extensive and penetrating discussion of Fichte's views in this respect, there is no better place than Nakhimovsky 2011.

51. Nakhimovsky 2011, especially 63–84.

52. See especially Friedrich von Gentz, *Fragments upon the Balance of Power in Europe*, M. Peltier: London, 1806 (orig. *Fragmente aus der neusten Geschichte des politischen Gleichgewichts in Europa*, Johann Friedrich Hartkoch, St. Petersburg 1806).

53. Gollwitzer 1951, 128–145.

54. Paternó 2009.

55. Kater 2006, 10–13.

56. Spreen 2006, 135–156.

4 Peace during the Concert

1. Richard Cobden, *The Political Writings of Richard Cobden*, with a Preface by Lord Welby, Introductions by Sir Louis Mallet, C.B., and William Cullen Bryant, Notes by F.W. Chesson and a Bibliography, 2 vols. (London: T. Fisher Unwin, 1903), vol. 1, 214 (http://oll.libertyfund.org/titles/173, 22 October 2014).

2. Especially, Henry Kissinger 1957 is responsible for the positive image of the Concert's 'realist' power balance. See also Soutou 2000. For a strident critique of this appreciation, see Anderson 2007. The standard assessment is Jarrett 2013. See also Duchhardt 2013.
3. Cf. supra, 36–37, 47.
4. Cf. supra, 37.
5. Karsh and Karsh 2001, 17.
6. Quoted in Bély 2007, 663.
7. Jarrett 2014, 184–197.
8. Soutou 2000. Compare Jarrett 2014.
9. Leopold von Ranke, *Über die Epochen der neueren Geschichte*, München/Leipzich, 1921 (orig. 1854), 143, quoted by Kaelble 2001, 56.
10. Nakhimovsky 2001 discusses the issue in detail. On Constant, however, see Dicke 2006, 39–41.
11. Especially in his *De l'état de la France, à la fin de l'an VIII* (1800). See Nakhimovsky 2007, 84–98.
12. On List's ideas and reception see Wendler, 2013 and 1996.
13. Stråth 2008, 171–183. See also the references in note 12. On Mitteleuropa see more extensively Brechtefeld 1996; Elvert 2003; Mommsen 1995; Schmidt 2001; Stirk 1994. On List, see Henderson 1983; Szporluk 1988.
14. The German concept Mitteleuropa diverges considerably from the English 'Central Europe' (or the French *Europe centrale*), which in German is rather called *Zwischeneuropa*. Okey 1992; Sinnhuber 1954, 27.
15. See Konrad von Schmidt-Phiseldeck, *Europa und Amerika oder die künftigen Verhältnisse der zivilisierten Welt*, 1820 (written in German but translated into Danish, Dutch, French and Swedish); *Der europäische Bund*, 1821 and *Die Politik nach den Grundsätzen der heiligen Allianz*, 1822. See Bech-Petersen 1998, 441–460 (especially 446–447); Borodziej et al. 2005, vol. 2, 38–49; Cavallar 2006, 49–55.
16. Mattli 2001, 108–128; Hahn 1984.
17. For a recent overview of different ways to conceive of the relationship between religion and nationalism, see Brubaker 2012, 2–20 and Kennedy 2009.
18. Wojciech Jastrzębowski, *Traktat o Wiecznym Przymierzu Miedzy Narodami Ucywilizowanymi: Konstytucja dla Europy* [The treatise on the Eternal Union between the Civilized Nations: the Constitution for Europe], Warsaw, 1831. Parts of it are translated and edited in Loew 2004, 59–91. See Morawiec 2012.
19. Loew 2004; *Europe of Free Nations* 2008.
20. Recchia and Urbinati 2013, 14.
21. Bayly and Biagini 2008; Hobsbawm 1990, 31.
22. See in particular the discussion in Mazower 2012, 48–54.
23. Krejčí 2007, 217–220. Compare Fitzpatrick 2011, 1–24.
24. Thompson 1994.
25. Loew 2004; *Europe* 2008.
26. Romsics 2005, 137–142.
27. Horel 2007; 2009; Krejčí 2005, 217–220; Romsics 2005 143–145; Timms 1991; Vermeersch 2004.
28. Krejčí 2005, 198–226.
29. Cf. Grossi 2003 and Ousselin 2006.

30. Durchhardt 2005.
31. Julius Fröbel, 'Wien, Deutschland und Europa' (1848) in Borodziej et al. 2005, vol. III, 45–72 (51).
32. Kaelble 2001, 55.

5 Between Empire, Market and Nation

1. Richard Cobden, *Speeches on Questions of Public Policy by Richard Cobden, M.P.*, ed. John Bright and J.E. Thorold Rogers [...], London: T. Fisher Unwin, 1908, vol. 1, 41.
2. J.R. Seeley, 'The United States of Europe', *Macmillan's Magazine*, 23 (1871) 441–444 (443).
3. Charles-Henri Vergé, 'Le droit des gens avant et depuis 1789', xlvi, in Georg Friedrich Martens, *Précis du droit des gens moderne de l'Europe* [...], Guillaumin et Cie: Paris, 1864, quoted by Koskenniemi 2001, 28.
4. Durchhardt 2005, 24.
5. Langhorne 1984.
6. 'I have always found the word "Europe" in the mouths of those politicians who wanted from other powers something they did not dare to demand in their own name.' Bismarck, *Varziner Diktat*, 9 November 1876, quoted in Hildebrand 2008, 44.
7. Mattli 2001, 108–128; Hahn 1984.
8. Winifred Taffs, 'Conversations between Lord Odo Russell and Andrássy, Bismarck and Gorchakov in September, 1872', *The Slavonic and East European Review*, 8: 2 (1930) 701–707 (703–704), also quoted in Steinberg 2011, 328.
9. Quotations from Krüger 2006, 98.
10. Sieg 2007, 173ff.
11. The distinction has been famously coined by Hans Kohn, but is ideal-typical at best. See Gat 2013, 260ff. for a recent reappraisal, as well as Ther 2011, 24–49.
12. Weber, 1976.
13. Horel 2009, 67–84.
14. See Burbank and Cooper 2010, for a general discussion.
15. Maleševića 2012, 31–63.
16. For this paragraph, see Fink 2004, 3–66; Ther 2011, 29–64.
17. Fink 2004, 3–38.
18. Ther 2011, 57–64.
19. Ther 2011, 69–86. On the minorities question, see Fink 2006.
20. The question has generated much debate. See for a recent state of the art Berghahn 2006; Kühne 2013; Stratton 2003.
21. McLeod 2000.
22. Ther 2011.
23. McLeod 1998.
24. Clark and Kaiser 2003.
25. On the 'Black International', see Lamberts 2002.
26. On the integration of Catholics see especially Bennette 2012; Kennedy 2008, 104–134, 561–562.

27. Kalyvas 1993. See also Clark and Kaiser 2003.
28. Gustav von Blome, *Wo ist Europas Zukunft?* Herder: Freiburg im Bresgau, 1871. On Blome and the Black International, see Lamberts 2012 (on Blome's European view 199–201) and Lamberts 2002. For the continuing legacy of Christendom, see Perkins 2004.
29. Blaschke 2002; Clark and Kaiser 2003.
30. McLeod 1998.
31. Anderson 2001, 231–238; Altermatt 1999; Blaschke 1997; Hanebrink 2006.
32. Reinalda 2009; Lyons, 1963; Sluga, 2013.
33. Strikwerda 1993.
34. Strikwerda 1998.
35. Flandreau 2000.
36. Berend 2012, 288–314.
37. Michel Chevalier, 'La guerre et la crise européenne', *Revue des Deux Mondes*, 36:63 (1866) 758–785; Arcidiacono 2005.
38. Marsh 1999, 191.
39. Marsh 1999; Mattli 2001, 129–138 (quotation 135).
40. Joseph R. Seeley, *The Expansion of England*, The University of Chicago Press: Chicago and London, 1971(orig. 1883), 62. On Seeley's view on a federal 'Greater Britain', see Bell 2007.
41. Jules Huret, *En Amérique: De New-York à la Nouvelle-Orléans*, Bibliothèque-Charpentier/ Eugène Fasquelle: Paris, 1907, 107; Du Rhéau 1996, 67.
42. Mattli 2001, 129–138 (quotation 135).
43. Walther Rathenau, *Gesammelte Schriften in fünf Bänden*, vol. 1, S. Fischer, Berlin, 1918, 276–278. See Mattli 2001, 129–138 and Stevenson 2012, 843. On Rathenau see Gall 2009; Volkov 2012.
44. Norman Angell, *Europe's Optical Illusion*, London: Simpkin, Marshall, Hamilton, Kent & Co., 1909 (subsequent editions carry the title of *The Great Illusion*).
45. J.R. Seeley, 'The United States of Europe', *Macmillan's Magazine*, 23 (1871) 441–444. See also Burgess 2000, 133.
46. Guieu 2007, 387–388.
47. On Victor Hugo's Europeanism, see Grossi 2003, 49–74 and Ousselin 2006. Quotation in Victor Hugo, 'L'Avenir', 1867 (Victor Hugo, *Oeuvres complètes, Actes et Paroles*, vol. IV, p. 295).
48. Charles Lemonnier, *Les Etats-Unis d'Europe*, Paris: Librairie de la bibliothèque démocratique, 1872 (http://gallica.bnf.fr/ark:/12148/bpt6k114580t.r=.langFR .swf); Anteghini, Petricioli and Cherubini 2003.
49. Kuk 2003.
50. James Lorimer, 'Le Problème Final du Droit International', *Revue de Droit International*, 9:2 (1877) 161–206.
51. Francis Lieber, *Fragments of Political Science on Nationalism and Inter-Nationalism*, Charles Scribner & Co.: New York, 1868.
52. Johann Caspar Bluntschli, 'Die Organisation des Europäischen Staatenvereines', *Gesammelte kleine Schriften*, vol. II, Beck: Nördlingen, 1881. See the discussion in Arcidiacono 2005, 18–22; 2012; 13–26; Koskenniemi 2001, 42–53 and Röben 2003.
53. Sheehan 2008, 42–44.

54. Koskenniemi 2001, 67–76; Mazower 2012, 65–93. See also Anghie 2005 for an analysis of the development of international law in relation to colonial realities.

55. Jean-Baptiste-André Godin, *Le Gouvernement, ce qu'il a été, ce qu'il doit être et le vrai socialisme en action*, Guillaumin & cie/Auguste Ghio: Paris, 1883, 335–345 (art. 32, 342)

56. Paul d'Estournelles de Constant, 'La Chine et la diplomatie européenne', *Le Temps*, 7 July 1900.

57. Victor Hugo, 'Discours sur l'Afrique', 1879 (*Actes et Paroles*, Volume 4: www.gutenberg.org/etext/8490#sthash.8xGrzf8K.dpuf).

58. Camparini 2003, 240–261. Jaurès would soon lose hope, however, especially after the Russo-Japanese war of 1906.

59. Chabot 2005, 37–42.

60. Koskenniemi 2001, 216 ff.

61. For example, the international conference of political sciences in Paris in 1900 (*Institut des sciences politiques*): *Les Etats-Unis d'Europe*, Paris: Société d'imprimerie et de librairie, 1901 (rapport de synthèse); Anatole Leroy-Beaulieu, *Les Etats-Unis d'Europe*; André Fleury, *Y-a-t-il des intérêts spéciaux à l'Europe?*; René Dollot, *Comment les intérêts spéciaux à l'Europe ont-ils été jusqu'à présent sauvegardés?*; Paul Lefébure, *Y-a-t-il lieu de modifier la situation actuelle?*; Henry de Montardy, *Peut-on trouver un mode particulier de trancher les litiges internationaux?*; and Gaston Isambert, *Projet d'organisation politique d'une confédération européenne*.

62. Pierre-Joseph Proudon, *Du Principe fédératif et de la nécessité de reconstituer le Parti de la Révolution*, Paris: E. Dentu, 1863, 88. See extensively Voyenne 1973.

63. Adler 2003.

64. Constantin Frantz, *Untersuchungen über das europäische Gleichgewicht*, 1859; *Die Weltpolitik unter besonderer Bezugnahme auf Deutschland*, 3 vol., 1882. See Durchhardt 2005, 26–27; Stråth 2008, 179–180; Mommsen 1995; Schmidt, 55–56 2001; Brechtefeld 1996; Elvert 2003. On Frantz, see Ehmer 1988; Weitzmann, 1998, 36–60 and on his anti-Semitic ideas, elsewhere largely ignored, Dreyer 2009.

65. Vermeiren 2013, 140–141.

66. Schulze Wessel 2011; von Hirschhausen 2009.

67. Borodziej, Brzostek and Górny 2005, 69–72; Górny 2005, 189–196.

68. Aurel Popovici, *Die Vereinigten Staaten von Groß-Österreich. Politische Studien zur Lösung der nationalen Fragen und staatrechtlichen Krisen in Österreich-Ungarn*, B. Elischer: Leipzig, 1906.

69. Romsics 2005, 148–151.

70. Berki 1989; Berger and Smith 1999; Pasture and Verberckmoes 1998, 1–42.

71. Borodziej, Brzostek and Górny 2005, 74–81.

72. Otto Bauer, *The Question of Nationalities and Social Democracy*, ed. Ephraim Nimni, trans. by Joseph O'Donnell, University of Minnesota Press: Minneapolis, 2000, 414 (orig. *Die Nationalitätenfrage und die Sozialdemokratie*, 1907).

73. Nimni 1999; Sandner 2005; Strong 1992; Reifowitz 2009.

74. Hiden and Smith 2006, 389.

75. Said 1997, 123–148.

76. Simoni 2003.
77. Maleševića 2012; Reynolds 2011 (rectify the standard narrative that overemphasizes nationalism and bring imperial policies back into the analysis).
78. Nico van Schendelen, *Voorstel tot vorming van een Europeesche Stalenbond*, Amsterdam 1914; id. *Europa eendrachtig*, Amsterdam, 1915. Cf. Dumoulin and Stélandre 1992, 17–23 (extract).
79. Boleslaw Limanowski, *Naród i państwo. Studium socjologiczne*, Kraków 1906.
80. Chabot 2005, 38–42.

6 The Long War

1. Norman Angell, *The Fruits of Victory: A Sequel to 'The Great Illusion'*, The Century: New York, 1921, xxxi.
2. Chenaux 2007, 42–46.
3. Tooze 2014.
4. Cf. Pasture 2001.
5. Quoted by Stevenson 2012, 844.
6. Vermeiren 2013, 150–151.
7. Friedrich Naumann, *Mitteleuropa*, Georg Reimer: Berlin, 1915. On this publication and its impact, and WW I views on Mitteleuropa see Brechtefeld 1996; Elvert 2003; Kurlander 2012; Mommsen 1995; Schmidt 2001, 55–56; Stevenson 2012; Stråth 2008, 179–180.
8. Comp. Vermeiren 2013.
9. Mogk 1972.
10. Vermeiren 2013, 144–147.
11. Romsics 2005, 150–153.
12. Quotation from a confidential memorandum, written by Tomas G. Masaryk for British friends and members of the British government in April 1915, in Seton-Watson 1943, 117.
13. Thomas G. Masaryk, *The New Europe: The Slav Standpoint*, Bucknell University Press: Lewisburg, 1972, 77 (orig. London, Eyre and Spottiswoode, 1918).
14. Thomas G. Masaryk, *The Making of a State*, tr. H. W. Steed, Frederick A. Stokes: New York, 1927, 429–435.
15. Gottfried 2007; Krejčí 2005, 227–250; Timms 1991.
16. Soutou 1989; Stevenson 2012, 852–857. On the negotiations between France, Belgium and Luxemburg, see extensively Bussière 1992.
17. Schwarz 1995, 202–229.
18. Quoted in Jackson 2012, 169.
19. Mazower 2012, 116–153.
20. Richmond 2006, 376.
21. Borodziej, Brzostek and Górny 2005, 89–92; Morawiec 2012, 3–10.
22. A more positive evaluation in Namont 2009, 45–56.
23. Jackson 2012.
24. Fink 2006, 273–278 (and passim); Mazower 2012,159–162; Soutou 2000.
25. Cf. Manela 2007; Throntveit 2011.
26. Mazower 1989, 40 ff; Ther 2011, 69–89.
27. Fink 2006, 295 ff; Bailey 2013, 38–39.
28. Amato 2013 and Gioli 2007; Dini and D'Auria 2013.

29. Attilio Cabiati and Giovanni Agnelli, *Federazione European o Lega delle Nazioni*, Bocca: Torino, 1918. The book is discussed extensively in Pinder 1998.
30. Bariéty 2003.
31. Paul Otlet, *Constitution mondiale de la Société des Nations: Le nouveau droit des gens, Atar/G. Cres et Cie*: Genève and Paris, 1917, quoted in Guieu 2007, 391.
32. Jackson 2012, especially 133–162 and passim.
33. On the perceptions of the other in this context, see especially Kaelble 2001. The importance of these representations is particularly emphasized by Bailey 2013.
34. Dini and D'Auria 2013, 11–26.
35. Max Scheler, *Der Genius des Kriegs und der Deutsche Krieg*, Verlag der Weißen Bücher: Leipzig, 1915 (chapter 'Die geistichegeistige Einheit Europas und ihre politische Förderung', 251–441). See Gollwitzer 1951, 4–5.
36. Chenaux 2007, 42–43; Racine 1993, 52–69 (especially on René Guénon, *Orient et Occident*, Payot: Paris, 1924).
37. *Pour que l'Europe soit*, written in 1915 but published in 1930.
38. Chabot 2005, 59–61 (quotation from Joseph Caillaux, *Ma doctrine*, Flammarion: Paris, 1926, 237, quoted p. 61).
39. Koskenniemi, *Gentle Civilizer*, 266 ff.
40. See Berki 1989, 41–64; Chabot 2005, 99–103; Pasture 2001.
41. Griffin 2008, 136–138.
42. Godefroid Kurth, 'Les Etats-Unis d'Europe', handwritten note dated 1916, published in Duchenne 2001, 44 (as Kurth fell deathly ill at the end of December 1915 and passed away on 4 January 1916, the note must have been written earlier).
43. Müller 2005, 309–456; Gusejnova 2013, 111–133. On Rohan, the *Europäische Kulturbund* and the *Revue européenne* see furthermore Bailey 2013; Conze 2005; Schulz 2010; Gottfried 2007; Ziegerhofer-Prettenthaler 2013.
44. Karl Anton Rohan, *Europa*, Leipzig, 1923, 21–30.
45. Curzio Malaparte, *L'Europa vivente*, Roma, 1923 (I consulted the French translation *L'Italie contre l'Europe*, Félix Alcan: Paris, 1927).
46. Karl Anton Rohan, 'Die Utopie des Pazifismus', in Karl Anton Rohan, *Umbruch der Zeit, 1923–1930*, G. Stilke: Berlin, 1930, 23 (quoted in Ziegerhofer-Prettenthaler 2013, 167).
47. Certainly, the *Europäische Kulturbund* appealed particularly to conservatives but its members and supporters also included the liberal Heidelberg economist, geographer and cultural sociologist Alfred Weber (the brother of the famous sociologist Max Weber), the French writers Paul Valéry and Jules Romains, the Spanish essayist José Ortega y Gasset, the expressionist painter Max Beckmann, the German author and pacifist Anna Kolb, the Belgian socialist Jules Destrée, the physicist Marie Curie and the French radical-socialist Marcel Déat, who in the 1930s would become the leader of the neo-socialists. Incidentally, one should not overemphasize the French title of the association, though it does point to the continuing confusion between Europeanism and internationalism, illustrating the fundamentally Eurocentric and colonial perspective of these Europeanists.
48. Griffin 2008, quotation 151. See Lecarme 2001 for a critical biography.
49. Conze 2005, 27–110.

50. Carl Schmitt, *Römische Katholizismus und politische Form*, Hegner: Hellerau, 1923. For an assessment, see Untea 2012; McCormick 2003, 133–142. On Schmitt's life and significance, see Breuer 2012; Müller 2003.
51. Quoted in Vermeiren 2012, 135–154, 143. See also Guth 1973; Fossaluzza 2009 and Gutsche 2012.
52. Jackson 2012 (it is one of the main arguments and runs throughout the whole book).
53. Krüger 1989, 87; 1984.
54. Jackson 2012, 323–356; Jeannesson 1998.
55. Krüger 1989, 89–90.
56. On the failure of the conference of Genoa, see Petricioli 1995.
57. Kent 1992, quotation 376.
58. Manigand 2003.
59. Müller 2005, 54–80.
60. Schonfield 2012, 257–270.
61. On Coudenhove-Kalergi and Paneuropa, see Schöberl 2010; Ziegerhofer-Prettenthaler 2004; Ziegerhofer-Prettenthaler 2012, 89–109; Ziegerhofer-Prettenthaler 2013; Holl 2002, 11–73. For a French perspective, see Saint-Gille 2003 (French historiography gives a far more positive image of Coudenhove-Kalergi's personality, movement and influence than Germanic authors, who emphasize the authoritarian character of the man, the conflicts with other movements, his lack of success and his flirting with Austro-Fascism in the 1930s.
62. Richard Nicolaus Coudenhove-Kalergi, *Pan-Europe*, A. A. Knopf: New York, 1926 (orig. 1923), quotations 8 and xiv.
63. Alfred Hermann Fried and Lewis S. Gannet, 'Pan Americanism as a Lesson for Europe', *The Advocate of Peace*, 78:1 (1916) 17–18; Alfred Hermann Fried, *Pan-Amerika*, Orell-Füssli: Zürich, 1910. See also Alfred Hermann Fried, *The Restoration of Europe*, trans. by Lewis Stiles Gannett, New York, Macmillan, 1916.
64. Richard N. Coudenhove-Kalergi, *Praktischer Idealismus: Adel – Technik – Pazifismus*, Paneuropa-Verlag, Wien/Leipzig, 1925, 23, 50.
65. Holl 1974, 36–38.
66. Holl 1974; Conze 2005, especially 210–219.
67. Chenaux 2007, 18–35; 52 ff; Durand 1995, 143–161. The radical nationalism of the *Action française* constituted an element of its condemnation by the Holy See in 1926.
68. Chenaux 2007, 15–35.
69. Müller 2005, 59–65.
70. Lorenzini 2013; Barry 2012, 128–152.
71. Pasture 1999, 87–90.
72. See also supra, on socialist party politics towards Europe.
73. Léon Jouhaux, 'The Trade Union Movement and World Peace', *The International Trade Union Movement*, 2:6 (November–December 1922) 310–326; Pasture 2001.
74. Edo Fimmen, *Labour's Alternative: The United States of Europe or Europe limited*, preface A.A. Purcell, The Labour Publishing Company: London, 1924. The text was published in several European languages.
75. Pasture 2001; Pegg, 38–39. Comp. Bailey 2013, 88–96.

76. Collected writings in Jules Destrée, *Pour en finir avec la guerre par une organisation fédérative de l'Europe, la constitution d'une police internationale et la reconnaissance pour les citoyens du droit de refuser le service militaire pour le crime de la guerre d'agression*, L'Eglantine:Brussels, 1931. Cf. Duchenne 2008, 289–290 (and passim).
77. However, even if they foresaw arbitration procedures, they did not provide the same guarantees for the eastern states, which would prove a fatal mistake.
78. Similarly Cohrs 2006.

7   Hope and Deception

1. Gustav Stresemann, quoted in *The Times*, 2 December 1925, 16.
2. Bugge 2002.
3. See especially Keiger 2004, 95–107. Briand refers explicitly to this politics of détente in *Le Temps*, 18 October 1925.
4. Conze 2005, 40.
5. See the references in the previous chapter.
6. Chabot 2005, 52–55; 111–118 (and passim). Heerfordt's main publications include *Une Europe nouvelle, premier essai* (1924), *Une Europe nouvelle I* and *Une Europe nouvelle II* (1926).
7. Wladimir Woytinsky, *Les Etats-Unis d'Europe*, Brussels: L'Eglantine, 1927 (orig. in German, 1926); John Pepper, *Les États-Unis de l'Europe socialiste*, Paris: Librarie de l'Humanité, [1926]. See Chabot 2005, 199–201; 239–241; 372. For the unions see Pasture 2001.
8. Guérin 1996.
9. Guieu 2007.
10. Cherubini 2007, Pasture 2001.
11. Meffre 2009. See also Spiering 2002.
12. Barthel 2004; Conze 2005, 272–273; Müller 2005, 81–308.
13. Schonfield 2012. See also Bock 2013.
14. Holl, 'Europapolitik', 39–43.
15. Bartel 1999, Chapter IV (131–192); Guieu 1998; 2003.
16. Pinder 1998, 204–207.
17. See for example Emil Lederer, 'Russland in der Weltpolitik', *Neue Rundschau*, 37:1 (1926) 566, 570 in Bailey 2013, 32.
18. Ibidem. On Riou see Badel 1999, Chapter IV.
19. Renée Arcos, 'Patrie européenne', *Europe*, 15 February 1923, quoted in Racine 1993, 56.
20. Francis Delaisi, *Les contradictions du monde moderne*, Payot, Paris, 1925, 551. See the assessment of Chabot 2005, 217 ff, especially 253 ff (on Delaisi, 256). Strangely, Chabot limits his assessment to 'rightist' authors, but the same clearly holds true for socialists.
21. Borodziej, Brzostek and Górny 2005, 93–96; Goddeeris 2012, 127.
22. On the European orientation of economic sectors in France, see Badel 1999.
23. Gustav Stresemann, *Rapports sur l'oeuvre accomplie par la Société des Nations depuis la dernière session de l'assemblée*, SDN. Journal Officiel, Supplément spécial, 75, 1926, 70, quoted in Vittorio and D'Auria 2013, 11–26, 24.

24. See in this respect, the different volumes of the book series edited by Schot and Scranton, 2013–2015.
25. Fischer 2012; Hewitson 2012, 15–34; Jackson 2012, 431–513; Steiner 2005, 241–243; Tooze 2014, 462–486.
26. Signatories include the former Secretary of State for Finance and President of the Hungarian National Bank Elemér Hantos, the French economist Charles Gide, the German journalist Edgar Stern-Rubarth, the British writer Norman Angell and the Dutchman Anton van Gijn, a former minister of finance. See Chabot 2005, 78–87; Badel 1993, Chapter IV; Du Rhéau 1996, 89–90; Horel 2007.
27. Citation from the 'Appeal to the Europeans', 12 March 1925, quoted in Chabot 2005, 78.
28. John Maynard Keynes, *Essays in Persuasion*, London: Macmillan, 1931, 24 quoted in Gioli 2007, 196.
29. Noman Angell, *The Fruits of Victory: A Sequel to 'The Great Illusion'*, W. Collins Sons & Co.: London, 1921, xxvii.
30. See also Muet 1997, 62–63.
31. Francis Delaisi, *Les contradictions du monde moderne*, Payot: Paris, 1925, especially 469–470. Important works of Delaisi were *Les contradictions du monde moderne* (Paris: Payot, 1925) and especially *Les deux Europe* (Paris: Payot, 1929), but his influence started much earlier. Pasture 1992, 43.
32. Dini and D'Auria 2013, 11–26 (quotation Walter Leaf 18).
33. Müller 2010, 89–94; Sachse 2010.
34. Bussière 1997; Bussière and Dumoulin 1994, 67–105. See also Berger 2006; Stirk 1996, 31–33; Wurm 1989.
35. Bussière 1992, 257, 287–326.
36. Barthel 2006.
37. Pasture 2001. On the fascination of European trade unions with the US, see Van Goethem 2000, 117–118 and Boyce 1989, especially 71.
38. Clavin 2013, 42 ff; D'Alessandro 2007.
39. Schirmann 2000, 31–50; Schirmann 2007, 73–92; Clavin 2013, 39–46. On the ILO more below.
40. Mechi 2012, 19 ff; Guérin 1996; Van Daele et al. 2010.
41. Cf. Keiger 2004.
42. Quoted in Hewitson 2012, 17.
43. On the Turkish reaction see Barlas and Güvenç 2009.
44. Cf. Kent 1992.
45. Prettenthaler-Ziegerhofer 2013, 173.
46. Telegram of Card. Marchetti-Selvaggiani to François Charles-Roux, (new) French Ambassador to the Holy See, 11 July 1932 quoted in Chenaux 2007, 35.
47. Quoted in Jansen and Van Hecke 201, 9–10. See also Kaiser 2007, 107–108.
48. Guieu 2007.
49. Pinder 1998, 204–207. The article of Winston Churchill, 'United States of Europe', *Saturday Evening Post* (New York), 15 February 1930.
50. Fischer 2012; 2011, 87–91. For the classic opposing view Krüger 1998, 289–306.
51. Kaelble 2001, 128–218.
52. Richard Coudenhove-Kalergi, 'Afrika', *Paneuropa* 5, 2 (1929) 3.

53. Jules Destrée, *Pour en finir avec la guerre par une organisation fédérative de l'Europe, la constitution d'une police internationale et la reconnaissance pour les citoyens du droit de refuser le service militaire pour le crime de la guerre d'agression*, L'Églantine: Brussels, 1931, quoted in Muet 1997, 122. See also Dumoulin and Stelandre 1992, 83–85 and Hansen and Johnson 2011, 450 (referring to E. L. Guernier, *L'Afrique: champ d'expansion de l'Europe*, 1933).
54. Antonsich 1997; Deschamps 1996.
55. Gall 1998; Hansen and Jonsson 2014, 60–64.
56. Hans Zache, *Für oder gegen Kolonien, Eine Diskussion in zehn Aufsätzen von Freuden und Gegnern des kolonialen Gedankens* (1928), quoted in Ageron 1975, 453.
57. Ageron 1975.
58. Schaeffer 2003, 367–387; Schirmann 2007; 2000, 95–122; Bussière 1992, 338–400.
59. Müller 2010, 102–104.
60. Guérin 1996; Mechi, 2012, 19 ff.
61. See especially Marcel Déat, *Perspectives socialistes*, Valois: Paris, 1930. A discussion in Lewis 1996, 26–37.
62. Pasture 2001.
63. Bailey 2013, 36–40.
64. The MWT would replace the MEWT (since 1926 *Mitteleuropäischen Wirtschaftstag*) in 1931. See Freytag 2012; Sachse 2010.
65. For example, Wilhelm Gürge und Wilhelm Grotkopp (eds), *Großraumwirtschaft, der Weg zur europäischen Einheit: ein Grundriss*, 'Organisation': Berlin, 1931.
66. Schirmann 2000, 109–122.
67. Romscics 2005, 156–165.
68. Horel 2007.
69. Gużkowski 2005, 247–268; Borodziej, Brzostek and Górny 2005, 96–99; Morawiec 2012, 10–12.
70. On the Customs Truce Conference and the Oslo Convention, see Bussière 1992, 405–413; Schirmann 2000, 109–122 and Van Roon 1989.
71. Bussière 1992, 423–454 provides a detailed analysis of the process which led to the failure of what he calls 'the first experience of a regional economic entente in Western Europe'.
72. Asvero Gravelli, quoted in Griffin 2008, 143.
73. Cofrancesco 1983, 5; Giustibelli 2002; 2006.
74. I borrow the term 'Eurofascism' from Lewis 1996, ix–x, though I do not follow all of Lewis' distinctions. 'Eurofascism', also labelled 'universal fascism' in the Italian case, and Euronazism (see below) should be considered ideal-typical.
75. Bauerkämper 2007; Griffin 2008, 132–180; Lewis 1996.
76. Bauerkämper 2007, 55.
77. Extensive discussions in Giustibelli 2006; 2002; Müller 2005, 424–436.
78. 'Voce Europa', a cura di E. Sestan, in *Enciclopedia italiana di scienze, lettere ed art*, Istituto G. Treccani, Milano 1932, vol. XIV, 645, quoted in Giustibelli 2002, 187–188.
79. See the discussion in Giustibelli 2006, 111–118.

80. Chenaux 2007, 54. See also Gonzague de Reynold, *L'Europe tragique*, Spes: Paris, 1934.
81. C. Dawson, 'The interracial cooperation as a factor in European culture', in *Atti dei convegni. Convegno di scienze morali e storiche, 14–20 novembre 1932*, XI. Tema: *L'Europa*, Reale Accademia d'Italia Fondazione Volta: Roma, 1933, 98–99, quoted in Giustibelli 2002, 232, note 79.
82. Bailey 2013, 38–40; Müller 2002, 385–456.
83. Conze 2005, 27–110.
84. Elvert 2003, 239 ff; Grunert 2012, 52–53; Schmoeckel 1994.
85. McCormick 2003; Untea 2012.
86. Bailey 2013, 42–45.
87. Extensively discussed in Koskenniemi 2001, 236 ff. See also Ferraro 2013.
88. Cf. Lewis 1996, ix.
89. Griffin 2008, 153.
90. *Documents*, vol. I, 12–13.
91. Vermeiren 2013, 152–155.
92. Hansen and Johnson 2001, 444.
93. Lewis 1996, 30–61.
94. Koskenniemi 2001, 418 ff; Stirk 1998.
95. Carl Schmitt, *Völkerrechtliche Großraumordnung mit Interventionsverbot für raumfremde Mächte: Ein Beitrag zum Reichsbegriff im Völkerrecht*, [1938] 1941, Duncker & Humblot: Berlin 1991; Stirk 1998.
96. Werner Daitz, *Der Weg zur völkischen Wirtschaft und zur europäischen Großraumwirtschaft*, Meinhold: Dresden, 1941; *Der weg zur vo¨lkischen Wirtschaft: europa¨ischen Großraumwirtschaft und gerechten Weltordnung*; Meinhold: Dresden, 1943.
97. Ageron 1975; Deschamps 1996.
98. Joachim von Ribbentrop, 'European Confederation, 1943', in *Documents*, vol. I, 122–127 (124).
99. Vermeiren 2013, 152–155.
100. Lewis 1996, 155 ff.
101. [Cécil von Renthe-Fink], 'Note for the Reich Foreign Minister', 1939, in *Documents*, vol. I, 55.
102. Ageron 1975.
103. A summary in Pasture 2007.
104. This whole section relies largely on the detailed assessment of Lewis 1996.
105. Francis Delaisi, *La Révolution européenne*, Les Éditions de la Toison d'Or: Brussels/Paris, 1942. See also Laughland 1997, 44–46.
106. Pierre Laval, radio speech on 22 June 1942 (*Les Nouveaux Temps*, 24 juin 1942, http://www.fonjallaz.net/MLH/Laval%20collaboration.html).
107. Lewis 1996, 37–40. On Abetz, see especially Ray 2000; Lambauer 2001.
108. Deakin 1962, 289–307; 323–50; Lewis 1996, 242–243.
109. Pulzer 2004.
110. For the personalists and the 'Non-Conformists of the 1930s' as well as their federalist ideas, see Loubet del Bayle 2001; Roy 1999; Vayssière 2003; Chenaux 2007, 59–81; Loughlin 1998; Laughland 1997, 663.
111. See especially Kaiser 2011, 61–71 and 119–162.
112. D'Auria 2013.
113. Bailey 2013, 92–103; 2010; Schilmar 2003.

114. For example, Minion 1998. See infra, 170–172 and 187.
115. Gillingham 2003, 10–11.
116. See especially Pinder 2005a.
117. Ernest Bevin, 'Impressions of the British Commonwealth Relations Conference, 1938,' *International Affairs*, 18 (1938), pp. 56–76 (quoted in Deighton 2006, 838).
118. Clarence K. Streit, *Union Now: A Proposal for a Federal Union of the Democracies of the North Atlantic*, Harper & Brothers: New York, 1939; George Orwell, 'Not Counting Niggers', *The Adelphi*, July 1939 (http://ebooks.adelaide.edu.au/o/orwell/george/not-counting-niggers/ retrieved 18 July 2014). I owe this reference to an anonymous contributor to the Wikipedia article on 'Union Now'.
119. Orwell, 'Not Counting Niggers', 5.

8 Pacification by Division

1. Ash 1999, 181 (the quote actually applies to the 1990s).
2. See even Winter 2008, 119.
3. Conway 2001; Lagrou 1997; 2000, 285.
4. Maurice Duverger, 'Naissance ou enterrement de l'Europe', *Le Monde*, 9 August 1949 (*Documents*, vol. 3, Doc. 34, 107–108).
5. *Documents*, Vol. I; Lipgens 1968. For recent assessments of the role of Lipgens c.s., see Kaiser and Varsori 2010.
6. http://www.altierospinelli.org/manifesto/en/manifesto1944en_en.html.
7. Blum 1941, 188.
8. Bailey 2010; 2013, 92–96.
9. Willy Brandt, *Stormaktenes krigsmal og det nye Europa*, 1940, quoted in Schilmar 2003, 210.
10. Mary Saran, *The Future Europe: Peace or Power Politics*, London, 1943, 24; 'The Old World and the New Order', *Socialist Commentary*, 18 April 1942, 9, quoted in Minion 1998, 11–12.
11. Minion 1998.
12. Loth 1995; WA Visser 't Hooft, *Memoirs*, SCM Press/Westminster Press: London and Philadelphia, 1971, 175–181.
13. Mioche 1995, 307–323.
14. Shlaim 1981; Gates 1981.
15. Grosbois 2007, 22; Goddeeris 2012; Lane and Wolanski 2009, 18–34.
16. Bianchini 2002, 197–210.
17. Delwit 1995.
18. Mastny 2002.
19. Bianchini 2002; Pavlovitsch 2002; Valdevit 2002.
20. Mastny 2002 and Borhi 2002, 171–183.
21. Petracchi 2002, 123–137.
22. At different points different political modalities were suggested for each of these regions – occupation by French and Belgians of the Ruhr, Allied control of the Rhineland and independence/association with France for the Sarre. See Guillen 1995; Lynch 1995, 459–467; Soutou 2002; Young 1995.
23. Quoted in Bossuat 1992, 76.

24. René Massigli. *Une comédie des erreurs 1943–1956: Souvenirs et réflexions sur une étape de la construction européenne*, Plon: Paris, 1978, 29, referring to a meeting on 17 July 1943. See also Guillen 1995, 153; Greenwood 1992; Lynch 1995; Soutou 2002; Young 1984; 1990; 1995.
25. Brugmans 1970, 91; Groisbois 1997, 106; Kent 2002, 40–58; Laptos 2003, 185.
26. This was an argument with a long history. See Laqua 2013.
27. On Belgian views of post-war Europe, see Grosbois 1994.
28. Groisbois 1997, 121.
29. The following assessment largely follows Schwabe 2002.
30. Bhambra 2009, 69–85; Dussel 2000, 465.
31. Sheehan 2008, 162–166.
32. Lundestad 2005.
33. Ther 2011 (quot. 144); Ther and Siljak 2001.
34. Cf. Weiner 2005.
35. Schroeder 2013; He 2009.
36. Mazower 2012, 212.
37. For example, Arne Jørgensen, 'Europaeisk Union' [European Union], *Freds-Bladet*, 57:2 (15 February 1948) 11–12 in Lipgens, vol. III, 584.
38. Di Biagio 2002, 297–305.
39. Leboutte 2008, 57; Samuels 1948.
40. Leboutte 2008, 111.
41. Soutou 2002.
42. Lane 2002, 219–228.
43. See extensively Mazower 1998.
44. Schwabe 2002.
45. Cox and Kennedy-Pipe 2005 and Trachtenberg 2005.
46. Ludlow 1977, 34 ff and supra, note xxx.
47. For example, Minion 1998.
48. Deighton 2007; Greenwood 1993; Young 2000, 6–16. On the colonial dimension see below, Chapter 9.
49. Arcidiacono 2002, 93–103.
50. Greenwood 1995. On British policies Kent 2002.
51. Quoted in Adamthwaite 2005, 122 and Kent 1992, 147, n. 70.
52. Griffiths 2014, 55–88, 57.
53. Narinskii 2002.
54. See especially Bossuat, 1992, 145–151.
55. Bianchini 2002, 197–210; Nathanaili 2003. On the Stalin–Tito split see Perović 2007, 32–63.
56. Rathkolb 2002, 306–318.
57. Leboutte 2008, 19–121.
58. Bossuat 1992, 141–175; Guillen 1995.
59. Griffiths, 2014, 55–88. Kaplan and Schleiminger 1998.
60. Di Nolfo 2002.
61. On the importance of such networks see the pioneering volumes of Gehler, Kaiser and Leucht 2009 and Kaiser, Leuch, and Gehler 2010.
62. Di Biagio 2002, 297–305.
63. Pistone 2008.
64. In *Temps Présent*, 19 October 1945, quoted in Durantin 1994, 347.

65. Quoted in Bailey 2013, 179–180.
66. Van Kemseke 2006, 39–41.
67. See especially Bailey 2013, 174–179. On Christian democracy in the beginning of the European integration process and the role of the NEI and the Geneva circle, see Kaiser 2007, 163–190, 209 and passim; Chenaux 1990; 2007; Jansen and Van Hecke 2011; Van Kemseke 2006, 37–46.
68. The importance of prewar Christian democratic connections is easily overstated, for example by Judt 2005, 157.
69. See especially Chenaux 1990.
70. Ibidem.
71. Bailey 2013, 179–183; Kaiser 2007, 178–179; Van Kemseke 2006, 37–49.
72. Leboutte 2008, 120–121.
73. Dumoulin and Dutrieue 1993.
74. Gillingham 2003, 6–15.
75. Bayley 2013, 172–183; Lundestad 2003, 78–81; *Congress of Europe: The Hague-May, 1948: Resolutions*, International Committee of the Movements for European Unity: London-Paris, 1948, 5–7. For the history of the Council of Europe, see Wassenberg, *Histoire*.
76. Buchanan 2010, 160–164. For a revisionist view on the ECHR, see Duranti 2013.
77. Bossuat 1997, 647.
78. Leboutte 2008, 107–162. For the reaction against American pressure, see Trachtenberg and Gehrz 2003.
79. Schuman Declaration, 9 May 1950 (http://europa.eu/about-eu/basic -information/symbols/europe-day/schuman-declaration/index_en.htm). The literature on the ECSC is extensive. Leboutte 2008, 107–162 integrates different perspectives. It should be complemented by the assessment of transnational interactions, as discussed in Gehler, Kaiser and Leucht 2009 and Kaiser, Leucht and Gehler 2011; Guilbert 2010.
80. Massigli 1978, 143.
81. Griffiths 2013, 154.
82. Cf. Knudsen 2009.

9 Epilogue: The EC's Colonial Empire

1. Victor Hugo, 'Discours sur l'Afrique', 1879 (*Actes et Paroles*, Volume 4: www .gutenberg.org/etext/8490#sthash.8xGrzf8K.dpuf).
2. De Bruin 2011. I was not able to consult De Bruin's published PhD dissertation on time for this book.
3. Quotations in Deighton 2007, 840–844.
4. On post-war British policies towards their empire and decolonization, see Heinlein 2013. For their policies towards European integration in general, see Young 1984; 2000 and the references quoted in the following notes.
5. Heinlein 2013, 137–43. On 'Plan G' see Ellison 1996; Schaad 1998.
6. Wall 2005, 133.
7. See Bossuat 1992, 521–611.
8. Moser 2000, 147–280. The issue of Eurafrica has received much scholarly attention in recent years: see especially Moser 2005; Bitch and Bossuat 2005 and Hansen and Jonson 2005; 2011; 2012; 2014.

9. Quoted in Hick 1991, 16.
10. Hansen and Johnson 2012, 1034.
11. Council of Europe, 1952, quoted in Hansen and Johnson 2012, 1034 (emphasis added PP).
12. Vandenweyer 2012.
13. Paul-Henri Spaak, *Combats Inachevés*, Fayard: Paris, 1969, vol. 2, 234–238; Vandenweyer 2012, 40.
14. Leikam 2009; Heinlein 2002.
15. Thiemeyer 2005.
16. Adamthwaite 2005; Wall 2005.
17. Not all colonies were lost, however: even the Netherlands maintained a colonial presence in Suriname and the Antilles, for example. Other examples include Portuguese Macau and British Hong Kong, to name but a few. France and the United Kingdom continued to include territories overseas, granting them different statuses.
18. See also Hansen and Johnsson 2013; Lagrou 2009. Bhambra 2009, Bossuat and Garavini 2010; 2012 indicate the turn.
19. Cf. Mishra 2012 (who, however, has an eye for the complexities of this inspiration).
20. L.-S. Senghor, 'L'Eurafrique, unité économique de l'avenir', *Nation et voie africaine du socialisme (Liberté II)*, Le Seuil: Paris, 1971, 93 (quoted in Dramé and Saul 2004, 7).
21. For a thorough revisionist critique of European human rights discourse, see Moyn 2010.
22. Tusan 2014.
23. *Congress of Europe: The Hague-May, 1948: Resolutions*. London-Paris: International Committee of the Movements for European Unity, 1948, 5–7.
24. Schuman declaration, 9 May 1950 (http://europa.eu/about-eu/basic-information/symbols/europe-day/schuman-declaration/index_en.htm).
25. Quoted in Vandenweyer 2012, 13–14.
26. Quoted in Moser 2000, 126. Comp. Hansen and Johnson 2011.
27. Kaiser 1996, especially 121–22; 129–130; Leikam 2009, 102 ff.
28. Monnet 1963.
29. Garavini 2010, 196. For a start of such a discussion, see Garavini 2012; Hansen 2002; Hansen and Johnson 2014. A publication on the continuity of this discourse is in the making, based on the excellent master's theses of Veronica Raszler (MAES, KULeuven, 2013), Helena Van Roosbroek (MAES, 2013) and Koen Vandenweyer (LSE, 2013).
30. Comp. Patel 2013 for some similar observations.
31. Keukeleire and Delreux 2014, 245–246.
32. Bickerton 2012.
33. A separate publication on this subject is in the making.
34. For a summary, see Keukeleire and Delreux 2014 (especially the conclusion 321–333).

Conclusion: In Search of European Unity

1. Dirk U. Stikker, *Men of Responsibility: A Memoir*, Murray: London, 1966, 156.

2. Herman Van Rompuy and José Emmanuel Barroso, 'From War to Peace: A European tale', Acceptance speech of the Nobel Peace Award to the European Union, Oslo, 10 December 2012 (http://ec.europa.eu/news/pdf/131120_en.pdf).
3. Brague 2009.
4. Illustrative are the many textbook overviews, including very recent ones such as Dinan 2014; Krüger 2006; Prettenthaler-Ziegerhofer 2012. Things are changing though, as illustrated by the publications of Gurminder Bhambra, Gerard Bossuat, Giuliano Garavini, Peo Hansen, et al. Studies on European identity seem more attentive to colonial issues, for example Pedersen 2008; Schmale 2008.
5. Collins 2013.
6. On the evolution of the different perceptions of the US, see Kaelble 2001.
7. Guilbert 2010.
8. Zielonka 2006. The term is not well chosen, as this model of empire was not introduced in Münster in 1648, but much later, with the First French Empire of Napoleon Bonaparte as first example.
9. For an informed discussion on empires in a global historical perspective, see Burbank and Cooper 2010. With regard to European empires, see also Ghervas 2014.
10. Van Middelaar 2013.
11. Bickerton 2012.
12. Gilbert 2007; Patel 2013.
13. Sassatelli 2009, 19 ff.
14. Compare Nirenberg 2013.
15. Kraus and Sciortino 2014; Sassatelli 2009, 41; Stråth 2002, 390.
16. John Hume, 'Nobel Lecture', Oslo, 10 December 1998. http://www.nobelprize.org/nobel_prizes/peace/laureates/1998/hume-lecture.html (consulted 24 November 2014).
17. Lucassen 2005 discusses these issues of continuity and discontinuity.
18. Landfried 2011.
19. Cf. supra, 52.
20. Not any longer, it seems: see Jarausch and Lindenberger 2007; Müller 2002.

Literature

Abu-Lughod, Janet L. *Before European Hegemony: The World System A.D. 1250–1350*. Oxford, 1989.

Adamthwaite, Anthony. 'Britain, France, the United States and Euro-Africa, 1945–1949', in Bitsch and Bossuat 2005, 118–132.

Adler, Jasna. 'Comment faire régner la paix dans les Balkans? "Les Etats-Unis d'Europe" et les Balkans, 1867–1913', in Anteghini, Petricioli and Cherubini 2003, 345–368.

Ageron, Charles-Robert. 'L'idée d'Eurafrique et le débat colonial franco-allemand de l'entre-deux-guerres', *Revue d'histoire moderne et contemporaine*, 22:3 (1975) 446–475.

Al-Azmeh, Aziz. 'Epilogue: Romancing the Word', in Persson and Stråth 2007, 349–376.

Alesina, Alberto, Arnaud Devleeschauwer, William Easterly, Sergio Kurlat and Romain Wacziarg. 'Fractionalization', *Journal of Economic Growth*, 8:2 (2003) 155–194.

Altermatt, Urs. *Katholizismus und Antisemitismus: Mentalitäten, Kontinuitäten, Ambivalenzen. Zur Kulturgeschichte der Schweiz 1918–1945*. Frauenfeld, 1999.

Amato, Annamaria. 'Einaudi, Agnelli and Cabiati: Between Criticism of the League of Nations and Ideas of European Unification', in Dini and D'Auria 2013, 105–116.

Anderson, Margaret Lavinia. 'From Syllabus to Shoah?' (review article), *Central European History*, 34:2 (2001) 231–238.

Anderson, Sheldon. 'Metternich, Bismarck and the 'Myth of the "Long Peace": 1815–1914', *Peace Change*, 32:3 (2007) 301–328.

Anghie, Antony. *Imperialism, Sovereignty and the Making of International Law*. Cambridge, 2005.

Anteghini, Alessandra, Marta Petricioli and Donatella Cherubini (eds), *Les Etats-Unis d'Europe: Un Projet Pacifiste*. Bern, 2003.

Antonsich, Marco. 'Eurafrica. Dottrina Monroe del fascism', *Limes: Rivista Italiana di Geopolitica*, 3 (1997) 261–266.

Archibugi, Daniele. 'Models of International Organization in Perpetual Peace Projects', *Review of International Studies*, 18:4 (1992) 295–317.

Arcidiacono, Bruno. 'Great Britain, the Balkans and the Division of Europe, 1943–1945', in Varsori and Calandri 2002, 93–103.

Arcidiacono, Bruno. 'Les projets de réorganisation du système international au XIXe siècle (1871–1914)', *Relations Internationales*, 3:123 (2005) 11–24.

Arcidiacono, Bruno. 'La paix par le droit international, dans la vision de deux juristes du XIXe siècle: Le débat Lorimer-Bluntschli', *Relations Internationals*, 149 (2012) 13–26.

Ash, Timothy Garton. *History of the Present: Essays, Sketches, and Dispatches from Europe in the 1990s*. New York, 1999.

Ash, Timothy Garton. *Free World: America, Europe and the Surprising Future of the West*. New York, 2005.

Augustyn, Wolfgang (ed.), *Pax: Beitrage zu Idee und Darstellung des Friedens*. München, 2003.

Ayako Bennette, Rebecca. *Fighting for the Soul of Germany: The Catholic Struggle for Inclusion after Unification*. Cambridge, MA, 2012.

Badel, Laurence. *Un milieu libéral et européen: Le grand commerce français (1925–1948)*. Paris, 1999.

Bailey, Christian. 'The European Discourse in Germany 1939–1950: Three Case Studies', *German History*, 28:4 (2010) 453–478.

Bailey, Christian. *Between Yesterday and Tomorrow: German Visions of Europe in Germany, 1926–1950*. Oxford, 2013.

Balibar, Etienne. *Nous, citoyens d'Europe: Les frontières, l'état, le people*. Paris, 2001.

Balzaretti, Ross. 'The Creation of Europe', *History Workshop Journal*, 33 (1992) 181–196.

Barbero, Alessandro. *Charlemagne: Father of a Continent*. Berkeley, 2004.

Bariéty, Jacques. 'La paix par le droit, la prospérité et l'entente européenne. *Les Etats Unis d'Europe* 1919–1933', in Anteghini, Petricioli and Cherubini 2003, 419–433.

Barlas, Dilek and Serhat Güvenç. 'Turkey and the Idea of a European Union during the Inter-war Years, 1923–1939', *Middle Eastern Studies*, 45:3 (2009) 425–446.

Barry, Gearóid. *The Disarmament of Hatred: Marc Sangnier, French Catholicism and the Legacy of the First World War, 1914–1945*. Houndmills, 2012.

Barthel, Charles. 'Émile Mayrisch et les dirigeants de l'Arbed entre la Belgique, la France et l'Allemagne. Rivalités et complicités (1918–1925)', in Dumoulin 2004, 125–143.

Barthel, Charles. 'Emile Mayrisch et le pacte international de l'acier des années vingt', *Journal of European Integration History*, 1:1 (2006) 43–65.

Bartlett, Robert. *The Making of Europe: Conquest, Colonization and Cultural Change, 950–1350*. Princeton, 1994.

Bauerkämper, Arnd. 'Ambiguities of Transnationalism: Fascism in Europe between Pan-Europeanism and Ultra-Nationalism', *Bulletin of the German Historical Institute London*, 29:2 (November 2007) 43–67.

Bayly, C.A. and E.F. Biagini (eds), *Giuseppe Mazzini and the Globalization of Democratic Nationalism, 1830–1920*. Oxford, 2008.

Beaulac, Stephane. *The Power of Language in the Making of International Law: The Word Sovereignty in Bodin and Vattel and the Myth of Westphalia*. Leiden, 2004.

Beaune, Colette. 'Chrétienté et Europe: Le projet de Georges de Podiebrad au XV siècle', *Chrétiens et Sociétés XVIe-XXIe siècles*, 1 (1994) 35–56.

Bech-Petersen, Ole. 'Destination U.S.A.: The Mid Nineteenth-Century Danish Intellectual Encounter with the United States', *Scandinavian Studies*, 70:4 (1998) 441–460.

Behr, Hartmut. 'The European Union in the Legacies of Imperial Rule? EU Accession Politics Viewed from a Historical Comparative Perspective', *European Journal of International Relations*, 13:2 (2007) 239–262.

Beiser, Frederick C. *The Early Political Writings of the German Romantics*. Cambridge, 1992.

Bell, Duncan. *The Idea of Greater Britain: Empire and the Future of World Order, 1860–1900*. Princeton, 2007.

Bellomo, Manlio. *The Common Legal Past of Europe: 1000–1800*. Washington, DC, 1995.

Bély, Lucien. *L'art de la paix en Europe: Naissance de la Diplomatie Moderne XVIe-XVIIIe siècle*. Paris, 2007.

Beneke, Chris. *Beyond Toleration: The Religious Origins of American Pluralism*. Oxford, 2008.

Bennette, Rebecca Ayako. *Fighting for the Soul of Germany: The Catholic Struggle for Inclusion after Unification*. Cambridge, MA, 2012.

Berend, Ivan. *An Economic History of Nineteenth-Century Europe: Diversity and Industrialization*. Cambridge, 2012.

Berend, Nora. 'Violence as Identity: Christians and Muslims in Hungary in the Medieval and Early Modern Period', *Austrian History Yearbook*, 44 (April 2013) 1–13.

Bergami, Carol. 'Des lignes proudhonniennes? Sur les raciness et sur la portée d'un européisme "à la française"', in Morten Rasmussen and Ann-Christina Knudsen (eds), *The Road to a United Europe: Interpretations of the Process of European Integration*. Brussels, 2009, 23–38.

Berger, Françoise. 'Milieux économiques et États vis-à-vis des tentatives d'organisation des marchés européens dans les années trente', in Éric Bussière, Michel Dumoulin and Sylvain Schirmann (dir.), *Europe Organisée, Europe du Libre-Échange: Fin XIXe siècle – Années 1960*. Bruxelles, 2006, 222–242.

Berger, Stefan and Angel Smith (eds), *Nationalism, Labour and Ethnicity 1870–1939*. Manchester, 1999.

Berghahn, Volker. *Europe in the Era of Two World Wars: From Militarism and Genocide to Civil Society*. Princeton, 2006.

Berki, R.N. 'Marxism and European Unity', in Stirk 1989, 41–64.

Bhambra, Gurminder K. *Rethinking Modernity: Postcolonialism and the Sociological Imagination*. Houndmills, 2007.

Bhambra, Gurminder K. 'Postcolonial Europe: Or, Understanding Europe in Times of the Postcolonial', in Chris Rumford (ed.), *Sage Handbook of European Studies*. London, 2009, 69–85.

Bianchini, Stefano. 'Relations between East European Countries: The Balkan Federation (1942–1949)', in Varsori and Calandri 2002, 197–210.

Bickerton, Christopher J. *European Integration: From Nation-States to Member States*. Oxford, 2012.

Bideleux, Robert and Richard Taylor (eds), *European Integration and Disintegration: East and West*. New York, 1996.

Bitsch, Marie-Thérèse and Gérard Bossuat (eds), *L'Europe unie et l'Afrique: De l'idée d'eurafrique à la convention de Lomé I*. Brussels, 2005.

Blanning, T.C.W. *The French Revolution in Germany: Occupation and Resistance in the Rhineland, 1792–1802*. Oxford, 1983.

Blaschke, Olaf. *Katholizismus und Antisemitismus im Deutschen Kaiserreich*. Göttingen, 1997.

Blaschke, Olaf (ed.), *Konfessionen im Konflikt: Das zweiten konfessionelle Zeitalter Zwischen 1800 und 1970*. Göttingen, 2002.

Bock, Hans Manfred. 'Das "Locarno intellectuel". Pierre Bertaux als teilnehmender Beobachter', *La revue de l'Association Pierre Bertaux*, 2 (July 2013). www. Asnières+à+Censier+-+Hans+Manfred+Bock.pdf.

Bond, M.A. 'The Political Conversion of Friedrich von Gentz', *European History Quarterly*, 3 (January 1973) 1–12.

Borhi, László. 'Soviet Economic Imperialism and the Sovietization of Hungary' in Varsori and Calandri 2002, 171–183.

Borodziej, Włodzimierz, Blazej Brzostek and Maciecj Górny. 'Polnische Europa-Pläne des 19. Und 20. Jahrhundrerts', in Borodziej et al. 2005, vol. 1, 43–134.

Borodziej, Włodzimierz, Heinz Duchhardt, Małgorzata Morawiec and Ignác Romsics (eds), *Option Europa: Deutsche, polnische und ungarische Europapläne des 19. und 20. Jahrhunderts*. Göttingen, 2005, 3 vols.

Bossuat, Gerard. *La France, l'aide américaine et la construction européenne, 1944–1954*. Paris, 1992, 2 vols.

Bossuat, Gerard. *Faire l'Europe sans défaire la France: 60 ans de politique d'unité européenne des gouvernements et des présidents de la République française (1943–2003)*. Brussels and Bern, 2005.

Bossuat, Gerard. *L'Europe et la mondialisation*. Paris, 2006.

Bossuat, Gérard. *La France et la construction de l'unité européenne: De 1919 à nos jours*. Paris, 2012.

Bossuat, Gérard and Georges Saunier coll. (eds), *Inventer l'Europe: Histoire nouvelle des groupes d'influence et des acteurs de l'unité européenne*. Brussels, 2003.

Boyarin, Jonathan. *The Unconverted Self: Jews, Indians, and the Identity of Christian Europe*. Chicago, 2009.

Boyce, Robert. 'British Capitalism and the Idea of European Unity Between the Wars', in Stirk 1989, 65–83.

Brague, Rémi. *Europe, la voie rmaine*. Paris, 1992.

Brechtefeld, Jörg. *Mitteleuropa and German Politics: 1848 to the Present*. Houndmills, 1996.

Breuer, Stefan. *Carl Schmitt im Kontext: Intellektuellenpolitik in der Weimarer Republik*. Berlin, 2012.

Broers, Michael. *Europe under Napoleon, 1799–1815*. Oxford, 1996.

Broers, Michael, Peter Hicks and Agustin Guimera (eds), *The Napoleonic Empire and the New European Political Culture*. Houndmills, 2012.

Brown, Peter. *The Rise of Western Christendom: Triumph and Diversity, AD 200–1000*. Chichester, 2013, 408–433.

Brubaker, Rogers. 'Religion and Nationalism: Four Approaches', *Nations and Nationalism*, 18:1 (2012) 2–20.

Bruce, Steve. *Religion in the Modern World: From Cathedrals to Cults*. Oxford, 1996.

Brugmans, Hendrik. *L'idée européenne 1920–1970*. Brugge, 1970.

Buchanan, Tom. 'Human Rights, the Memory of War and the Making of a "European" Identity, 1945–1975', in Conway and Patel 2010, 157–171.

Budzik, Stanislaw. *Doctor Pacis: Theologie des Friedens bei Augustinus*. Innsbruck, 1988.

Bugge, Peter. ' "Shatter Zones": The Creation and Re-creation of Europe's East', in Spiering and Wintle 2002, 47–68.

Bukovansky, Mlada. *Legitimacy and Power Politics: The American and French Revolutions in International Political Culture*. Princeton, 2009.

Burbank, Jane and Frederick Cooper. *Empires in World History: Power and the Politics of Difference*. Princeton, 2010.

Burgdorf, Wolfgang. 'Imperial Reform and Visions of a European Consitution in Germany around 1800', *History of European Ideas*, 19:1–3 (1994) 401–408.

Burgess, Michael. *Federalism and European Union: The Building of Europe 1950–2000*. London, 2000.

Bussière, Eric. *La France, la Belgique et l'Organisation Économique de l'Europe, 1918–1935*. Paris, 1992.

Bussière, Eric. 'Les milieux économiques face à l'Europe au XXième siècle', *Journal for European Integration History*, 3:2 (1997) 5–21.

Bussière, Eric and Michel Dumoulin et al., 'L'émergence de l'idée d'identité européenne d'un après-guerre à l'autre', in René Girault (ed.), *Identité et conscience européennes au XXe siècle*. Paris, 1994, 67–105.

Camparini, Aurelia. 'La conception du socialisme international dans la pensée et l'œuvre de Jean Jaurès', in Anteghini, Petricioli and Cherubini 2003, 240–261.

Cavallar, Georg. *Die europäische Union – von der Utopie zur Friedens- und Wertegemeinschaft*. Berlin, 2006.

Chabot, Jean-Luc. *Aux origines intellectuelles de l'Union européenne: L'idée d'Europe unie de 1919 à 1939*. Grenoble, 2005.

Chaudhuri, K.N. *Asia before Europe: Economy and Civilization of the Indian Ocean form the Rise of Islam to 1750*. Cambridge, 1990.

Chenaux, Philippe. *Une Europe vaticane? Entre le Plan Marshall et les Traités de Rome*. Louvain-la-Neuve, 1990.

Chenaux, Philippe. *De la chrétienté à l'Europe: Les catholiques et l'idée européenne au XXe siècle*. Tours, 2007.

Cherubini, Donatella. 'Guiseppe Emanuele Modigliani: From the *paix quelconque* to the Europeanisation of the League of Nations', in Petricioli and Cherubini 2007, 307–340.

Claggett-Borne, Elisabeth. 'Definitions of Peace and Reconciliation', in K. Malley-Morrisson et al. (eds), *International Handbook of Peace and Reconciliation*. New York, 2013, 11–21.

Clark, Christopher. *The Sleepwalkers: How Europe Went to War in 1914*. London, 2012.

Clark, Christopher and Wolfram Kaiser (eds), *Culture Wars: Secular-Catholic Conflict in Nineteenth-Century Europe*. Cambridge, 2003.

Clavin, Patricia. *Securing the World Economy: The Reinvention of the League of Nations, 1920–1946*. Oxford, 2013.

Cofrancesco, Dino. 'Il mito europeo del fascismo (1939–1945)', *Storia Contemporanea*, 14:1 (1983) 5–46.

Cohrs, Patrick O. *The Unfinished Peace after World War I: America, Britain and the Stabilisation of Europe, 1919–1932*. Cambridge, 2006.

Collins, Michael. 'Decolonisation and the "Federal Moment"', *Diplomacy & Statecraft*, 24 (2013) 21–40.

Conway, Martin. 'Legacies of Exile: The Exile Governments in London and the Politics of Post-War Europe', in Martin Conway and José Gotovitch (eds), *Europe in Exile: Refugee Communities in Great Britain, 1940–1945*. New York and Oxford, 2001, 255–274.

Conway, Martin and Kiran Klaus Patel (eds), *Europeanization in the Twentieth Century: Historical Approaches*. Houndmills, 2010.

Conze, Vanessa. *Das Europa der Deutschen: Ideen von Europa in Deutschland Zwischen Reichstradition und Westorientierung (1920–1970)*. München, 2005.

Cox, Michael and Caroline Kennedy-Pipe. 'The Tragedy of American Diplomacy? Rethinking the Marshall Plan', *Journal of Cold War Studies*, 7:1 (2005) 97–134.

Crom, Georges. *L'Europe et le mythe de l'Occident: La construction d'une histoire.* Paris, 2009.

Crouzet, Denis. *Les guerriers de Dieu: La violence au temps des guerres de religion vers 1525-vers 1610.* Paris, 1990.

D'Alessandro, Michele. 'Seeking governance for world markets: The League of Nations between corporatism and public opinion, 1925–1929', *European Business History Association – XIth Annual Conference,* Geneva, 13–15 September 2007. http://www.ebha.org/ebha2007/pdf/Alessandro.pdf (2 January 2014).

Damberg, Wilhelm and Patrick Pasture. 'Restoration and Erosion of Pillarized Catholicism in Western Europe', in Leo Kenis, Jaak Billiet and Patrick Pasture (eds), *The Transformation of Christian Churches in Europe.* Leuven, 2010, 55–76.

D'Auria, Matthew. ' "Against the State": Carlo Rosselli and the Social Space of European Federalism', in Dini and D'Auria 2013, 117–134.

De Bruin, Robin. 'Dutch politics in the 1950s and the myth of inevitable Europeanization', in Jolán Róka (ed.), *Globalisation, Europeanization and Other Transnational Phenomena: Description, Analyses and Generalizations.* Budapest, 2001, 382–390.

De Rougemont, Denis. *The Idea of Europe.* London, 1966.

Deakin, Frederick W.D. *The Brutal Friendship: Mussolini, Hitler and the Fall of Italian Fascism.* New York, 1962.

Deighton, Anne. 'Entente Neo-Coloniale?: Ernest Bevin and the Proposals for an Anglo–French Third World Power, 1945–1949', *Diplomacy Statecraft,* 17:4 (2006) 835–852.

Delanty, Gerard. *Formations of European Modernity: A Historical and Political Sociology of Europe.* Houndmills, 2013.

Delwit, Pascal. 'Les conceptions de l'Europe dans le mouvement communiste entre 1940 et 1947', in Dumoulin 1995, 215–231.

Den Boer, Pim. 'Europe to 1914: The Making of an Idea', in Wilson and van der Dussen 1993, 13–82.

Deschamps, Eugène. 'L'Eurafrique, le fascisme et la collaboration francophone belge', *Cahiers de l'histoire du temps présent,* 1 (1996) 141–161.

Di Biagio, Anna. 'The Cominform as the Soviet Response to the Marshall Plan', in Varsori and Calandri 2002, 297–305.

Di Nolfo, Ennio. 'The United States, Europe, and the Marshall Plan', in Varsori and Calandri 2002, 288–296.

Dicke, Klaus. 'Friedensvorstellungen in der deutschen philosophischen Diskussion um 1800', in Thomas Kater (ed.), *'Der Friede ist keine leere Idee...': Bilder und Vorstellungen vom Frieden am Beginn der politischen Moderne.* Essen 2006, 33–46.

Dickinson, Edward Ross. 'The German Empire: An Empire?', *History Workshop Journal,* 66:1 (2008) 129–162.

Dini, Vittorio and Matthew D'Auria (eds), *The Space of Crisis: Shifting Spaces and Ideas of Europe. 1914–1945.* New York, 2013.

Dini, Vittorio and Matthew D'Auria. 'Introduction: Spatial Crisis and Ideas of Europe. 1914–1945', in Dini and D'Auria 2013, 11–26.

Documents on the History of European Integration, ed. Walter Lipgens, 4 vols. Berlin, 1985–1991.

Dorn, Barbara. *Friedrich von Gentz und Europa: Studien zu Stabilität und Revolution 1802–1822.* PhD, Universität Bonn, 1993.

Dramé, Papa and Samin Saul. 'Le projet d'Eurafrique en France (1946–1960): quête de puissance ou atavisme colonial?', *Guerres mondiales et conflits contemporains*, 4:216 (2004) 95–114.

Dreyer, Michael. 'Constantin Frantz: der Außenseiter des Antisemitismus', in Werner Bergmann and Ulrich Sieg (eds), *Antisemitische Geschichtsbilder*. Essen, 2009, 39–59.

Du Rhéau, Elisabeth. *L'idée d'Europe au XXe siècle*. Brussels, 1996.

Duchêne, François. 'The European Community and the Uncertainties of Interdependence', in Max Kohnstamm and W. Hager (eds), *A Nation Writ Large? Foreign-Policy Problems before the European Community*. London, 1973, 1–21.

Duchenne, Geneviève. *Visions et projets belges pour l'Europe: De la Belle Epoque aux Traités de Rome (1900–1957)*. Brussels, 2001.

Duchenne, Geneviève. *Esquisses d'une Europe nouvelle: L'européisme dans la Belgique de l'entre-deux-guerres (1919–1939)*. Brussels, 2008.

Duchenne, Geneviève and Michel Dumoulin (eds), *Générations de fédéralistes européens depuis le XIXe siècle: Individus, groups, espaces et réseaux*. Brussels, 2012.

Duchhardt, Heinz. *Der Wiener Kongress: Die Neugestaltung Europas 1814–1815*. München, 2013.

Duchhardt, Heinz. 'Model Europe', *European History Online* (EGO). http://www.ieg-ego.eu/duchhardth-2010a-en URN: urn:nbn:de:0159-20101025191 (retrieved 15 February 2014).

Dumoulin, Michel (ed.), *Plans de temps de guerre pour l'Europe d'après guerre, 1940–1947 – Wartime Plans for Postwar Europe, 1940–1947*. Brussels, 1995.

Dumoulin, Michel and Anne-Myriam Dutrieue. *La Ligue Européenne de Coopération Économique, 1946–1981: un groupe d'étude et de pression dans la construction européenne*. Bern, 1993.

Dumoulin, Michel and Yves Stélandre. *L'idée européenne dans l'entre–deux-guerres*. Louvain-la-Neuve, 1992.

Dumoulin, Michel, René Girault and Gilbert Trausch (eds), *L'Europe du patronat: De la guerre froide aux années soixante*. Bern, 1993.

Durand, Jean-Dominique. *L'Europe de la Démocratie chrétienne*. Brussels, 1995.

Durantin, Jean-François. 'Les conceptions européennes des neutralistes français vis-à-vis du conflit Est-Ouest au début de la guerre froide', in Vaïsse 1994, 347–371.

Durchhardt, Heinz. 'Der deutsche Europa-Diskurs des 19. und frühen 20. Jahrhunderts', in Borodziej et al. 2005, vol. 1, 15–42.

Dussel, Enrique. 'Europe, Modernity and Eurocentrism', *Neplanta: Views from the South*, 1:3 (2000) 465–478.

Ehmer, Manfred. *Constantin Frantz: Die politische Gedankenwelt eines Klassikers des Föderalismus*. Rheinfelden, 1988.

Ellison, James R.V. 'Perfidious Albion? Britain, Plan G and European Integration, 1955–1956', *Contemporary British History*, 10:4 (1996) 1–34.

Elvert, Jürgen. ' "Irrweg Mitteleuropa". Deutsche Konzepte zur Neugestaltung Europas aus der Zwischenkriegszeit', in Heinz Duchhardt and Małgorzata Morawiec (eds), *Vision Europa: Deutsche und polnische Föderationspläne des 19. und frühen 20. Jahrhunderts*. Mainz, 2003, 117–137.

Englund, Steven. 'Monstre Sacré: The Question of Cultural Imperialism and the Napoleonic Empire', *The Historical Journal*, 51 (2008) 215–250.

Europe of Free Nations: Idea of an Integrated Continent in Polish Nineteenth Century Thought, The Sejm Exhibition, 10–21 May 2008. http://oide.sejm.gov.pl/oide/images/files/wystawa1/leaflet.pdf.

Eze, Emmanuel Chukwudi. 'The Color of Reason: The Idea of "Race" in Kant's Anthropology', in Emmanuel Chukwudi Eze (ed.), *Postcolonial African Philosophy: A Critical Reader*. Cambridge, MA, 1997, 103–140.

Fenet, Alain. 'Emeric Crucé aux origines du pacifisme et de l'internationalisme modernes', *Miskolc Journal of International Law*, 1:2 (2004) 21–34.

Ferraro, Francesca. 'The Kelsen/Schmitt Debate. Heller's Solution and the Future of Europe', in Dini and D'Auria 2013, 181–195.

Fink, Carole. *Defending the Rights of Others: The Great Powers, the Jews, and International Minority Protection, 1878–1938*. Cambridge, 2006.

Fischer, Conan. 'The Failure of Détente? German-French Relations between Stresemann and Hitler, 1929–1932', in Frank McDonough (ed.), *The Origins of the Second World War: An International Perspective*. London 2011, 87–91.

Fischer, Conan. 'The Failed European Union: Franco-German Relations during the Great Depression of 1929–1921', *The International History Review*, 34:4 (2012) 705–724.

Fischer, Jürgen. *Oriens–Occidens–Europa. Begriff und Gedanke 'Europa' in der späten Antike und im frühen Mittelalter*. Mainz, 1957.

Fitzpatrick, Matthew P. 'Introduction: Particular or Universal? Historicizing Liberal Approaches to Empire in Europe', in Matthew P. Fitzpatrick (ed.), *Liberal Imperialism in Europe*. Houndmills, 2011, 1–24.

Flandreau, Marc. 'The Economics and Politics of Monetary Unions: A Reassessment of the Latin Monetary Union, 1865–71', *Financial History Review*, 7 (April 2000) 25–44.

Fleury, Antoine and Lubor Jilek (eds), *Le Plan Briand d'Union fédérale européenne*. Bern, 1998.

Fontana, Biancamarria. 'The Napoleontic Empire and the Empire of Nations', in Anthony Pagden (ed.), *The Idea of Europe: From Antiquity to the European Union*. Cambridge, 2002, 116–128.

Forrest, Allan. 'La Révolution française et l'Europe', in François Furet and Mona Ozouf (eds), *Dictionnaire critique de la Révolution française*. Paris, 1988, 146–155.

Fossaluzza, Cristina. 'Phönix Europa? Krieg und Kultur in Rudolf Pannwitz' und Hugo von Hofmannsthals Europa-Idee', in Sascha Bru et al. (eds), *Europa! Europa? The Avant-Garde, Modernism and the Fate of a Continent*. Berlin and New York, 2009, vol. 1, 113–125.

Frevert, Ute. 'Europeanizing German History', *GHI Bulletin*, 36 (2005) 9–24.

Freytag, Carl. *Deutschlands "Drang nach Südosten" – Der Mitteleuropäische Wirtschaftstag und der "Ergänzungsraum Südosteuropa" 1931–1945*. Vienna and Göttingen, 2012.

Gall, Alexander. *Das Atlantropa-Projekt: Die Geschichte einer gescheiterten Vision. Herman Sörgel und die Absenkung des Mittelmeers*. Frankfurt, 1998.

Gall, Lothar. *Walther Rathenau: Portrait einer Epoche*. München, 2009.

Garavini, Giuliano. 'Foreign Policy beyond the Nation-State: Conceptualizing the External Dimension', in Kaiser and Varsori 2010, 190–208.

Garavini, Giuliano. *After Empires: European Integration, Decolonization, and the Challenge from the Global South 1957–1986*. Oxford, 2012.

Gat, Azar. *Nations: The Long History and Deep Roots of Political Ethnicity and Nationalism*. Cambridge, 2013.

Gates, Eleanor M. *End of the Affair: The Collapse of the Anglo-French Alliance, 1939–1940*. London, 1981.

Gehler, Michael. 'The Geneva Circle of West European Christian Democrats', in Michael Gehler and Wolfram Kaiser (eds), *Christian Democracy in Europe since 1945*. London and New York, 2004, 207–220.

Gehler, Michael, Wolfram Kaiser and Brigitte Leucht (eds), *Netzwerke im europäischen Mehrebenensystem. Von 1945 bis zur Gegenwart. Networks in European multi-level Governance. From 1945 to the Present*. Vienna, 2009.

Georges-Henri, Soutou. 'De Gaulle's Plans for Postwar Europe', in Varsori and Elena Calandri 2002, 49–58.

Germond, Carine and Henning Türk (eds), *A History of Franco-German Relations in Europe: From 'Hereditary Enemies' to Partners*. Houndmills, 2008.

Geyer, Michael. 'War and Terror in Contemporary and Historical Perspective: An Outlook', in Michael Geyer (ed.), *War and Terror in Contemporary and Historical Perspective*. Washington, DC, 2003, 129–139.

Geyer, Michael. 'The Subject(s) of Europe', in Konrad H. Jarausch and Thomas Lindenberger (eds), *Conflicted Memories: Europeanizing Contemporary History*. Oxford, 2011, 254–280.

Ghervas, Stella. 'Antidotes to Empire: From the Congress System to the European Union', in John W. Boyer and Berthold Molden (eds), *EUtROPEs: The Paradox of European Empire*. Chicago, 2014, 49–81.

Gilbert, Mark. 'Delusions of Grandeur: New Perspectives on the History of the European Community', *Contemporary European History*, 16:4 (2007) 545–553.

Gilbert, Mark. 'Partners and Rivals: Assessing the American Role', in Kaiser and Varsori 2010, 169–189.

Gioli, Gabriela. 'Before Bretton Woods: Italian Economists on Peace and Economic Cooperation', in Petricioli and Cherubini 2007, 191–207.

Giustibelli, Simona. 'L'Europa nella riflessione del convegno della Fondazione Volta (Roma, 16–20 novembre 1932)', *Dimensioni e problemi della ricerca storica*, 1 (2002) 181–233.

Giustibelli, Simona. *Europa, paneuropa, antieuropa: Il dialogo tra Italia fascista e Francia democratica nell'epoca del memorandum Briand (1929–1934)*. Soveria Mannelli, 2006.

Goddeeris, Idesbald. 'Poland towards European Integration Projects', in Duchenne and Dumoulin 2012, 125–139.

Gollwitzer, Heinz. *Europabild und Europagedanke: Beiträge zur deutschen Geistesgeschichte des 18. und 19. Jahrhunderts*. München, 1951.

Górny, Maciej. 'Das ethnografische Motiv in den polnischen Föderationsplänen des 19. Jahrhunderts', in Borodziej et al. 2005, vol. 1, 189–196.

Gottfried, Paul. 'Hugo von Hofmannsthal and the Interwar European Right', *Modern Age*, 49:4 (Fall 2007) 508–519.

Greenwood, Sean. *Britain and European Cooperation Since 1945*. Oxford, 1992.

Greenwood, Sean. 'The Third Force in the late 1940s', in Brian Brivati and Harriet Jones (eds), *From Reconstruction to Integration: Britain and Europe since 1945*. Leicester, 1993, 59–70.

Greenwood, Sean. 'The Third War Force of Ernest Bevin', in Dumoulin 1995, 419–439.

Gregory, Brad S. *The Unintended Reformation: How a Religious Revolution Secularized Society*. Cambridge, MA, 2012.

Grell, Ole Peter and Bob Scribner (eds), *Tolerance and Intolerance in the European Reformation*. Cambridge, 2002.

Griffin, Roger. *A Fascist Century: Essays by Roger Griffin*, ed. Matthew Feldman. Houndmills, 2008.

Griffiths, Richard T. *Thank You M. Monnet: Essays on the History of European Integration*. Leiden, 2014.

Grosbois, Thierry. *L'idée européenne en temps de guerre dans le Benelux 1940–1944*. Louvain-la-Neuve, 1994.

Grosbois, Thierry. 'Les projets des petites nations de Benelux pour l'après-guerre 1941–1945', in Dumoulin 1997, 95–125.

Grosbois, Thierry. 'The Activities of Józef Retinger in Suport of the European Idea (1940–1946)', in Thomas Lane and Marian Wolański (eds), *Poland and European unity: Ideas and Reality*. Wroklaw, 2007, 13–51.

Grossi, Verdiana. 'Victor Hugo et sa perception des Etats-Unis d'Europe', in Anteghini, Petricioli and Cherubini 2003, 49–74.

Grunert, Robert. *Der Europagedanke westeuropäischer faschistischer Bewegungen 1940–1945*. Paderborn, 2012.

Guérin, Denis. *Albert Thomas au BIT 1920–1932: de l'internationalisme à l'Europe*. Geneva, 1996.

Guida, Fransesca. 'Federal Projects in Interwar Romania: An Overvaulting Ambition?', in Petricioli and Cherubini 2007, 229–257.

Guieu, Jean-Michel. 'L'engagement européen d'un grand mathématicien français: Émile Borel et la "coopération européenne", des années vingt aux années quarante', *Bulletin de l'Institut Pierre Renouvin*, 5 (Summer 1998). http://www.univ-paris1.fr/autres-structures-de-recherche/ipr/les-revues/bulletin/tous-les-bulletins/bulletin-n-05/emile-borel-et-la-cooperation-europeenne/, (retrieved 3 January 2014).

Guieu, Jean-Michel. 'Le Comité fédéral de Coopération européenne: L'action méconnue d'une organisation internationale privée en faveur de l'union de l'Europe dans les années trente (1928–1940)', in Sylvain Schurmann (ed.), *Organisations internationales et architectures européennes (1929–1939)*. Paris, 2003, 73–91.

Guieu, Jean-Michel. 'Les Congrès universels de la Paix et la question de l'unité européenne, 1921–1939', in Petricioli and Cherubini 2007, 387–406.

Guieu, Jean-Michel. 'Editorial: L'Europe et la paix. Jalons pour une relecture de l'histoire européenne des XIXe-XXIe siècles', *Matériaux pour l'histoire de notre temps*, 108:4 (2012) 1–6.

Guieu, Jean-Michel and Christophe Le Dréau (dir.), *Le "Congrès de l'Europe' à La Haye (1948–2008)*. Bruxelles and Bern, 2009.

Guillen, Pierre. 'Le projet d'union économique entre le France, l'Italie et le Benelux', in Raymond Poidevin (ed.), *Histoire des débuts de la construction européenne Mars 1948–mai 1950*. Brussels, 1986, 143–164.

Guillen, Pierre. 'La France Libre et le projet de fédération ouest-européenne 1943–1944', in Dumoulin 1995, 153–173.

Gusejnova, Dina. 'Noble Continent? German-Speaking Nobles as Theorists of European Identity in the Interwar Period', in Dini and D'Auria 2013, 111–133.

Guth, Alfred. *Rudolf Pannwitz, un européen, penseur et poète allemand en quête de totalité (1881–1969)*. Paris, 1973.

Gutsche, Verena. '*SOS Europa*: Cultural Pessimism in the German Discourse on Europe during the Interwar Years', in Teresa Pinheiro, Beata Cieszynska and José Eduardo Franco (eds), *Ideas of/for Europe: An Interdisciplinary Approach to European Identity*. Bern, 2012, 121–145.

Gużkowski, Stefan. 'Das Iagiellonische Imperium: Über die osteuropäischen Union', in Borodziej et al. 2005, vol. 3, 247–268.

Habermas, Jürgen and Jacques Derrida. 'February 15, or What Binds Europeans Together: A Plea for a Common Foreign Policy, Beginning in the Core of Europe', *Constellations*, 10:3 (2003) 291–297.

Hahn, Hans-Werner. *Geschichte des Deutschen Zollvereins*. Göttingen, 1984.

Hanebrink, Paul A. *In Defense of Christian Hungary: Religion, Nationalism and Anti-Semitism*. Ithaca, 2006.

Hansen, Peo. 'European Integration, European Identity and the Colonial Connection', *European Journal of Social Theory*, 5:4 (2002) 483–498.

Hansen, Peo and Stefan Jonsson. 'Bringing Africa as a "Dowry to Europe": European Integration and the Eurafrican Project, 1920–1960', *Interventions: International Journal Postcolonial Studies*, 13:3 (2011) 443–463.

Hansen, Peo and Stefan Jonsson. 'Imperial Origins of European Integration and the Case of Eurafrica', *Journal of Common Market Studies*, 50:6 (2012) 1028–1041.

Hansen, Peo and Stefan Jonsson. 'A Statue to Nasser? Eurafrica, the Colonial Roots of European integration, and the 2012 Nobel Peace Prize', *Mediterranean Quarterly*, 24:4 (2013) 5–18.

Hansen, Peo and Stefan Jonsson. *Eurafrica: The Untold History of European Integration and Colonialism*. London, 2014.

Hay, Denys. *Europe: The Emergence of an Idea*. Edinburgh, 1968 (2).

He, Yinan. *The Search for Reconciliation: Sino-Japanese and German-Polish Relations since World War II*. Cambridge, 2009.

Heather, Peter. *Empires and Barbarians: Migration, Development and the Birth of Europe*. Oxford, 2010.

Heinlein, Frank. *British Government Policy and Decolonisation, 1945–1963: Scrutinising the Official Mind*. London, 2013.

Helfers, James P. (ed.), *Multicultural Europe and Cultural Exchange in the Middle Ages and Renaissance*. Turnhout, 2005.

Henderson, W.O. *Friedrich List: Economist and Visionary 1789–1846*. London, 1983.

Hewitson, Mark. 'The United States of Europe: The European Question in the 1920s', in Hewitson and D'Auria 2012, 15–34.

Hewitson, Mark and Matthew D'Auria (eds), *Europe in Crisis: Intellectuals and the European Idea, 1917–1957*. Oxford, 2012.

Heywood, Robert W. 'West European Community and the Eurafrica Concept in the 1950s', *Journal of European Integration*, 4:2 (1981) 199–210.

Hick, Alan. 'The "European Movement" ', in *Documents*, Vol. 4 ed. Walter Lipgens and Wilfried Loth, 1991, 318–324.

Hiden, John W. and David J. Smith. 'Looking beyond the Nation State: A Baltic Vision for National Minorities between the Wars', *Journal of Contemporary History*, 41:3 (2006) 387–399.

Hildebrand, Klaus. *Das vergangene Reich: Deutsche Außenpolitik von Bismarck bis Hitler 1871*. München, 2008.

Hobsbawm, Eric. *Nation and Nationalism Since 1790: Programme, Myth, Reality*. Cambridge, 1990.

Höfert, Almut. 'Europe and Religion in the Framework of Sixteenth-Century Relations between Christian Powers and the Ottoman Empire', in Hans-Åke Persson and Bo Stråth (eds), *Reflections on Europe: Defining a Political Order in Time and Space*. Bern, 2007, 211–230.

Holl, Karl. 'Europapolitik im Vorfeld der deutschen Regierungspolitik. Zur Tätigkeit proeuropäischer Organisationen in der Weimarer Republik', *Historische Zeitschrift*, 219 (1974) 33–94.

Holl, Karl. 'Richard Nikolaus Graf Coudenhove-Kalergi und seine Vision von "Paneuropa"', in Heinz Duchhardt (ed.), *Europäer des 20. Jahrhunderts*. Mainz, 2002, 11–73.

Horel, Catherine. 'La pensée fédéraliste en Hongrie', in Petricioli and Cherubini 2007, 209–227.

Horel, Catherine. *Cette Europe qu'on dit centrale: Des Habsbourg à l'intégration européenne 1815–2004*, Paris, 2009.

Huistra, Pieter, Marijn Molema and Daniel Wirt. 'Political Values in a European Museum', *Journal of Contemporary European Research*, 10:1 (2014) 124–136.

Isac, Iulian Nicusor. 'The United States of Greater Austria – A step towards European Union?', in *Europe as viewed from the Margins: An East-Central European Perspective During the Long Nineteenth Century*, Centrul de Cercetare a Istoriei Relatiilor Internationale si Studii Culturale 'Grigore Gafencu', s.d. http://www.centrulgafencu.ro/products.htm (retrieved 28 December 2013).

Jackson, Peter. *Beyond the Balance of Power: France and the Politics of National Security in the Era of the First World War*. Cambridge, 2012.

Jacobs, Jaap. *The Colony of New Netherland: A Dutch Settlement in Seventeenth-Century America*. Ithaca, 2009.

Jansen, Thomas and Steven Van Hecke. *At Europe's Service: The Origins and Evolution of the European People's Party*. Brussels, 2011.

Jarausch, Konrad H. and Thomas Lindenberger (eds), *Conflicted Memories: Europeanizing Contemporary Histories*. New York and Oxford, 2007.

Jarrett, Mark. *The Congress of Vienna and Its Legacy: War and Great Power Diplomacy After Napoleon*. New York, 2013.

Jeannesson, Stanislas. 'L'Europe de Jacques Seydoux', *Revue historique*, 122:1 (1998) 123–144.

Johnson, Gaynor (ed.), *Locarno Revisited: European Diplomacy 1920–1929*. London, 2004.

Judt, Tony. *Postwar. A History of Europe Since 1945*. London, 2005.

Judt, Tony. *A Grand Illusion? An Essay on Europe*. New York and London, 2011.

Kaelble, Hartmut. *Europaer über Europa: Die Entstehung des europäischen Selbstverständnisses im 19. und 20. Jahrhundert*. Frankfurt, 2001.

Kaelble, Hartmut and Martin Kirsch (eds), *Selbstverständnis und Gesellschaft der Europäer: Aspekte der sozialen und kulturellen Europäisierung im späten 19. und 20. Jahrhundert*. Bern, 2007.

Kaiser, Wolfram. *Using Europe, Abusing the Europeans: Britain and European Integration 1945–63*. London, 1996.

Kaiser, Wolfram. *Christian Democracy and the Origins of European Union.* Cambridge, 2007.

Kaiser, Wolfram and Antonio Varsori (eds), *European Union History: Themes and Debates.* Houndmills, 2010.

Kaiser, Wolfram, Brigitte Leucht and Michael Gehler (eds), *Transnational Networks in Regional Integration: Governing Europe 1945–1983.* Houndmills, 2010.

Kalyvas, Statys. *The Rise of Christian Democracy in Europe.* Ithaca, 1993.

Kaplan, Benjamin J. *Divided By Faith: Religious Conflict and the Practice of Toleration in Early Modern Europe.* Cambridge, MA, 2007.

Kaplan, Jacob J. and Gunther Schleiminger. *European Payments Union: Financial Diplomacy in the 1950s.* Oxford, 1989.

Karsh, Efraim and Inari Karsh. *Empires of the Sand: The Struggle for Mastery in the Middle East, 1789–1923.* Cambridge, MA, 2001.

Kater, Thomas. 'Zur Transformation von Friedensbildern am Beginn der Moderne', in Thomas Kater (ed.), *'Der Friede ist keine leere Idee . . . ': Bilder und Vorstellungen vom Frieden am Beginn der politischen Moderne.* Essen, 2006, 9–29.

Keiger, John. 'Poincaré and Briand: Continuity in French Diplomacy in the 1920s', in Johnson 2004, 95–107.

Kennedy, James C. 'Religion, Nation and European Representations of the Past', in Stefan Berger and Chris Lorenz (eds), *The Contested Nation: Ethnicity, Class, Religion and Gender in National Histories.* Houndmills, 2009, 104–134.

Kent, Bruce. *The Spoils of War: The Politics, Economics, and Diplomacy of Reparations 1918–1932.* New York, 1992.

Kent, John. *The Internationalization of Colonialism: Britain, France, and Black Africa, 1939–56.* Oxford, 1992.

Kent, John. 'British Postwar Planning for Europe 1942–1945', in Varsori and Calandri 2002, 40–58.

Keukeleire, Stephan and Tom Delreux. *The Foreign Policy of the European Union.* Houndmills, 2014.

Kissinger, Henry. *A World Restored: Metternich, Castlereagh and the Problems of Peace 1812–1822.* London, 1957.

Kleingeld, Pauline. 'Kant's Second Thoughts on Race', *The Philosophical Quarterly,* 57 (2007) 573–592.

Kleingeld, Pauline. 'Romantic Cosmopolitanism: Novalis' Christianity or Europe', *Journal of the History of Philosophy,* 46 (2008) 269–84.

Knudsen, Ann-Christina L. *Farmers on Welfare: The Making of Europe's Common Agricultural Policy.* Ithaca, 2009.

Knutsen, Torbjørn L. 'The Rise of Balance-of-Power as an Ordering Institution', paper presented at the International Studies Association, Chicago, 28.02.07–02.03.07. http://turin.sgir.eu/uploads/Knutsen-The%20Rise2%20of%20Balance-of%20Power%20as%20an%20Ordering%20Institution.pdf

Kooi, Christine. *Calvinists and Catholics during Holland's Golden Age: Heretics and Idolaters.* Cambridge, 2012.

Koskenniemi, Martti. *The Gentle Civilizer of Nations: The Rise and Fall of International Law 1870–1960.* Cambridge, 2001.

Kraus, Peter and Giuseppe Sciortino. 'The Diversities of Europe: From European Modernity to the Making of the European Union', *Ethnicities,* 14:4 (2014) 485–497.

Krejčí, Oskar. *Geopolitics of the Central European Region: The View from Prague and Bratislava*. Bratislava, 2005.

Krüger, Peter. 'Die Ansätze zu einer europäischen Wirtschaftsgemeinschaft in Deutschland nach dem Ersten Weltkrieg', in Helmut Berding (ed.), *Wirtschaftliche und Politische Integration im 19. und 20. Jahrhundert*. Göttingen, 1984, 149–168.

Krüger, Peter. 'European Ideology and European Reality: European Unity and German Foreign Policy in the 1920s', in Stirk 1989, 84–98.

Krüger, Peter. 'Der abgebrochene Dialog: Die deutschen Reaktionen auf die Europavorstellungen Briands in 1929', in Fleury and Jilek 1998, 289–306.

Krüger, Peter. *Das unberechenbare Europa: Epochen des Integrationsprozesses vom späten 18. Jahrhundert bis zur Europäischen Union*. Stuttgart, 2006.

Kühne, Thomas. 'Colonialism and the Holocaust: Continuities, Causations, and Complexities', *Journal of Genocide Research*, 15:3 (2013) 339–362.

Kuk, Leszek. 'La Ligue internationale de la Paix et de la Liberté et la "question polonaise"', in Anteghini, Petricioli and Cherubini 2003, 325–344.

Kurlander, Erik. 'Between Völkisch and Universal Visions of Empire: Liberal imperialism in Mitteleuropa, 1890–1918', in Matthew Fitzpatrick (ed.), *Liberal Imperialism in Europe*. Houndmills, 2012, 141–166.

Kymlicka, Will and Baogang He (eds), *Multiculturalism in Asia*. Oxford, 2005.

Labrie, Arnold. *Zuiverheid en decadentie: Over de grenzen van de burgerlijke cultuur in West-Europa, 1870–1914*. Amsterdam, 2011.

Lagrou, Pieter. 'La résistance et les conceptions de l'Europe, 1945–1965: Anciens résistants et victimes de la persécution face à la Guerre froide, au problème allemand et à l'intégration Européenne', *Cahiers d'Histoire du Temps Présent*, 2 (1997) 155–197.

Lagrou, Pieter. *The Legacy of Nazi-occupation: Patriotic Memory and National Recovery in Western Europe, 1945–1965*. Cambridge, 2000.

Lagrou, Pieter. 'Europe in the World: Imperial Legacies', in Mario Telo (ed.), *The European Union and Global Governance*. London, 2009, 306–326.

Lambauer, Barbara. *Otto Abetz et les Français ou l'envers de la Collaboration*. Paris, 2001.

Lamberts, Emiel (ed.), *The Black International: The Holy See and Militant Catholicism in Europe*. Leuven, 2002.

Lamberts, Emiel. *Het gevecht met Leviathan: Een verhaal over de politieke ordening in Europa, 1815–1965*. Amsterdam, 2012.

Landes, Richard, Andrew Gow and David C. Van Meter (eds), *The Apocalyptic Year 1000: Studies in the Mutation of European Culture*. Oxford, 2003.

Landfried, Christine. 'The Concept of Difference', in Kolja Raube and Annika Sattler (eds), *Difference and Democracy: Exploring Potentials in Europe and Beyond*. Frankfurt, 2001, 15–45.

Lane, Ann. 'British Perceptions of the Sovietization of Eastern Europe, 1947–1948', in Varsori and Calandri 2002, 219–228.

Lane, Thomas and Marian Wolanski. *Poland and European Integration: The Ideas and Movements of Polish Exiles in the West, 1939–1991*. Houndmills, 2009.

Langhorne, Richard. *The Collapse of the Concert of Europe: International Politics, 1890–1914*. New York, 1984.

Laptos, Józef. 'Jozef Retinger, "le père de l'ombre" de l'Europe. Le rôle de Jósef Retinger et de ses réseaux personnels dans les débuts de la construction européenne', in Gerard Bossuat and Georges Saunier (eds), *Inventer l'Europe: Histoire nouvelle des groupes d'influence et des acteurs de l'unité européenne*. Brussels, 2003, 179–195.

Laqua, Daniel. *The Age of Internationalism and Belgium, 1880–1930: Peace, Progress and Prestige*. Manchester, 2013.

Laughland, John. *The Tainted Source: The Undemocratic Origins of the European Idea*. London, 1997.

Leboutte, René. *Histoire économique et sociale de la construction européenne*. Brussels, 2008.

Lecarme, Jacques. *Drieu la Rochelle ou la bal des maudits*. Paris, 2001.

Leikam, Ferdinand. 'A Strategy that Failed – Great Britain, Commonwealth Africa and EEC Association Policy, 1957–1963', in Morten Rasmussen and Ann-Christina Knudsen (eds), *The Road to a United Europe: Interpretations of the Process of European Integration*. Brussels, 2009, 101–118.

Lesaffer, Randall (ed.), *Peace Treaties and International Law in European History. From the Late Middle Ages to World War One*. Cambridge, 2008.

Lesaffer, Randall. *European Legal History: A Cultural and Political Perspective: The Civil Law Tradition in Context*. Cambridge, 2012.

Lewis, David Charles. *European Unity and the Discourse of Collaboration: France and Francophone Belgium: 1938–1945*, Unpublished PhD thesis in Philosophy, Graduate Department of History, University of Toronto, 1996.

Lewis, M. Paul (ed.), *Ethnologue: Languages of the World*. Dallas, 2009.

Lieberman, Benjamin. *Remaking Identities: God, Nation, and Race in World History*. Lanham, 2013.

Lipgens, Walter. 'European Federation in the Political Thought of Resistance Movements during World War II', *Central European History*, 1:1 (March 1968) 5–19.

Loew, Peter Oliver. *Polen denkt Europa: Politische Texte aus zwei Jahrhunderten*, ed. and transl. by Peter Oliver Loew. Berlin, 2004.

Lorenzini, Sara. 'The White International and Peace in Europe, 1925–1932', in Petricioli and Cherubini 2003, 367–385.

Loriaux, Michael. *European Union and the Deconstruction of the Rhineland Frontier*. Cambridge, 2008, 138–147.

Loth, Wilfried. 'Die Résistance und die Pläne zu europäischer Einigung', in Dumoulin 1995, 47–57.

Loubet del Bayle, Jean-Louis. *Les non-conformistes des années 30: Une tentative de renouvellement de la pensée politique française*. Paris, 2001.

Loughlin, John. 'French Personalist and Federalist Movements in the Interwar Period', in Stirk 1998, 188–200.

Louthan, Howard, Gary B. Cohen and Franz A.J. Szabo (eds), *Diversity and Dissent: Negotiating Religious Difference in Central Europe, 1500–1800*. Oxford, 2011.

Lucassen, Leo. *The Immigrant Threat: The Integration of Old and New Immigrants in Western Europe since 1850*. Urbana and Chicago, 2005.

Ludlow, Peter. 'The Unwinding of Appeasement', in Lothar Kettenacker (ed.), *Das 'Andere Deutschland' im Zweiten Weltkrieg: Emigration und Widerstand in internationaler Perspektive*. Stuttgart, 1977, 9–40.

Lundestad, Geir. *The United States and Western Europe since 1945: From 'Empire' by Invitation to Transatlantic Drift*. Oxford and New York, 2005.

Lützeler, Paul Michael. *Europa: Analysen und Visionen der Romantiker*. Frankfurt, a. M. 1982.

Lynch, Frances. 'A Missed Opportunity to Plan the Reconstruction of Europe? Franco-British Relations 1945–1947', in Dumoulin 1995, 459–467.

Lyons, Francis S.L. *Internationalism in Europe 1815–1914*. Leiden, 1963.

Malešević, Siniša. 'Wars that Make States and Wars that Make Nations: Organised Violence, Nationalism and State Formation in the Balkans', *European Journal of Sociology*, 53:1 (2012) 31–63.

Mamdani, Mahmood. *When Victims Become Killers: Colonialism, Nativism and Genocide in Rwanda*. Princeton, 2001.

Manela, Erez. *The Wilsonian Moment: Self-Determination and the International Origins of Anticolonial Nationalism*. Oxford, 2007.

Manigand, Christine. 'Projets genevois et projets d'unité européenne à travers l'Europe Nouvelle de Louise Weiss', in Gérard Bossuat (dir.), *Histoire des groupes d'influence et des acteurs de l'idée européenne*. Brussels, 2003, 125–138.

Mann, Golo. *Friedrich von Gentz. Geschichte eines europäischen Staatsmannes*. Zürich, 1947.

Mann, Michael. *The Dark Side of Modernity: Explaining Ethnic Cleansing*. Cambridge, 2005.

Manners, Ian. 'Normative Power Europe: A Contradiction in Terms?', *Journal of Common Market Studies*, 40 (2002) 235–258.

Mansfield, Andrew. 'Émeric Crucé's "Nouveau Cynée" (1623), Universal Peace and Free Trade', *Journal of Interdisciplinary History of Ideas*, 2:4 (2013) 2:1–2:23.

Marsh, Peter T. *Bargaining on Europe: Britain and the First Common Market 1860–1892*. New Haven, 1999.

Marshall, John. *John Locke, Toleration, and Early Enlightenment Culture: Religious Intolerance and Arguments for Religious Toleration in early Modern and 'Early Enlightenment' Europe*. Cambridge, 2006.

Martin, Guy. 'Africa and the Ideology of Eurafrica: Neo-Colonialism Or Pan-Africanism?', *The Journal of Modern African Studies*, 20 (1982) 221–238.

Mastny, Vojtech. 'Soviet Plans for Postwar Europe', in Varsori and Calandri 2002, 59–75.

Mattli, Walter. *The Logic of Regional Integration: Europe and Beyond*. Cambridge, 2001.

Mazower, Mark. *Dark Continent: Europe's Twentieth Century*. New York, 1998.

Mazower, Mark. *Governing the World: History of an Idea*. New York, 2012.

McCarthy, Thomas. *Race, Empire and the Idea of Human Development*. Cambridge, 2008.

McCormick, John P. 'Carl Schmitt's Europe. Cultural, Imperial and Spatial Proposals for European Integration, 1923–1955', in Christian Joerges, Navraj Singh Ghaleigh and Michael Stolleis (eds), *Darker Legacies of Law in Europe: The Shadow of National Socialism and Fascism over Europe and its Legal Traditions*. Portland, 2003, 133–142.

McLeod, Hugh. *Religion and the People of Western Europe, 1789–1989*. Oxford, 1998.

McLeod, Hugh. *Secularisation in Western Europe, 1848–1914*. Houndmills, 2000.

Mechi, Lorenzo. *L'Organizzazione Internazionale del Lavoro e la ricostruzione europea: Le basi sociali dell'integrazione economica (1931–1957)*. Rome, 2012.

Meffre, Liliane. 'Europa: Une manifestation des avant-gardes européennes', in Bru et al. 2009, 153–160.

Mergel, Thomas. 'Die Sehnsucht nach Ähnlichkeit und die Erfahrung der Verschiedenheit. Überlegungen zu einer Europäischen Gesellschaftsgeschichte im 20. Jahrhundert', *Archiv für Sozialgeschichte*, 49 (2009) 417–434.

Middell, Matthias and Katja Naumann, 'Global History and the Spatial Turn: From the Impact of Area Studies to the Study of Critical Junctures of Globalization', *Journal of Global History*, 5:1 (2010): 149–170.

Milward, Alan Steele. *The Reconstruction of Western Europe*. London, 1984.

Milward, Alan Steele. *The European Rescue of the Nation State*. London, 1992.

Minion, Mark. 'The Labour Party and Europe during the 1940s: The strange case of the Socialist Vanguard Group', South Bank European Institute Working Papers – Centre for International Business Studies, 4.98, 1998. http://bus.lsbu.ac.uk/resources/CIBS/european-institute-papers/papers2/498.pdf.

Mioche, Philippe. 'Une vision conciliante du futur de l'Europe: Le plan d'Alexis Aron en 1943', in Dumoulin 1995, 307–323.

Mishra, Pankaj. *From the Ruins of Empire: The Revolt against the West and the Remaking of Asia*. New York, 2012.

Mogk, Walter. *Paul Rohrbach und das 'Größere Deutschland': Ethischer Imperialismus im Wilhelminischen Zeitalter. Ein Beitrag zur Geschichte des Kulturprotestantismus*. München, 1972.

Mommsen, Wolfgang. 'Die Mitteleuropaidee und die Mitteleuropaplanungen im deutschen Reich vor und während des Ersten Weltkrieges', in R.G. Plaschka et al. (eds), *Mitteleuropa-Konzeptionen in der ersten Hälfte des 20. Jahrhunderts*. Vienna, 1995, 3–25.

Monnet, Jean. 'A Fervent of Change', *Journal of Common Market Studies*, 1 (1963) 203–2011.

Moore, R.I. *The Formation of a Persecuting Society: Authority and Deviance in Western Europe 950–1250*. Oxford, 2007 (2).

Moore, R.I. *The War on Heresy: Faith and Power in Medieval Europe*. Cambridge, MA, 2012.

Moravcsik, Andrew. *The Choice for Europe: Social Purpose and State Power from Messina to Maastricht*. Ithaca, 1998.

Morawiec, Małgorzata. 'Antiliberale Europäisierung? Autoritäre Europakonzeptionen im Polen der Zwischenkriegszeit', *Zeithistorische Forschungen/Studies in Contemporary History*, Online edition, 9 (2012), H. 3. http://www.zeithistorische-forschungen.de/16126041-Morawiec-3-2012 (retrieved 12 July 2014).

Moser, Thomas. *Europäische Integration, Dekolonisation, Eurafrika: Eine historische Analyse über die Entstehungsbedingungen der eurafrikanischen Gemeinschaft von der Weltwirtschaftskrise bis zum Jaunde-Vertrag, 1929–1963*. Baden-Baden, 2000.

Moyn, Samuel. *The Last Utopia: Human Rights in History*. Cambridge, MA, 2010.

Muchembled, Robert (ed. in chief), *Cultural Exchange in Early Modern Europe*. Cambridge, 4 vols. 2006–2007.

Muet, Yannick. *Le débat européen pendant l'entre-deux-guerres*. Paris, 1997.

Müller, Guido. *Europäische Gesellschaftsbeziehungen nach dem Ersten Weltkrieg. Das Deutsch-Französische Studienkomitee und der Europäische Kulturbund*. München, 2005.

Muller, Jan-Werner (ed.), *Memory and Power in Postwar Europe: Studies in the Presence of the Past*. Cambridge, 2002.

Muller, Jan-Werner. *A Dangerous Mind: Carl Schmitt in Post-War European Thought*. New Haven, 2003.

Müller, Nils. 'Die Wirtschaft als "Brücke der Politik". Elemér Hantos' wirtschaftspolitisches Programm in den 1920er und 1930er Jahren', in Sachse 2010, 87–114.

Muthu, Sankar. *Enlightenment against Empire*. Princeton, 2003, 172–209.

Nakhimovsky, Isaac. *The Closed Commercial State: Perpetual Peace and Commercial Society from Rousseau to Fichte*. Princeton, 2011.

Namont, Jean-Philippe. 'La Petite Entente, un moyen d'intégration de l'Europe Centrale?', *Bulletin de l'Institut Pierre Renouvin*, 2:30 (2009) 45–56.

Narinskii, Mikhail M. 'The Soviet Union and the Marshall Plan', in Varsori and Calandri 2002, 275–287.

Nathanaili, Petrit, 'Le projet de federation balkanique de Belgrade, Sofia et Tirana. Un grand dessein des années 1944–1948', in Bossuat and Saunier 2003, 223–240.

Nederman, Cary J. *Community and Consent: The Secular Political Theory of Marsiglio of Padua's Defensor Pacis*. Lanham, 1995.

Nederman, Cary J. *Worlds of Difference: European Discourses of Toleration, c. 1100–c. 1550*. University Park, 2000.

Nehring, Holger and Helge Pharo. 'Introduction: A Peaceful Europe? Negotiating Peace in the Twentieth Century', *Contemporary European History*, 17:3 (2008) 277–299.

Nexon, Daniel H. *The Struggle for Power in Early Modern Europe: Religious Conflict, Dynastic Empires, and International Change*. Princeton, 2009.

Nimni, Ephraim. 'Nationalist Multiculturalism in Late Imperial Austria as a Critique of Contemporary Liberalism: The Case of Bauer and Renner', *Journal of Political Ideologies*, 4:3 (1999) 289–314.

Nirenberg, David. *Communities of Violence: Persecution of Minorities in the Middle Ages*. Princeton, 1996.

Nirenberg, David. *Anti-Judaism: The Western Tradition*. New York, 2013.

Oberman, Heiko A. 'The Travail of Tolerance: Containing Chaos in Early Modern Europe' in Ole Peter Grell and Bob Scribner (eds), *Tolerance and Intolerance in the European Reformation*. Cambridge, 2002, 21–35.

Okey, Robin. 'Central Europe/Eastern Europe: Behind the Definitions', *Past Present*, 137 (1992) 102–133.

Onnekink, David (ed.), *War and Religion after Westphalia, 1648–1713*. Farnham, 2009.

Osiander, Andreas. 'Sovereignty, International Relations, and the Westphalian Myth', *International Organization*, 55:2 (2001) 251–287.

Ousselin, Edward. 'Victor Hugo's European Utopia', *Nineteenth-Century French Studies*, 34:1–2 (Fall–Winter 2005–2006) 32–43.

Pacifici, Lorenzo. 'La question de l'association des PTOM au cours des négociations pour la création de la CEE', in Bitsch and Bossuat 2005, 252–267.

Pagden, Anthony (ed.), *The Idea of Europe. From Antiquity to the European Union*. Cambridge, 1992.

Palayret, Jean-Marie. 'Les mouvements proeuropéens et la question de l'Eurafrique, du Congrès de La Haye à la Convention de Yaoundé (1948–1963)', in Bitsch and Bossuat 2005, 185–229.

Pasture, Michèle. 'Francis Delaisi et l'Europe, 1925–1929–1931 (extraits)', in Michel Dumoulin and Yves Stélandre (eds), *L'idée européenne dans l'entre-deux-guerres*. Louvain-la-Neuve, 1992.

Pasture, Patrick. *Histoire du syndicalisme chrétien international: La difficile recherche d'une troisième voie*. Paris and Montréal, 1999.

Pasture, Patrick. 'The Interwar Origins of International Labour's European Commitment (1919–1934)', *Contemporary European History*, 10:2 (July 2001) 221–237.

Pasture, Patrick. 'Christian Social Movements Confronted with Fascism in Europe: Consistency, Continuity, or Flexibility in Principles, Strategies, and Tactics towards Social and Economic Democracy', in Lieve Gevers and Jan Bank (eds), *Religion under siege. Vol.1: The Roman Catholic Church in occupied Europe (1939–1950)*. Leuven, 2007, 283–314.

Pasture, Patrick. 'Religious Globalization in Post-War Europe', *Archiv für Sozialgeschichte*, 51 (2011) 63–108.

Pasture, Patrick. '*Formations of European Modernity*: "Cosmopolitan Eurocentrism" and the Uses of History', *International Journal for History, Culture and Modernity*, forthcoming 2015.

Pasture, Patrick and Johan Verberckmoes, 'Working Class Internationalism and the Appeal of National Identity. Historical Dilemmas and Current Debates on Western Europe', in Patrick Pasture and Johan Verberckmoes (eds), *Working Class Internationalism and the Appeal of National Identity: Historical Dilemmas and Current Debates on Western Europe*. Oxford, 1998, 1–42.

Patel, Kiran Klaus. 'Provincialising European Union: Co-operation and Integration in Europe in a Historical Perspective', *Contemporary European History*, 22 (2013) 649–673.

Paternó, Maria Pia. 'Diplomacy of Treatises and Political Balance between XVIII and XIX Century', *Publikationsportal Europäische Friedensverträge*, Institut für Europäische Geschichte, Mainz 27.07.2009, Abschnitt 1–17. http://www.ieg-friedensvertraege.de/publikationsportal/paterno07200901/index.html (retrieved 1 December 2013).

Pavlowitch, Stevan K. 'The Balkan Union: And Instance in the Postwar Plans of Small Countries', in Varsori and Calandri 2002, 76–83.

Pedersen, Thomas. *When Culture Becomes Politics: European Identity in Perspective*. Aarhus, 2008.

Pegg, Carl H. *Evolution of the European Idea, 1914–1932*. Chapel Hill, 1983.

Pellegrino, Nicholas. 'Thy Will be Done: Divine Directive in Anglo-American Church-State Debates', *Journal of History and Cultures*, 2 (2013) 17–38.

Perkins, Mary Anne. *Christendom and European Identity: The Legacy of a Grand Narrative since 1789*. Berlin, 2004.

Pernot, François. 'Les physiocrates, l'Europe unie par l'économie: L'idée d'Europe chez les physiocrates, économistes et financiers de la fin du XVIIIe siècle', in Bossuat 2003, 27–39.

Perovič, Jeronim. 'The Tito-Stalin Split: A Reassessment in Light of New Evidence', *Journal of Cold War Studies*, 9:2 (Spring 2007) 32–63.

Persson, Hans-Åke and Bo Stråth (eds), *Reflections on Europe: Defining a Political Order in Time and Space*. Brussels, 2007.

Petracchi, Giorgio. 'Italy and Eastern Europe, 1943–1948', in Varsori and Calandri 2002, 123–137.

Petricioli, Marta (ed.), *Une occasion manquée? 1922: La reconstruction de l'Europe.* Bern, 1995.

Petricioli, Marta and Donatella Cherubini (eds), *For Peace in Europe: Institutions and Civil Society between the World Wars.* Bern, 2007.

Philpott, Daniel. *Revolutions in Sovereignty: How Ideas Shaped Modern International Relations.* Princeton, 2001.

Piguet, Marie-France. 'L'Europe des Européens chez le comte de Saint-Simon', *Mots*, 34 (March 1993) 7–24. http://www.persee.fr/web/revues/home/prescript/article/mots_0243-6450_1993_num_34_1_1771.

Pinder, John. 'Federalism in Britain and Italy', in Stirk 1998, 201–223.

Pinder, John. 'British Federalists 1940–1947: From Movement to Stasis', in Dumoulin 2005, 247–274.

Pistone, Sergio. *The Union of European Federalists: From the Foundation to the Decision on Direct Election of the European Parliament (1946–1974).* Milano, 2008.

Pitts, Jennifer. 'Empire and Legal Universalisms in the Eighteenth Century', *The American Historical Review*, 117:1 (February 2012) 92–121.

Povolo, Caudio. 'An Historical Dimension of European Cultural Heritage', *Acta Histriae*, 21:4 (2013) 1–14.

Prügl, Elisabeth and Markus Thiel (eds), *Diversity in the European Union.* Houndmills, 2009.

Pulzer, Peter. 'Nationalism and Internationalism in European Christian Democracy', in Michael Gehler and Wolfram Kaiser (eds), *Christian Democracy in Europe since 1945.* London, 2004, vol. 2, 10–24.

Racine, Nicole. 'La revue "Europe" et le pacifisme dans les années vingt', in Vaïsse 1993, 51–69.

Ragnow, Marguerite and William D. Phillips Jr. (eds), *Religious Conflict and Accommodation in the Early Modern World.* Minneapolis, 2011.

Rathkolb, Oliver. 'First Budapest, then Prague and Berlin, why not Vienna? Austria and the Origins of the Cold war, 1947–1948', in Varsori and Calandri 2002, 306–318.

Ray, Roland. *Annäherung an Frankreich im Dienste Hitlers? Otto Abetz und die deutsche Frankreichpolitik 1930–1942.* München, 2000.

Recchia, Stefano and Nadia Urbinati. 'Giuseppe Mazzini's International Political Thought', in Stefano Recchia and Nadia Urbinati (eds), *A Cosmopolitanism of Nations: Giuseppe Mazzini's Writings on Democracy, Nation Building, and International Relations.* Princeton, 2013, 1–30.

Reifowitz, Ian. 'Otto Bauer and Karl Renner on Nationalism, Ethnicity Jews', *Journal of Jewish Identities*, 2:2 (July 2009) 1–19.

Reinalda, Bob. *Routledge History of International Organizations: From 1815 to the Present Day.* Abingdon, 2009.

Rempe, Martin. 'Decolonization by Europeanization? The Early EEC and the Transformation of French-African Relations', *KFG Working Paper Series*, Nr. 27 (2011).

Reuter, Timothy. 'Medieval Ideas of Europe and their Modern Historians', *History Workshop Journal*, 33 (1992) 176–180.

Rey, Marie-Pierre. 'L'engagement européen du tsar Alexandre Ier', in Bossuat 2003, 41–53.

Reynolds, Michael A. *Shattering Empires: The Clash and Collapse of the Ottoman and Russian Empires, 1908–1918.* Cambridge, 2011.

Rich, Paul. 'European Identity and the Myth of Islam: A Reassessment', *Review of International Studies*, 25:3 (1999) 435–451.

Richmond, Oliver P. 'Patterns of Peace', *Global Society*, 20:4 (2006) 367–394.

Rietbergen, Peter. *Europe: A Cultural History*. London, 1998.

Righart, Hans. *De katholieke zuil in Europa: Het ontstaan van verzuiling onder katholieken in Oostenrijk, Zwitserland, België en Nederland*. Meppel, 1986.

Röben, Betsy. *Johann Caspar Bluntschli, Francis Lieber und das moderne Völkerrecht 1861–1881*. Baden-Baden, 2003.

Roberts, Penny. *Peace and Authority during the French Religious Wars*, c. 1560–1600. Houndmills, 2013.

Romsics, Ignác. 'Regionalismus und Europa-Gedanke im ungarischen politischen Denken des 19. Und 20. Jahrhunderts', in Borodziej et al. 2005, vol. I, 135–165 (137–142).

Roy, Christian. *Alexandre Marc et la Jeune Europe (1904–1934): L'Ordre Nouveau aux origines du personnalisme*. Nice, 1999.

Sachse, Carola (ed.), *'Mitteleuropa' und 'Südosteuropa' als Planungsraum. Wirtschafts- und kulturpolitische Expertisen im Zeitalter der Weltkriege*. Göttingen, 2010.

Sachse, Carola. 'Einleitung: "Mitteleuropa" und "Südosteuropa" als Planungsraum. Der Mitteleuropäische Wirtschaftstag im Kontext', in Sachse 2010, 13–45.

Said, Edward. *Orientalism*. New York, 1979.

Saint-Gille, Anne-Marie. *La 'Paneurope': Un débat d'idées dans l'entre-deux-guerres*. Paris, 2003.

Samuels, Nathaniel. 'The European Coal Organization', *Foreign Affairs*, July 1948. http://www.foreignaffairs.com/articles/70696/nathaniel-samuels/the-european-coal-organization (retrieved 18 July 2014).

Sandner, Gunther. 'Nations without Nationalism: The Austro-Marxist Discourse on Multiculturalism', *Journal of Language and Politics*, 4:2 (2005) 273–291.

Sassatelli, Monica. *Becoming Europeans: Cultural Identity and Cultural Policies*. Houndmills, 2009.

Schaad, Martin. 'Plan G – A "Counterblast"? British Policy Towards the Messina Countries, 1956', *Contemporary European History*, 7:1 (1998) 39–60.

Schaeffer, Patrick J. 'Les illusions de la coopération financière européenne au début de la crise des années 1930: l'exemple de la Société internationale de credit hypothécaire agricole', in Sylvain Schirmann (ed.), *Organisations internationales et architectures européennes 1929–1939*. Metz, 2003, 367–387.

Schilling, Heinz. *Konfessionalisierung und Staatsinteressen: Internationale Beziehungen 1559–1660*. Paderborn, 2007.

Schilmar, Boris. *Der Europadiskurs im deutschen Exil 1933–1945*. München, 2003.

Schirmann, Sylvain. *Crise, coopération économique et financière entre Etats européens, 1929–1933*. Paris, 2000.

Schirmann, Sylvain. 'Les comités économique et financier de la Société des Nations, l'ordre économique et monétaire et la paix en Europe, 1920–1939' in Petricioli and Cherubini 2007, 73–92.

Schmale, Wolfgang. *Geschichte und Zukunft der Europäischen Identität*. Stuttgart, 2008.

Schmidt, Rainer. *Die Wiedergeburt der Mitte Europas: Politisches Denken jenseits von Ost und West*. Berlin, 2001.

Schmoeckel, Mathias. *Die Großraumtheorie: Ein Beitrag zur Geschichte der Völkerrechtswissenschaft im Dritten Reich, insbesondere der Kriegszeit*. Berlin, 1994.

Schöberl, Verena. *'Es gibt ein großes und herrliches Land, das sich selbst nicht kennt...Es heißt Europa': Die Diskussion um die Paneuropaidee in Deutschland, Frankreich und Großbritannien 1922–1933*. Berlin, 2010.

Schonfield, Ernest. 'The Idea of European Unity in Heinrich Mann's Political Essays in the 1920s and 1930s', in Hewitson and D'Auria 2012, 257–270.

Schot, Johan and Phil Scranton (eds), *Making Europe: Technology and Transformations, 1850–2000*. Houndmills, 6 vol., 2013–2015.

Schröder, Jan. 'Is There a "European Law" of the Early Modern Period?', in Mónica García-Salmones and Pamela Slotte (eds), *Cosmopolitanisms in Enlightenment Europe and Beyond*. Brussels/Bern, 2013, 39–48.

Schröder, Peter. 'The Holy Roman Empire as Model for Saint-Pierre's *Projet pour rendre la Paix perpétuelle en Europe*', in R. Evans and P. Wilson (eds), *The Holy Roman Empire, 1495–1806: A European Perspective*. Leiden, 2012, 35–50.

Schroeder, Steven M. *To Forget It All and Begin Anew: Reconciliation in Occupied Germany, 1944–1954*. Toronto, 2013.

Schulz, Matthias. 'Der Europäische Kulturbund', *Europäische Geschichte Online* (EGO). http://www.ieg-ego.eu/schulzm-2010c-de (retrieved 14 September 2013).

Schulze Wessel, Martin. 'Religion, Politics and the Limits of Imperial Integration – Comparing the Habsburg Monarchy and the Russian Empire', in Ulrike von Hirschhausen and Jörn Leonhard (eds), *Comparing Empires: Encounters and Transfers in the Long Nineteenth Century*. Göttingen, 2011, 337–358.

Schwabe, Klaus. 'The United States and Europe from Roosevelt to Truman', in Varsori and Calandri 2002, 17–39.

Schwarz, Hans-Peter. *Konrad Adenauer: A German Politican and Statesman in a Period of War, Revolution and Reconstruction*. Providence, 1995–1997.

Semmel, Bernard. *The Liberal Ideal and the Demons of Empire: Theories of Imperialism from Adam Smith to Lenin*. Baltimore, 1993.

Sen, Amartya. *The Argumentative Indian: Writings on Indian History, Culture and Identity*. New York, 2005.

Seton-Watson, R.W. *Masaryk in England*. Cambridge and New York, 1943.

Sheehan, James. *Where Have All the Soldiers Gone?* New York, 2008.

Shlaim, Avi. 'Prelude to Downfall: The British Offer of Union to France, June 1940', *Journal of Contemporary History*, 3:9 (July 1974) 27–63.

Shlapentokh, Dmitry. 'Slavic, European, or Asiatic? F. H. Duchinski on the Origins of the Russian People', *The European Legacy*, 19:1 (2014) 60–71.

Shore, Chris. *Building Europe: The Cultural Politics of European Integration*. London, 2000.

Shorto, Russell. *The Island at the Center of the World: The Epic Story of Dutch Manhattan and the Forgotten Colony that Shaped America*. New York, 2004.

Sieg, Ulrich. *Deutschlands Prophet: Paul de Lagarde und die Ursprünge des modernen Antisemitismus*. München, 2007.

Siendentop, Larry. *Inventing the Individual: The Origins of Western Liberalism*. New York, 2014.

Simoni, Marcella. 'The Inner Frontier: Jews in *Les Etats Unis d'Europe*', in Anteghini, Petricioli and Cherubini 2003, 151–172.

Sinnhuber, Karl A. 'Central Europe: Mitteleuropa: Europe Centrale: An Analysis of a Geographical Term', *Transactions of the Institute of British Geographers*, 20 (1954) 15–39.

Sluga, Glenda. *Internationalism in the Age of Nationalism.* Philadelphia, 2013.

Smith, Anthony D. *Nationalism and Modernism.* London, 1998.

Smith, Julia M.H. *Europe after Rome: A New Cultural History 500–1000.* Oxford, 2005.

Soutou, Georges-Henri. *L'Or et le sang – Les buts de guerre économiques de la Première Guerre mondiale.* Paris, 1989.

Soutou, Georges-Henri. 'La Première Guerre mondiale: Une rupture dans l'évolution de l'ordre européen', *Politique étrangère*, 3–4 (2000) 841–855.

Soutou, Georges-Henri. 'Was There a European Order in the Twentieth Century? From the Concert of Europe to the End of the Cold War', *Contemporary European History*, 9:3 (November 2000) 329–353.

Spector, Céline. 'L'Europe de l'abbé de Saint-Pierre', in C. Dornier and C. Poulin (eds), *Les Projets de l'abbé Castel de Saint-Pierre (1658–1743).* Caen, 2011, 39–49.

Spector, Céline. 'Who Is the Author of the Abstract of Monsieur l'Abbé de Saint-Pierre's "Plan for Perpetual Peace"? From Saint-Pierre to Rousseau', *History of European Ideas*, 39:3 (2013) 371–393.

Spiering, Menno. 'Engineering Europe: The European Idea in Interbellum Literature, the Case of Panropa', in Spiering and Michael 2002, 177–200.

Spiering, Menno and Michael Wintle (eds), *Ideas of Europe since 1914: The Legacy of the First World War.* Houndmills, 2002.

Spreen, Dierk. 'Friedensbildlichkeit und Gesellschaftsbegriff zur Zeit der Romantik', in Kater 2006 135–156.

Stein, Peter. *Roman Law in European History.* Cambridge, 1999.

Steinberg, Jonathan. *Bismarck: A Life.* Oxford, 2011.

Steiner, Zara. *The Lights That Failed: European International History, 1919–1933.* Oxford, 2005.

Stepan, Alfred. 'Multiple Secularisms of Modern Democratic and Non-Democratic Regimes', in Craig Calhoun, Mark Juergensmeyer and Jonathan van Antwerpen (eds), *Rethinking Secularism.* Oxford, 2011, 114–144.

Stern, Philip J. *The Company-State: Corporate Sovereignty and the Early Modern Foundations of the British Empire in India.* Oxford, 2011.

Sternhell, Zeev. *Neither Right Nor Left: Fascist Ideology in France.* Princeton, 1996.

Stevenson, David. 'The First World War and European Integration', *International History Review*, 43:4 (December 2012) 841–863.

Stirk, Peter M.R. 'Autoritarian and National Socialist Conceptions of Nation, State and Europe', in Stirk 1989, 125–148.

Stirk, Peter M.R. (ed.), *European Unity in Context: The Interwar Period.* London and New York, 1989.

Stirk, Peter M.R. *A History of European Integration since 1914.* London, 1996.

Stirk, Peter M.R. (ed.), *Mitteleuropa: History and Prospects.* Edinburgh, 1994.

Stirk, Peter M.R. 'Integration and Disintegration before 1945', in Desmond Dinan (ed.), *Origins and Evolution of the European Union.* Oxford, 2006, 9–28.

Stråth, Bo. 'A European Identity: To the Historical Limits of a Concept', *European Journal of Social Theory*, 5 (2002) 387–401.

Stråth, Bo. 'Mitteleuropa: From List to Naumann', *European Journal of Social Theory*, 11:2 (May 2008) 171–183.

Stratton, Jon. ' "It Almost Needn't Have Been the Germans". The State, Colonial Violence and the Holocaust', *European Journal of Cultural Studies*, 6 (2003) 507–527.

Strikwerda, Carl. 'The Troubled Origins of European Economic Integration: International Iron and Steel and Labour Migration in the Era of World War I', *American Historical Review*, 98 (1993) 1106–42.

Strikwerda, Carl. 'Reinterpreting the History of European Integration: Business, Labor and Social Citizenship in Twentieth Century Europe', in Jytte Clausen and Louise A. Tilly (eds), *European Integration in Social and Historical Perspective*. Lanham, 1998, 51–70.

Strong, Georg. 'German-Austrian Social Democracy and the Nation-State Idea: 1889–1918', *History of European Ideas*, 15:4–6 (1992) 583–588.

Svenungsson, Jayne. 'Christian Europe: Borders and Boundaries of a Mythological Conception', in S. Lindberg, S. Prozorov and M. Ojakangas (eds), *Transcending Europe: Beyond Universalism and Particularism*. Houndmills, 2014, 120–134.

Swedberg, Richard. 'The Idea of "Europe" and the Origin of the European Union: A Sociological Approach', *Zeitschrift für Soziologie*, 23 (1994) 378–387.

Szporluk, Roman. *Communism and Nationalism: Karl Marx versus Friedrich List*. Oxford, 1988.

Ther, Philip. *Die dunkle Seite der Nationalstaaten: 'Ethnische Säuberungen' im modernen Europa*. Göttingen, 2001.

Ther, Philipp. 'Imperial Instead of National History: Positioning Modern German History on the Map of European Empires', in Alexei Miller and Alfred J. Rieber (eds), *Imperial Rule*. Budapest, 2004, 47–66.

Ther, Philipp and Ana Siljak (eds), *Redrawing Nations: Ethnic Cleansing in East-Central Europe, 1944–1948*. Totowa, 2001.

Thiemeyer, Guido. 'West German Perceptions of Africa and the Association of the Overseas Territories with the Common Market 1956–1957', in Bitsch and Bossuat 2005, 269–286.

Thiemeyer, Guido. 'Internationalismus als Vorläufer wirtschaftlicher Integration? Otto von Bismarck, das Phänomen der Supranationalität und die Internationalisierung der Wirtschaft im 19. Jahrhundert', in Ulrich Lappenküper and Guido Thiemeyer (eds), *Europäische Einigung im 19. und 20. Jahrhundert. Akteure und Antriebskräfte*. Paderborn, 2013, 71–94.

Thompson, Martyn P. 'Ideas of Europe during the French Revolution and Napoleonic Wars', *Journal of the History of Ideas*, 55:1 (1994) 37–58.

Throntveit, Trygve. 'The Fable of the Fourteen Points: Woodrow Wilson and National Self-Determination', *Diplomatic History*, 35:3 (2011) 445–481.

Tielker, Wilhelm. *Europa – Die Genese einer politischen Idee: Von der Antike bis zur Gegenwart*. Münster, 1998.

Timms, Edward. 'National Memory and the "Austrian Idea" from Metternich to Waldheim', *The Modern Language Review*, 86:4 (1991) 898 –910.

Tooze, Adam. *The Deluge: The Great War and the Remaking of Global Order 1916–1931*. New York, 2014.

Trachtenberg, Marc. 'The Marshall Plan as Tragedy', *Journal of Cold War Studies*, 7:1 (Winter 2005) 135–140.

Trachtenberg, Marc and Christopher Gehrz, 'America, Europe, and German Rearmament, August-September 1950: A Critique of a Myth', in Marc Trachtenberg (ed.), *Between Empire and Alliance: America and Europe during the Cold War*. Lanham, 2003, 1–31.

Tschubardjan, Alexander. *Europakonzepte von Napoleon bis zum Gegenwart. Ein Beitrag aus Moskau*. Berlin, 1992.

Tuck, Richard. 'Scepticism and Toleration in the Seventeenth Century', in Susan Mendus (ed.), *Justifying Toleration: Conceptual and Historical Perspectives*. Cambridge, 1988, 21–35.

Tusan, Michelle. ' "Crimes against Humanity": Human Rights, the British Empire and the Origins of the Response to the Armenian Genocide', *American Historical Review*, 119:1 (February 2014) 47–77.

Untea, Ionut. 'New Middle Ages or New Modernity? Carl Schmitt's Interwar Perspective on Political Unity in Europe', in Hewitson and D'Auria 2012, 155–168.

Vahsen, Urban. *Eurafrikanische Entwicklungskooperation. Die Assozierungspolitik der EWG gegenüber dem subsaharischen Afrika in den 1960er Jahren*. Stuttgart, 2010.

Valdevit, Giampaolo. 'Yugoslavia between the Two Emerging blocs 1943–1948', in Varsori and Calandri 2002, 184–196.

Van Daele, Jasmien, Magaly Rodríguez García, Geert Van Goethem and Marcel van der Linden (eds), *ILO Histories: Essays on the International Labour Organization and Its Impact on the World during the Twentieth Century*. Bern, 2010.

Van De Haar, Edwin. 'David Hume and International Political Theory: A Reappraisal', *Review of International Studies*, 34:2 (2008) 225–242.

Vandenweyer, Koen. 'Europese integratie en dekolonisatie: België, Congo and de associatie van de overzeese gebieden met de gemeenschappelijke markt (1955–1957)', Unpublished MA thesis History KU Leuven, 2012.

Van Goethem, Geert. 'Conflicting Interests: The International Federation of Trade Unions 1919–1945', in Andrew Carew et al. (eds), *The International Confederation of Free Trade Unions*. Bern, 2000, 73–163.

van Heerikhuizen, Annemarie. 'How God Disappeared from Europe: Visions of a United Europe from Erasmus to Kant', *The European Legacy*, 13:4 (2008) 401–411.

Van Kemseke, Peter. *Towards an Era of Development: The Globalization of Socialism and Christian Democracy 1945–1965*. Leuven, 2006.

van Meurs, Wim, Robin de Bruin, Carla Hoetink, Karin van Leeuwen and Carlos Reijnen et al., *Europa in alle staten. Zestig jaar geschiedenis van de Europese integratie*. Nijmegen, 2013.

van Middelaar, Luuk. *The Passage to Europe: How a Continent Became a Union*. New Haven, 2013.

van Rooden, Peter. *Religieuze regimes: Over godsdienst en maatschappij in Nederland, 1570–1990*. Amsterdam, 1996.

van Roon, Ger. *Small States in Years of Depression: The Oslo Alliance 1930–1940*. Assen, 1989.

Varsori, Antonio and Elena Calandri (eds), *The Failure of Peace in Europe, 1943–48*. Houndmills, 2002.

Vayssière, Berrtand. 'Alexandre Marc: Les idées personnalistes au service de l'Europe', in Bossuat 2003, 383–401.

Vermeersch, Peter. 'Het principe van het deugdzame midden: Duitse, Hongaarse en Tsjechische versies van "Centraal-Europa"', in Idesbald Goddeeris (ed.), *De Europese Periferie*. Leuven, 2004, 139–156.

Vermeiren, Jan. '*Imperium Europaeum*: Rudolf Pannwitz and the German Idea of Europe', in Hewitson and D'Auria 2012, 135–154.

Vermeiren, Jan. 'Nation-State and Empire in German Political Thought: Europe and the Myth of the Reich', in Dini and D'Auria 2013, 135–160.

Vian, Giovanni Maria. *La donazione di Costantino*. Bologna, 2004.

Virk, Zacharia. 'Muslim contributions to European Renaissance'. https://www .academia.edu/6431705/Muslim_Contributions_to_European_Renaissance (retrieved 17 August 2014).

Volkov, Shulamit. *Walter Rathenau: Weimar's Fallen Statesman*. New Haven, 2012.

von Greyerz, Kaspar. *Religion and Culture in Early Modern Europe, 1500–1800*. Oxford, 2008.

von Hirschhausen, Ulrike. 'From Imperial Inclusion to National Exclusion: Citizenship in the Habsburg Monarchy and in Austria 1867–1923', *European Review of History*, 16:4 (2009) 551–573.

Voyelle [Vovelle?], Michel. 'Anticipations de l'idée européenne sous la révolution', in *L'idée de Communauté européenne de l'histoire*, University of Athens, 2003. http://www.pro-europa.eu/fr/index.php/espace/57-voyelle-anticipations-de-l-idee-europeenne.

Voyenne, Bernard. *Histoire de l'idée européenne*. Paris, 1964.

Voyenne, Bernard. *Le fédéralisme de P.J. Proudhon*. Lyon, 1973, 3 vols.

Wall, Irwin M. 'Les États-Unis et la décolonisation de l'Afrique. Le mythe de l'Eurafrique', in Bitsch and Bossuat 2005, 133–147.

Wangerman, Ernst. 'Confessional Uniformity, Toleration, Freedom of Religion: An Issue for Enlightened Absolutism in the Eighteenth Century', in Howard Louthan, Gary B. Cohen and Franz A.J. Szabo (eds), *Diversity and Dissent: Negotiating Religious Difference in Central Europe, 1500–1800*. New York and Oxford, 2011, 209–218.

Weber, Eugen. *Peasants into Frenchmen: The Modernization of Rural France, 1870–1914*. Palo Alto, 1976.

Weiner, Amir. *Making Sense of War: The Second World War and the Fate of the Bolshevik Revolution*. Princeton, 2005.

Weitz, Eric D. *A Century of Genocide: Utopias of Race and Nation*. Princeton, 2005.

Weitzmann, Walter R. 'Constantin Frantz, Germany and Central Europe: An Ambiguous Legacy', in Stirk 1994, 36–60.

Welsh, Jennifer. 'Edmund Burke and the Commonwealth of Europe: The Cultural Bases of International Order', in Ian Clark and Iver Neumann (eds), *Classical Theories of International Relations*. London, 1996, 173–192.

Wendler, Eugen (ed.), *'Die Vereinigung des europäischen Kontinents': Friedrich List: Gesamteuropäische Wirkungsgeschichte seines ökonomischen Denkes*. Stuttgart, 1996.

Wendler, Eugen. *Friedrich List (1789–1846): Ein Ökonom mit Weitblick und sozialer Verantwortung*. Wiesbaden, 2013.

Wickham, Chris. *The Inheritance of Rome: Illuminating the Dark Ages 400–1000*. New York, 2009.

Wilson, Kevin and Jan van der Dussen (eds), *The History of the Idea of Europe*. London and New York, 1993.

Wimmer, Andreas. *Nationalist Exclusion and Ethnic Conflict: Shadows of Modernity*. Cambridge, 2002.

Wimmer, Andreas. *Waves of War: Nationalism, State Formation, and Ethnic Exclusion in the Modern World*. Cambridge, 2012.

Wimmer, Andreas. *Ethnic Boundary Making: Institutions, Power, Networks*. New York and Oxford, 2013.

Winter, Jay R. *Dreams of Peace and Freedom: Utopian Moments in the Twentieth Century*. New Haven, 2008.

Wintle, Michael. 'Europe as Seen from the Outside: A Brief Visual Survey', in Michael Wintle (ed.), *Imagining Europe: Europe and European Civilisation as Seen from its Margins and by the Rest of the World, in the Nineteenth and Twentieth Centuries*. Brussels, 2008, 23–48.

Wintle, Michael. 'The History of the Idea of Europe: Where are we now?', *Perspectives on Europe*, 43:1 (2013) 8–12.

Wolf, Kenneth Baxter. *Conquerors and Chroniclers of Early Medieval Spain*. Liverpool, 1990.

Wolff, Larry. *Inventing Eastern Europe: The Map of Civilization on the Mind of the Enlightenment*. Stanford, 1994.

Wurm, Clemens A. *Internationale Kartelle und Aussenpolitik: Beiträge zur Zwischenkriegszeit*. Wiesbaden, 1989.

Yapp, Malcolm E. 'Europe in the Turkish Mirror', *Past and Present*, 137 (1992) 134–155.

Young, John W. *Britain, France and the Unity of Europe: 1945–1951*. Leicester, 1984.

Young, John W. *France, the Cold War and the Western Alliance, 1944–1949: French Foreign Policy and Post-War Europe*. Houndmills, 1990.

Young, John W. 'France's European Policy in the Aftermath of the War 1945–1947', in Dumoulin 1995, 437–458.

Young, John W. *Britain and European Unity 1945–1999*. Houndmills, 2000 (2).

Ziegerhofer-Prettenthaler, Anita. *Botschafter Europas: Richard Nikolaus Coudenhove-Kalergi und die Paneuropa-Bewegung in den zwanziger und dreißiger Jahren*. Vienna, 2004.

Ziegerhofer-Prettenthaler, Anita. *Europäische Integrationsgeschichte: Unter Berücksichtigung der österreichischen Integration*. Innsbruck, 2012.

Ziegerhofer-Prettenthaler, Anita. 'Richard Nikolaus Coudenhove-Kalergi, founder of the Pan European Union and the Birth of a "New" Europe', in Hewitson and D'Auria 2012, 89–109.

Ziegerhofer-Prettenthaler, Anita. 'Eurotopias: Coudenhove-Kalergi's Pan-Europa and Rohan's Europäischer Kulturbund', in Dini and D'Auria 2013, 161–177.

Zimmermann, Harro. *Friedrich Gentz: Die Erfindung der Realpolitik*. Paderborn, 2012.

Index

Note: Locators with 'ff' refer to following folios.

Printed by Printforce, the Netherlands